A DISNEY MONASTIC

a theme park travel guide for the God-seeker

Kevin M. Goodman

A Disney Monastic: a theme park travel guide for the God-seeker
©2014 by Kevin M. Goodman

A Digital Monastics Media Book
ISBN-13: 978-0-61587-654-2 (Digital Monastics Media)
ISBN-10: 0-61587-654-4

Author: Kevin M. Goodman; Designer: Constance Wilson; Photographer: Charlie Simokaitis;
Editor: Ginna Frantz; Copy: Margaret Goodman; Proof: Karla Kate; Forward: Sarah K. Fisher

CONTENTS } *A Disney Monastic*

FORWARD } *A Disney Monastic*

the Christian call

I remember my first trip to Disneyland. I was an adult, in my thirties. However, standing before the Main Gate, I felt every bit a seven-year-old, filled with energy, anticipation, and hope. The Magic Kingdom was about to wake up, fling open her gates, and invite me in to experience and be part of the magic. Kevin Goodman stood beside me. He had insisted we arrive early, with plenty of time to get our tickets and our bearings. I remember trying to take it all in, almost bouncing, feeling a bit like Tigger, whom I was hoping to meet. As we stood outside those iconic gates, staring at the precise landscape and intentional architecture that beckoned to us, talking to people I did not know, but whom I recognized as fellow travelers, all of us waiting for the pilgrimage that was before us, I understood. This was about more than just a theme park. This was about an experience of transformation. What Disney promised, as I stood on the cusp of his magic world, was something outside the ordinary, outside the expected. Disney offered me a chance, for a few hours, a few days, to live in, to experience something wholly other. There's a reason Disney's parks have tag lines like "The Happiest Place on Earth" and the place "Where Dreams Come True."

Of course, the monikers "The Happiest Place on Earth" and "Where Dreams Come True" are a lot to live up to. Ask anyone who has ever traveled to Disneyland or Walt Disney World with small children and you'll hear that the Disney moments of dreamy happiness are often interrupted by the realities of hungry bellies, tired tantrums and having to wait just a little too long in line. So it is with life. We have moments of joy and hope, and then hardship, sorrow or just the truth of daily life interrupts. Suddenly the happily-ever-after we hoped for seems to have disappeared and we find ourselves not in a magic castle, but lost in the woods, missing a slipper, trying hard to avoid the lady with the poisoned apples. In those moments of unknowing and fear, of isolation and loneliness, we can find ourselves wondering where God is in the midst of our lives.

What I love about Kevin's book, this spiritual travel guide through Walt Disney World, is that it acknowledges both the wonder and magic of the world and the sometimes harsh realities of living in it. Kevin skillfully develops and articulates the metaphor of Disney as a place where we learn what it means to wait for God's voice, to explore the story of God in our lives and in our world, and to find our own place in God's creation, ourselves part of the story that our Creator is constantly writing in us and through us. Kevin invites us to be pilgrims, sojourners, not by the usual retreat into stillness and quiet, but instead by stepping forward into the noise, traffic and congestion of the world, trusting that even, or perhaps especially, in the midst of the chaotic realities of human beings, God can be found and known, that God's voice can be heard speaking our name, if we are willing to seek and listen.

This book is an invitation to do just that— to stop, to seek, to be pilgrims. The power of pilgrimage is that by our very willingness to take the journey, we physically, emotionally and spiritually open ourselves into a place of willingness, a posture of openness to journeying with God.

Join Kevin on a pilgrimage to an unlikely spot, not Rome or Jerusalem or Mecca, but to the magical world of Disney. And though, at first glance, it may seem somewhat counterintuitive to imagine a pilgrimage to and through a theme park, Kevin offers a way for us to fully enter into the spiritual life and depth of a true faith sojourner. What's more, if we are willing to enter through Disney's gates not merely as tourists, but truly as pilgrims, we cannot help but leave transformed. And as we leave, we take with us more than t-shirts and tote bags, we take a life that is open to listening at a deeper level, a life that is actively seeking relationship with the Divine.

Step through the gate into the land that promises that dreams will come true, where magic and hope and awe are alive and waiting for us. Come. Step into the lines, the crowds, the busyness, the wonder and in the midst of the noise, hear God speak unexpected words. Come. Be in community. Be in prayer. Be. The gates are open, the music is playing, the parade is coming. Come. All of it waits for you.

The Rev. Sarah K. Fisher
Decatur, Georgia
September 2, 2013

INTRODUCTION } *A Disney Monastic*

Is it possible to have a religious experience, to discover the truth about God, to deepen your relationship with Christ, and to discern how to respond to the call of the Spirit at the Walt Disney World Resort?

I believe the answer is yes. A modern-day monastic lives, works and plays in the world but creates a spiritual window, an intentional space, looking into the situations and circumstances that are so often taken for granted. By becoming a modern-day monastic, you can transform your spiritual, work and play life. A Disney Monastic is someone who believes this transformation can occur at the place where dreams come true.

Are you a Disney Monastic? The answer to that question can be found as you work through the spiritual exercises in this guide to everyday monastic living

As a person of faith, I believe that we are able to encounter God in new and powerful ways when we create intentional space, holy space, sacred space. We go to Walt Disney World to retreat, yes? Walt Disney once said, "Our heritage and ideals, our code and standards - the things we live by and teach our children - are preserved or diminished by how freely we exchange ideas and feelings."[1] Taking the time to figure out what we are retreating from, and for what reasons, can provide incredible insight into the vitality of one's spiritual and religious life. A Disney Monastic believes the window of the world's most popular theme park is the ideal backdrop for this kind of spiritual discernment. For me, Walt Disney World is sacred space. As we enter into sacred space, we realize that everything we say and do matters. If we remember that we are inhabiting sacred space, every single moment of our lives, everything we say and everything we do has the potential for deep meaning.

Many may choose to work through this pilgrim's guidebook while at the Walt Disney World Resort. Others may be at home, on the beach, at work, or even at worship hoping to spend an intentional moment learning something about their relationship with God. Some may work through this guidebook starting with the first chapter and finishing up with the last chapter. Others may choose to work through one section during each visit to a Disney theme park. The spiritual journey is constantly ongoing, a prayer without ceasing.

STARTING THE SPIRITUAL JOURNEY

It is easy to compartmentalize, to divide life into segments, to separate "this" from "that," attempting to make the scattered pieces of life manageable. Family. Friends. Work. Play. Church.

School. Vacation. Vocation. All the pieces matter. The difficult work of the spiritual sojourner is praying them, living them, redeeming them, integrating them, synergizing all of it, during every moment of every day.

Like anything in life that matters, intentionality, discipline, awareness, passion and fun is the key to offering it all to God. If you believe God is constantly working, constantly transforming and constantly reaching out to you, right here, right now, wherever you are, you will discover joy, inspiration and spiritual opportunity on the pages that follow. It is difficult to accept, sometimes it is impossible to believe, that God is with you every moment of your life, especially when you find yourself in a crisis of faith. But I believe if you practice spiritual intentionality, you can live into this truth. To truly accept this means there are implications to every choice you make and the importance of future actions you take.

Our spiritual journey is how we seek to find and to recognize our place in the spiritual story. For Christians, this context is beyond the pages of the Hebrew Scriptures, the Gospels and the New Testament. Can I discover how to follow the Gospel call of Jesus, feeding my spiritual hunger and feeding others? Finding inspiration in Judith, I wonder if I have what it takes to lead others to success and victory? Following in the footsteps of Peter, am I stuck in my insecurities, preventing me from accepting how God is working through me in everything I do? Trying to live into challenges written about in Paul's letters, will I ever be able to articulate my relationship with God through Jesus Christ so that it makes sense to me and to others? I believe through prayer and intentionality the answer is a qualified yes!

It is easy to get lost and forget everything that God shares with us. As we move through our everyday lives, we get overwhelmed, distracted, and exhausted, often forgetting who we are and why we were created and for what purpose. We numb out. We run on automatic. We compartmentalize. We disengage. We fall asleep. But the sleeper must awaken. To be awake, fully alive and present to the possibilities of life, we must pray and we must claim space to develop a prayerful awakedness. This may seem overwhelming, but to pray without ceasing is to step into the figments of the imagination that we often ignore and discard as invaluable.

I believe if we walk through life developing this spiritual state of mind, we will encounter God in the most unusual and surprising cracks and crevices of this world. God delights in us. God delights in this world. God calls us to live and move and have our being in the incredible vastness of the people created by God's command. Where we feel the most alive is where God is working, calling and reaching out to us the most. We must be fully present, looking around, praying to discover the fingerprint of God in the midst of this energy rush.

We live in a world where we settle for security. We want to take care of our families. We want to spend time with our friends. We seek out community in hopes of smoothing out the rough edges within ourselves. It is easy for us to trade our passions for security and survival. We get caught in a rut.

A Disney Monastic tries to get out of the quicksand and go on living. Retreats call us to remember. Vacations call us to escape and relax. When retreats and vacations are over, we often find ourselves back where we started. We left our prayers at the retreat. We left our passions on the beach, at the mountaintop, or in the amusement park where we vacationed. Depression sets in as we return to "real life." But "real life" is everywhere. We never escape it.

My prayer is that you discover your passions, see how they connect with your spiritual beliefs, and then find a way to incorporate these realities into the rhythm of everyday life. Rhythm is the key. Understanding the chances and changes of that rhythm is fundamental.

The monastic life is all about rhythm. Prayer is on schedule. Eating times are consistent. Monastics sleep and wake with the rhythm of time of day. Monastics dress, move and work in accordance with the seasons of the year. Your task is to discover the rhythm of a modern-day monastic. That rhythm has been done in the past. You can do it. You can do it today, right here, right now.

I have discovered Walt Disney World to be a place of spiritual retreat, challenge and empowerment. My friends think I am nuts! My colleagues think I am out of my mind! But then we talk, share, take a rest, and sit in the moment. As I share my passions for the world that Disney built, they get a temporary glimpse of a spiritual spark that occurs when I move about the resort.

My family has been traveling to the Walt Disney World Resort every year since it opened. It has been a place where we have gathered to dream, to celebrate, to mourn, to forget, to reclaim and to remember. I have vacationed there during times of great joy. I have traveled there during times of great sorrow. For me, it has always been a place to imagine a world beyond the circumstances of my present reality, to hear the story, to get lost in wonder, to wish upon a star, and to ultimately claim and remember who I am and what God prays that I will accomplish in this world.

Many of us save for days, months and years to afford a Walt Disney World vacation. We surrender some of our experiences based on the economic choices we have made. When we are trying to get the most for our money, we often enter the parks at the crack of dawn, running and playing and eating and drinking all day, hardly pausing, until the parks close at night. We return to our rooms exhausted, tired, unfulfilled, and probably totally unaware of the experiences we have just had.

My prayer for you is that this travel guide will help you to enter the resort, to create intentional time and space, so your response will be to act in a new and different way. Then, and only then, can you experience the true magic that is Walt Disney World. Dream, imagine, listen and hear the story, then act like it all matters. It does.

For example, notice the partner's statue with Walt and Mickey at the castle intersection. Sit with Roy and Minnie just beyond the train station and look out at the world of dreams. Fly with Aladdin. Dive with Ariel. Travel with the Yeti. Drive with Aerosmith. It is all there, and you can experience it to the fullest, with God's help.

On July 17, 1955, Walt Disney welcomed all to the theme park experience with the following words: "To all who come to this happy place, Welcome. Disneyland is your land. Here, age relives fond memories of the past, and here youth may savor the challenge and promise of the future. Disneyland is dedicated to the ideals, the dreams, and the hard facts that have created America, with the hope that it will be a source of joy and inspiration to all the world."

Take the first step. It matters.

How to Use This Travel Guide

The fourteen chapters that follow work through familiar but challenging spiritual questions that often disrupt our journey with God. These questions are often overwhelming or ignored because we do not know how to create the space or time with God to examine them. When our faith is challenged, if we are lucky, we have prayed, studied and examined these questions before. If we have considered these questions before, when we bump up against them, we don't get thrown totally out of whack. We have created a foundational resource to sustain us during these challenging moments.

Whether you are at home, at work, or at the Walt Disney World Resort, this book is designed to help you create a spiritual foundation so that you can move through spiritually challenging times, maintaining some sense of strength, rhythm and normality while feeling the presence of God.

Following each question are reflections to help you live intentionally through the unique experiences of your spiritual journey. Just because you have moved through a crisis of faith doesn't mean you won't come up against it again. In fact, it may even reappear within the hour! But, intention, space, awareness and discipline help us to find the power of God through repetition and familiarity. This is what a monastic life is all about.

The reflection methods for the Disney Monastic begin at the "Main Gate." We read the focusing question that may even bring up more questions. In "In the Queue" we learn what to do while we wait, hoping to discover how to move forward, to react and to respond. We often examine where we have been, where we are and where we are going. Next, we look to scripture to see the answers that others on the journey with God have discovered. In "Ride the Attraction," if we are lucky enough to be at the Walt Disney World Resort, we ride the ride to discover and see how our spiritual questions are portrayed and addressed through images created by popular culture. Often, we seek out and listen to the experiences of others and how they have reflected on the same questions we are working on. "The E-Ticket" is where we combine all of what we have discovered and learned and come up with our own answers. We create a personal theological reflection. As we write our reflection, we look at the spiritual question; we examine how our faith tradition answers that question; we look at answers offered in book, film, television, drama, and any and all cultural sources. We conclude the reflection stating what we believe so that we can pray and hope to discover how to act. The final section of each chapter is in "The Collect," where we ask God to be continually with us on the journey.

This is how this book is set up.

You may choose to move through the book from start to finish. You may relate to the "Main Gate" and choose to do some work with the material in that section of each chapter. You may want to learn how to feel comfortable praying so you may want to just focus on "The Collect." You may want to create a Rule of Life and decide to move through the work found in the "E-Ticket." You may need help writing your personal spiritual autobiography. This is the work "In the Queue."

However you choose to move forward, my prayer is that you do step out, be intentional, discover you life's context and create new meaning, encountering God in powerful and exciting ways.

I suggest that you work through the "Sojourners" chapter from start to finish, then pray about how you want to move through the book.

Many have journeyed this way before, some seeking adventure, others seeking fortune while still others seek blessing. No matter what they seek, all wanted to know God.

May God be with you on your journey. If you can dream it, you can do it.

The Rev. Kevin M. Goodman
Chicago, Illinois
December 1, 2013

Endnotes

[1] (Smith, 1994, p. 3)

SOJOURNERS } *Where Am I Going?*

 ## MAIN GATE

Where am I going?

A journey at Walt Disney World begins once you enter the Main Gate. Within the midst of several intersecting highways, there are several gates allowing access to the 48-square mile resort. You determine how you wish to enter. It could be by going through the gate that is most convenient, perhaps closest to your ultimate park destination. To keep traffic around the resort moving, highway transportation controls attempt to manage crowds efficiently and effectively so you may not really have a choice about how you enter. But, once you pass through the Main Gate, you need to know where you are going.

Am I going to The Magic Kingdom? Am I eating at the California Grill atop the Contemporary Resort? Am I heading over to The Living Seas to dive with the dolphins? Am I hoping to celebrate life with Cirque du Soleil at Downtown Disney?

As you pass through the Main Gate at the Walt Disney World Resort, a sign of greeting with Mickey Mouse and Minnie Mouse welcomes you to the place "where dreams come true."

What do you dream for?

A place where dreams come true conjures up many images, most of them exciting. Some dreams are seductive and seem impossible to live into. Others lead to some dark spaces. Often we spend a significant amount of time recovering from dashed dreams so we become determined not to dream anymore. But the reality is, in order to live life to the fullest, you must be moving somewhere towards something. Dare to dream.

A spiritual journey begins with a vision of what happens at the end. You can envision a journey that will take an hour, a day, a week, a month, a year or even a lifetime. You might be mapping out several journeys at once. Or you might have only enough energy to focus on one. But in order to go somewhere, you must have an idea of where you are going.

In order to develop a vital spiritual self, you must have some vision of what a spiritual self looks like, if not within yourself, at least in someone else.

As Christians, we are given a vision of the resurrected Jesus - a promise held out to us by God proclaiming new life after death. But, we do have to step into death to get there. This is a challenging Main Gate. We have to move from Step A to Step B. Our resurrection hope is that God will fulfill God's promise to us, a promise of new life beyond death.

That is what I believe. What do you believe? What you believe shapes your vision of yourself. Pray carefully.

Once you know where you are going, you must figure out how to get there using maps, spiritual guides, measurable benchmarks, immeasurable faith.

You need vision, a plan, and discipline to get there. You cannot move without vision. We cannot take a spiritual journey if we don't have a vision of ourselves at the other end.

Disney Monastics are spiritual pilgrims on a journey to discover God in the midst of everyday, common life.

What is your vision of yourself at the end of this life? Is your vision a resurrected body? Does your vision include an entrance to the gates of heaven?

Where are you going?

Ask yourself, "Where am I going?"

IN THE QUEUE

At the Walt Disney World Resort, we spend a lot of time in line. A friend of mine once pointed out that there are very few places in this world that teach us more about the rhythm of life than a Disney Park queue line. We wait in line to experience an attraction or a show, to eat, and to go to the bathroom.

At the entrance, we must pass through the gate without knowing exactly where we are going or what we are getting into. Perhaps we have heard from others what awaits us on the other side of the line. Maybe we enter the Queue without really knowing anything.

Once we enter, the queue line travels back and forth, back and forth, and back and forth. We loose a sense of space. Context drops away as a sea of faces and shoulders surrounds us. We must be patient. We must stand. We must wait. We breathe. We move. We walk. As we round the bend, we feel as if we are getting nowhere. But we are getting somewhere even when we feel we are stuck in Never Never Land.

At *Peter Pan's Flight,* we simply move back and forth, sometimes not moving at all. The roof is right above us and people we do not know are right beside us. Our personal space disappears.

In *Ellen's Energy Adventure*, we are invited into a pre-show area where we are provided the context of the story and what the ride experience will expose us to. There are several screens. The auditorium is dark. We meet Ellen in her apartment where she is watching *Jeopardy*. She falls asleep and we are invited to ride "Ellen's dream."

At *Expedition Everest*, we are presented with a story that enables us to discover our place within the attraction about to unfold. We are fully immersed. We are explorers. We want to meet the Yeti. Will we find the courage to move forward?

In *Soaring*, we play interactive video games to distract ourselves from time spent in the queue. The games presented seem to have little relation to what the ride will be about. There is no context here, just the hope that we haven't spent wasted, unproductive time that may ultimately have no payoff.

While waiting in line, we realize that we are moving somewhere. Later we discover that we are at the front of the line. We are called out of a dream state when a Disney cast member asks, "How many in your party?" Perhaps we will have made it to the front of the line realizing that we do not have what it takes to get on the ride. What will we do? Often, we proceed with hesitation and fear.

With intentionality, we can get work done while moving through the queue. As my friend pointed out, we learn patience. We learn to create space. We learn how to be with the other, even if it is uncomfortable. We talk to friends and family who are with us. We look at others in the line and we wonder what they are doing there. Like a spiritual journey, life in the queue is full of ambiguity. But with a wish and a little imagination, life in the queue is filled with possibility.

In the context of this travel guide, "In the

Queue" is where we pause to see how we got to where we are. We reflect on simple questions to remind us that we are in the presence of God. The questions we ask ourselves while "In the Queue" determine the outcome of our situation. We must choose our questions carefully. If our questions are about God, we will think about God. If our questions are about marriage, we will think about marriage. If our questions are about gambling, we will think about gambling. What we think about "In the Queue" shapes who we are and how we are, or are not, going to live into the vision we have of ourselves.

To do the work while waiting "In the Queue," you will need a journal. Questions "In the Queue" will hopefully encourage and empower your spirit to spend some of this in-between time thinking about God and how you have lived and are living your life.

"In the Queue" is where we will write our spiritual autobiography. In the "E-Ticket," we develop a personal "Rule of Life."

A spiritual autobiography is a journal, a diary of sorts, about our walk with God. It records major transitions of life. It may recall our baptism or marriage or when we first read the Bible or had a sense that we had encountered the risen Christ. It celebrates when God felt close, present and alive. It ponders the times when God felt absent, nonexistent, unresponsive, totally elusive.

There are several ways for us to create our spiritual autobiographies. We will record our lives using a timeline method. As we develop our timelines and as we recall our spiritual stories, we will become holy people and we will find ourselves in God's story. We create a vision of ourselves and then discern the steps we must take to live into that vision. This spiritual guide will primarily invite you to record your spiritual autobiography in a series of circumstantial timelines.

Following a Rule of Life is another way to live into our vision, God's vision, of ourselves. A Rule of Life is used by Monastic Communities to organize and order their common life. The Rule of St. Benedict was created around 500 AD by St. Benedict of Nursia to create community and to spell out the authority between the leader of the community, an abbot, and those who live in the community, the monks. Monastic communities throughout all time have adapted the Rule of St. Benedict. We will use this to develop a framework for our own.

A Rule of Life is a manuscript, a personal creed, that will help us get back on track when we forget who we are and for what purpose we were created. We use a Rule of Life to live into our vision of God's created person, our spiritual selves.

A Rule of Life is a guidebook that holds us accountable. This guidebook shows us how to live with God and God's people on our best days. It helps us remember who we are when the circumstances of life are getting the best of us and we are having a bad day. A Rule of Life empowers us to find rhythm, balance and health within a world begging for our attention and distracting us from the things that matter.

In 1997, the Society of Saint John the Evangelist (SSJE) made their Community Rule public, encouraging and inspiring people everywhere to create their own Rule. A personal rule establishes the relationship with the leader of the community, God, and those who were created by God to love God and to love each other.

How am I going to order my life so that I have a relationship accountable to God? How am I going to order my life so that I can successfully be in relationship with others?

I have drawn on the SSJE's rule for sections of "In the Queue." On the history of the rule, the SSJE says, "Although communities can flourish spontaneously and informally for a while, gathered under the leadership of charismatic founders or in response to an urgent purpose, the need soon arises for an instrument which will articulate the identity of the community, express its ruling values and ideas, and specify its practices…(I)t enables the Church to confirm and validate the vocation of the community and hold it accountable."[1]

To create a personal spiritual autobiography and a Rule of Life, you will need a journal. In this journal, you will do the work of "In the Queue." This journal will get a lot of use. I encourage you to see it as a living workbook, something you can change or rework as God's relationship with you becomes clear, fulfilling and sustainable.

In each chapter that follows, you will be given guidance in the "In the Queue" section to create a precept. Each precept becomes a part of your Rule of Life. If you work through every "In the Queue" section in this travel guide, you will have 18 precepts for your personal Rule of Life. This is an incredible tool for keeping you focused during your spiritual journey.

Let's begin.

On the first page of your journal write the words "Holy Story." Put your name beneath the words. Then, flip to the back page of the journal and write "My Rule of Life." Put your name beneath the words.

You will be working on your Rule from the back of your journal moving forward. You will be working on your spiritual autobiography or your "Holy Story" from the front backwards.

This is your work. I believe an active Rule creates a very large space for forgiveness and grace to work within you. Nothing written in your journal is definitive. You might consider writing in pencil. If you are brave, write in pen! But always remember, this is a workbook. It is a space to examine your spiritual journey with God and how that impacts your prayers and actions in the world.

"In the Queue" is the space where you begin

to move through and wait within and walk forward with others as you prepare for the attraction, the main event, the ride of a lifetime.

Each time you work "In the Queue," you must claim the time and space for the work. If you are at home or in a hotel or at work, intentionally set some time apart. You can do this in several ways. Light a candle. Burn some incense. Minimally, you must claim the space by shutting down all things that beg for your attention - phones, music, partners or spouses, and even children. Easier said than done! But do your best to claim the space and mark the time. Don't be discouraged if the things you love and take care of creep in occasionally!

If you are on the Walt Disney World property, in the theme park, hotel, or Downtown Disney, you may want to read some of the reflective questions before entering a Queue line. Then, move through the line, gathering thoughts and insights so you can write them down later.

After you have gathered your thoughts, find a place to sit comfortably. Chances are there is movement all around, sound busting through, color seducing the eyes and smell awakening your senses.

Sit with your journal. Take five minutes to claim the space by looking around. Be aware of what is going on. What are people doing? Are they riding an attraction? Are they waiting? Are they eating? Are they happy? Are they frustrated? Are they energetic? Are they tired? Are they aware of what is going on around them?

Claim the space by being very aware of what is going on around you. Notice the thoughts and feelings of others. Be aware of your thoughts and feelings. Are you comfortable? Why or why not?

Once you have set intentional time and claimed your space within your particular surroundings, begin the work of "In the Queue." Start with a prayer. Pray the following prayer:

"Holy God, author of life and lover of humankind, you imagined my sacred story when you created me. Help me recognize your presence in my journey of life. May your creative spirit empower me to claim and continue to write a Holy Story. May I be an instrument of your peace. Be with me where I worship, work, play and live. I ask this in your holy name. Amen."

Next "In the Queue" will ask you questions about your Story. Open your journal. Read the questions. Reflect. Record the answers in the "Holy Story" section of your workbook.

What is your first memory of God in your life? Where were you? What were you doing? Describe the scene in detail. What were you thinking? How were you feeling?

Is God knowable?

If your answer is yes, how do you know God? If not, what do you want from God?

Outside of worship in a gathered community, how else do you experience God in this world?

Next, "In the Queue" will ask you to reflect on how and why you act and react the way you do.

Read the questions.

Reflect.

Record your answers in the Rule of Life section of your journal.

As you begin to work on your Rule, consider the following questions to gather your thoughts.

Who is God to me? What types of prayer am I familiar with? What types of prayer do I practice? During the course of a week, ask yourself how much time you spend developing your relationship with God and is it enough?

After you have considered, reflected and prayed on these questions, write your first rule. Use the following as a guide.

GOD

"God is _____. I experience God best _____. I work on my relationship with God by _____. I dedicate my life to God by _____.

The work of "In the Queue" is designed to deepen your relationship with God and with others. I pray that you will be successful at integrating reflections and insights so that true transformation by the spirit occurs and is recognizable.

Walt Disney always kept things in perspective. "Let's remember that this all started with a mouse."

For God, for Christians, for Disney, the work "In the Queue" often ignited a creative spark, a burst of light, a separation of the waters, a creation of Paradise, and an awareness of God and the world around us.

 # FROM THE BOOK
The Revelation to John 1:8 & Proverbs 29:18

What does Holy Scripture have to say to me right here, right now, in the midst of my life?

The Bible is made up of the collected books of Hebrew Scripture, the Gospels and the collected letters of The New Testament. It offers us an incredible library covering the breadth and depth of God's relationship with God's people.

The Hebrew Scriptures repeatedly illustrate our personal distaste of listening to anyone else. Patriarchs and matriarchs, judges and kings, prophets and wisdom writers, none of them were held in high regard by the people God called them to serve. As Christians, we profess that it took God becoming one of us to get us to listen. In the person of Jesus Christ, we discover how to live, love and serve. By the power of the spirit, we still have to listen. Through the parables and ministry of Jesus, we see how to live.

I am always amazed with people who speak as if they know what the Bible has to say on one thing or another and have never read it. These "Bible thumpers" rid Holy Scripture of the power and truths about God. We must stop listening to them and look to the pages of the Bible itself. Like everything, we must discern context - cultural, historical and circumstantial - so that we understand what the living word is actually trying to say to us right here, right now.

The Bible is powerful when it calls us to hear what is being proclaimed and then to sit within the embracing arms of the spirit, recalling what the words meant to the people who first heard them thousands of years ago and to try to discover what these words mean in today's particular context. If I listen to the words of Scripture while calling upon the power of the spirit, I can act and react and bring about the kingdom of God with the help of God and of God's people.

In this travel guide, "From the Book" invites us to study and engage with Holy Scripture. Biblical passages are included to help us answer some of life's difficult questions and to claim our place in God's holy story.

Scripture is important as we reflect and create our spiritual autobiography and formulate our Rule of Life. Each chapter that follows contains a scripture passage, encouraging us to find context and meaning in our lives. If we are lucky enough to be using this travel guide at the Walt Disney World Resort, we discover that these scripture passages have been paired with a ride at one of the Theme Parks. We ride the ride and ponder how Scripture and Culture speak, how they are similar and how they are different.

"From the Book" begins with a brief contextual introduction. You will be introduced to the cultural setting of the scripture passage and the theological context of the work we are doing today.

Let's begin the work "From the Book."

Where am I going?

We have two brief scripture passages to help us to reflect on this simple question.

The Book of Revelation is a colorful and complex book of images often used by Christians today to scare people from loving Christ. This was not the writer's intention. Our church's tradition asserts that John, the same author of "The Gospel of John," compiled its message. Scholarship suggests several other viable possibilities.

The Book of Revelation was actually written as a piece of encouragement and hope, inviting Christians and anyone who discovers they are trapped in persecution and inequality that Christ is with them always. Christ was there in the beginning at the creation of the world. Christ is here now, in the stuff of everyday life. Christ will be there for us in the end, moving us forward into the presence of God in the resurrected life.

Tradition suggests that The Book of Proverbs is a collection of poems and teachings from Solomon. According to 2 Samuel, Solomon was David's son from Bathsheba. He became King after David.

Scholarship suggests that the book is made up of several collections, each containing moral teachings filtered through a system of values inspired by the spirit of Lady Wisdom. The collection can probably be dated around the sixth century, following the exile of the Hebrew people.

The Revelation to John 1:8
"I am the Alpha and the Omega," says the Lord God, who is and who was and who is to come, the Almighty. [2]

Proverbs 29:18
Where there is no prophecy, the people cast off restraint, but happy are those who keep the law. [3]

RIDE THE ATTRACTION
"Please Stand Clear of the Doors."

In "Ride the Attraction," we ride a popular

attraction at Walt Disney World to see how images from popular culture comment on our religious beliefs, spiritual questions, and holy traditions as we prepare for reflection. Within the context of this travel guide, culture speaks through the rides and attractions of the Disney Parks.

Walt Disney was fascinated with modes of transportation. Throughout the Walt Disney World Resort, guests have several choices to make about how to get from Point A to Point B.

Walt Disney began his love of transportation through a fascination with trains. "Trains held an almost mystical fascination for Walt Disney, dating back to his Missouri farm days when he waved to his engineer uncle. As an adult, it gave him pleasure to visit the Southern Pacific station in Glendale, a few miles from his Los Feliz home, to feel the vibration of the tracks and then watch the passenger trains pass on the route to San Francisco. He delighted in operating his electric train for visitors to his office. Among them were two Disney operators, Ward Kimball, who had a full-size railroad on his property, and Ollie Johnston, who was building a one-twelfth scale steam train at his home." [4] Inspired by his friends, Walt Disney would eventually build a train in his backyard. As you approach The Magic Kingdom, you hear the trains inviting you to climb aboard and explore the themed lands of fantasy and adventure.

Prior to arriving on the property of the Walt Disney World Resort, you will have to make several decisions about transportation. How am I going to get to where I want to go?

The Walt Disney World Resort in Florida is made up of 48 square miles of themed entertainment. The property was secretly acquired by purchasers made on behalf of the Walt Disney Company with names such as the Reedy Creek Ranch Corporation, Latin-American Development and Management Corporation, Bay Lake Properties, Inc. On May 4, 1965, the Orlando Sentinel reported a rumor that Walt Disney was buying this land for a new Disneyland. They were correct. Construction began and Walt would die a year later. His brother Roy would take up the charge to complete the vision.

To get around the expansive resort, guests choose to take several forms of transportation - car, bus, boat, tram and monorail - just to name a few. "From the stagecoaches of the Old West to the technological marvels of the future, Walt Disney spent his entire life fascinated with modes of travel, old and new. His theme-park vision incorporated numerous ways to transport visitors around without detracting from the scenery or polluting the environment. Whether by land, air, or water, there's always more than one way to journey." [5]

If you are traveling to the Magic Kingdom, you may choose to ride a monorail, a boat, a bus or you may choose to even walk. If you choose to board the monorail, the excitement begins as you prepare to depart for your journey and you hear "Please stand clear of the doors, por favor mantengase alejado de las puertas."

On the journey to The Magic Kingdom, guests pass through the lobby of the Contemporary Hotel. As a young boy, I would always feel a rush of excitement as the monorail entered the A-frame hotel and I glimpsed the beautiful lobby containing huge mural tributes to the Grand Canyon.

As soon as the monorail exited the Contemporary, I would get the latest glimpse of *Space Mountain, Splash Mountain* and Cinderella's Castle. Roy O. Disney dedicated the Magic Kingdom on October 1, 1971. He dedicated The Magic Kingdom on October 1, 1971 with a vision that Walt Disney World would bring joy and inspiration to all who visited, where the young at heart of all ages could laugh, play and learn together. The Magic Kingdom is located at the most northern part of the property.

Heading south from Cinderella's Castle, you move past Disney Springs on the eastern part of the property. This part of the property has also been known as Disney Village, Downtown Disney, Disney Marketplace and Disney Westside. It is now the resort's premier shopping district while hosting entertainment venues such as Cirque Du Soleil and House of Blues. The waterside mall draws on the inspiration of Florida's waterfront towns and is divided into four sections: the Town Center, the Landing, the Marketplace and West Side. Guests get to Disney Springs primarily by boat, car or bus.

Moving west just a bit, guests travel between Epcot Center and Disney's Hollywood Studios. Epcot opened in October 1982 and gets its name from the acronym of Experimental Prototype Community of Tomorrow. Walt Disney bought the Florida property primarily with the dream of building the city of tomorrow. With the vision of bringing together corporations and creative thinkers of tomorrow, Walt believed this about Epcot: "It's like the city of tomorrow ought to be. A city that caters to the people as a service function. It will be a planned, controlled community, a showcase for American industry and research, schools, cultural and educational opportunities." [6] Walt's vision evolved into Disney World's second theme park and it is my personal favorite. Epcot consists of two distinct areas - Future World and World Showcase. Future World is a celebration of technology, enterprise and ingenuity. World Showcase is a celebration of the nations and people of our planet home, Spaceship Earth. Guests arrive by monorail, boat, bus and car.

Beyond Disney's Hollywood Studios, far west, is Disney's Animal Kingdom. This is the largest theme park on the resort property. In incredibly understated restraint, it presents all the best that Walt Disney World has to offer - story, memories, technology, education and concern for all creatures. The Tree of Life beckons guests to journey deep into the forest and to visit the continents of Africa and Asia by climbing aboard safari vehicles and roller-coaster trains that climb to the highest peaks of the Himalayas. Time-traveling vehicles transport guests to the times of the dinosaurs and back, all within a matter a minutes.

The ESPN Sports Complex is the destination for athletes both young and old. Moving south across the multiple sports arenas, the resort continues south, across HWY 192, ending at the township of Celebration.

The Walt Disney Company all started with a mouse named Mickey, an animated character with stories to share. Then, from within California orange groves, Disneyland, where stories came to life in front of family and friends, was built. Ultimately, these characters inspired the building of a city in the middle of the Florida swamplands, an Experimental Prototype Community of Tomorrow, where, through the power of our imagination, we could be good stewards of the earth, utilizing technology to enhance urban life.

Building on Walt Disney's fascination with transportation, The Disney Imagineers created, designed and built imaginative ways of moving people from Point A to Point B. Monorails, boats, people movers, parking lot trams, a fleet of buses, and steam trains transport the traveler, comfort the journeyer and encourage the faithful to move forward and claim the moment. The pilgrim's spiritual journey is the same. We move from here to there in hopes of discovering something new about God and how God is involved in every choice we make and every moment of life we pass through.

As Christians, we hear comforting words from the Book of Revelation. "I am the Alpha and the Omega, says the Lord God, who was and is and is to come." God is with us, wherever we are on the journey of life, right here, right now. Jesus lived so that I might live more fully. Jesus died so that He could be with me in suffering. Jesus rose again to show me that new life is the sign of a powerful God.

Walt Disney World has been imagineered to control and shape our experiences. "Disney, with its bricolage of themes within themes, is also the muse of decontextualization. History, geography, politics, language, the present, nature, even nutrition are annihilated in WDW stories and practices. Through this process a huge space is opened up for a context-free vision of technology that if 'we' use 'our' imaginations, this will allow 'us' to control our 'fun' future." [7] Whenever we enter a controlled environment, our intentions are often forgotten and our perception of reality is replaced by someone else's. By creating intentional space as we ride the attraction, we can encounter and discover some of our faith tradition's most difficult questions as we move around the Walt Disney World Resort. As you move through this travel guide, you will have choices to make. Which questions do you want to work through? How do you want to live your life? What is God calling for you to do right here, right now? The themed attractions created by the Imagineers of the Walt Disney Company invite us to ponder love, life, death, action, reaction, imagination and resurrection.

Be intentional when deciding how you will move from Point A to Point B.

FOR REFLECTION

Daily reflection and prayer focused on our journey with God is an essential part of the spiritual journey. The experience gleaned from reflection will sustain and inform our experience when we find ourselves in a crisis of faith.

"For Reflection" is a theological meditation in which you consider everything that you have experienced in hopes of creating a reflection based on what you believe and why you believe it. Here, you will find my personal reflections to inspire and help you prepare to write your own in the "E-Ticket"

section, immediately following "For Reflection."

We cannot get anywhere without a vision. Philippe Petit had a vision: the year -1968, the city - Paris, France.

Philippe's vision would keep him up every night, for many years to come. The vision was breathtaking. The task seemed impossible. The steps needed to move from A to B seemed simply overwhelming.

But every vision begins with a first step.

Like most visions, it came to him unexpectedly and at the most inopportune time. Philippe was at the dentist's office sitting in the waiting room. An unbearable toothache had brought him to this moment. He couldn't think. He was unable to focus.

What could possibly calm a busy mind? How could he escape such miserable suffering? Philippe didn't know what to do.

He picked up a magazine, flipped through a few pages, and then it happened - a vision. It was a moment of much beauty. It was as if he were totally inspired. But how to respond? To live into a vision we must be willing to take the first step. He knew that in order to feel totally alive, he had to follow through. It would take six years of work to live into his dentist-office vision.

What is your vision of yourself? Who are you? Where have you been? Where do you want to go? Every vision begins with a first step.

John the Baptist had a vision. It was a vision of a God that wanted to know God's people.

John ran through villages, cried out in the desert, proclaimed his vision from the river's edge.

"Prepare the way of the Lord… Make the paths straight. Repent. Turn toward God. Bring everything you have to offer."

His call was issued with a sense of urgency. His message was daunting to those who were desperately trying to understand God. His enthusiasm to the spiritual traveler struggling to just put one foot in front of the other was probably a bit overwhelming.

Prepare now!

Prepare for God!

Prepare the way of the Lord.

We hear John's call. Jesus is coming. Get ready.

Whenever I hear John calling out to me, I always respond, "Who? Me? Me prepare?

Prepare the way of the Lord?"

What does that mean?

What do I have to do?

I am most frustrated and I feel the most anxiety when I am trying to figure out what to do.

While waiting to see the dentist, Philippe Petit was flipping through a magazine. He read a story about construction in lower Manhattan. The article contained architectural images of the plans to build the world's two tallest skyscrapers side by side. The construction site was the World Trade Center. The two main buildings were the Twin Towers.

Philippe drew a cable, connecting the two towers, and the vision to walk between them, man on wire, grew that very day.

It would take six years to make his vision a reality. First, Philippe learned everything he could about the towers. He traveled to New York several times visiting the construction site, breaking in and spending nights near the top, observing building crews, security personnel and reading and stealing tenant plans.

From his notes, he was able to create a fake ID so he could move about freely between the two towers, recording how much the buildings swayed in the wind and how to look at the sky in order to predict upcoming weather conditions.

At home in Paris, he practiced on a wire that mimicked the 200-foot distance between the Twin Towers. Walking. Balancing. Kneeling down. Resting. Standing up. Then walking across the wire some more.

After months of practice, he added wind, generated by jet engines approximating wind conditions 110 stories up. Looking ahead. Stepping out. The rush of the wind currents. The tossing about of the wire.

Finally, he began to design the rigging. How would he attach the wire to the towers? What about the cavaletti lines to steady the wire? How could they be rigged? Drawings. Calculations. Engineering. Practice. Stamina. Preparing the way.

Philippe's vision demanded a balanced response of planning, practice, and action.

"Prepare the way of the Lord, make the paths straight. Every valley shall be filled, and every mountain and hill shall be made low, and the crooked shall be made straight, and the rough ways made smooth; and all flesh shall see the salvation of God."

John the Baptist had a vision. It was a vision of a spiritual journey, inviting us to turn away from everything that separates us from God and to turn away from everything that separates us from God's people. It is a daunting task. It is an overwhelming vision. It is an invitation to go on a journey.

You must be willing to step out, to recognize the barriers that have been placed between you and God's people because these are the same barriers that are ultimately separating you from God.

If you listen to John's call, if you say "yes" to Jesus' invitation to follow Him, with God's help you will begin to discern the steps of your spiritual journey.

Every vision begins with a first step. You must ask yourself, do I really want to take this journey? Do I want to be a follower of Jesus? Do I have what it takes to be called a Christian?

If you say "yes" and take the first step, you will be changed forever.

Like Philippe's vision of walking the wire, God's vision for us demands waiting, discipline, practice and action. Do you want to step out on the wire and discover how to live and to love, to eat and to feed, to heal and to give, to receive and to serve, to walk into death and know that there is life beyond death's valley, to love God and to love God's people?

A spiritual journey with Jesus is often a tightrope walk between here and there. It is the struggle between who you think you are and who God knows you to be.

Do you trust God enough to say "yes"?

Mountains. Valleys. Rocky roads. Crooked paths. There is a lot standing between you and God.

You must start with a vision of what your life with Jesus looks like. You must have a vision of what you want your journey with God to be. Without this vision, you will sit alone in a waiting room feeling the pain of despair and the anxiety about a future you have no vision for.

How can you prepare for a life with God if you have no vision of what it looks like?

After months of preparation, following many years of visioning, French wirewalker Philippe Petit walked into a vision. His amazing call to step out over an abyss of air, conquering the space between here and there, is captured in his book and in the documentary *Man on Wire*, directed by James Marsh.

At midnight, on the morning of August 7, 1974, Philippe's teams were 120 feet apart, on adjacent roofs of the Twin Towers. They attached a pull-string and shot it by arrow between the two buildings. Philippe retrieved the arrow, attached the pull-string to the tower then pulled the wire across 120 feet of sky, suspending it between the two towers.

The wire was 5/8ths of an inch thick.

As the sun began to rise on that foggy morning, Philippe grabbed his balancing pole and stepped out onto the wire.

An interviewer for *Psychology Today* asked Philippe about walking within the space in between the towers. Philippe responded, "I wonder if we can ever be prepared to face a void of such dimensions. I said yes to a vision and prepared as much as I could. That is all we can do. Death frames the high wire. But I don't see myself as taking a risk. I did all of the preparations that a non-death seeker would do. The WTC walk was terrifying. Still, I grabbed the balancing pole, not with the feeling of a man who is about to die, but of a man who was living into a dream that came in a vision."

As the sun was rising, people began stepping out into World Trade Center Plaza. An excited woman called out, "A man is walking on a wire between the two towers!"

Everyone looked up into the foggy Manhattan skyline. There was Philippe. He walked and danced and balanced on the wire for an entire hour.

Philippe shared later, after he was arrested, "As long as I stayed on the wire, I was free."

Do you have a vision of yourself with God? Are you willing to take that first step?

If you look at God face to face, God will demand that you take a step that leads into the streets, into the stable, wandering lost in the desert, calling for justice during the trial, entering a tomb at the time of death, and yelling at God to make it all right. Through the power of faith, and by the promises of God, you are given new life.

It is a vision of sitting in a stable with strangers, moving into the desert, being totally dependent on others, confronting injustices in the city square where entrenched systems loom grand over breaking hearts, and finally sitting with a friend at the time of death, with sure confidence that God has the power to deliver us all from the limitations of this body of flesh.

Are you prepared?

Can you accept this vision?

Every vision begins with a first step.

THE E-TICKET

The E-Ticket is your theological reflection. It takes its name from Disney's premier ticket label. "When Disneyland first opened its doors to the public on July 17, 1955, an adult ticket cost $1 and served as general admission to all areas of the park. Three months later, the park offered ticket books with A, B, and C coupons good for specific rides and attractions throughout Disneyland. The E-ticket entered the Disneyland ticket books in 1959, making its appearance the same year as the Matterhorn, Bobsleds, the Monorail, the Submarine Voyage, and Fantasyland's Autopia." [8]

Holy Story

Recall the major transitions in your life.

Where in your life have you moved from Point A to Point B?

In the "Holy Story" section of your workbook, record the major transitions in your life. What were the transitions? How did you make them? Was it easy or was it difficult? What were the months, dates and years that you associated with the transitions? With each transition, record your thoughts and your feelings.

Spend some time doing this.

Reflect on the two scripture passages - Revelation 1:8 and Proverbs 29:18. What do they each say about God? What do they say about you?

Spend some time in silence. Then reflect upon how you believe God is with you during the important transition times in your life. Write down your reflections.

Now, create a rule about transitions in your life. Move to the back of your journal.

Rule

We have many transitions. Transitions reflect big changes in our lives. I have heard people say that they do not like change. But the fact is, change occurs in every second of our lives. We are constantly changing. I suggest that we are better at dealing with change then we often realize.

Then, write down a rule about a way you handle the changes in this life. Begin with:

Transitions

God is the Alpha and the Omega, is the beginning and the end and is with me always. In the midst of the transitions of this life, God is…

Continue from there.

THE COLLECT

Each chapter ends with "The Collect." A Collect is a prayer that collects our thoughts based on our reflections, proclaiming who we think God is and suggesting how we believe God is present, acting in the world. Like different styles of writing or various forms of poetry and combining syntax and grammar, a Collect is created by using a very simple formula.

By writing a Collect, we gather our thoughts into a precise statement of belief while enhancing and expanding our prayer life.

Here is one of my favorite Collects from *The Book of Common Prayer* according to the use of The Episcopal Church.

"O Lord, you have taught us that without love whatever we do is worth nothing: Send your

Holy Spirit and pour into our hearts your greatest gift, which is love, the true bond of peace and of all virtue, without which whoever lives is accounted dead before you. Grant this for the sake of your only Son Jesus Christ, who lives and reigns with you and the Holy Spirit, one God, now and for ever. Amen."[9] Can you see the formula revealed in the Collect above?

A Collect begins by addressing God by one of God's divine names. In the Collect above, it begins "O Lord."

Then, we use words to describe the actions of God. "You have taught us that without love whatever we do is worth nothing."

Next, we ask God for something based on how we think God acts. "Send your Holy Spirit and pour into our hearts your greatest gift, which is love, the true bond of peace and of all virtue, without which whoever lives is accounted dead before you."

To conclude, we thank God. "Grant this for the sake of you only Son Jesus Christ, who lives and reigns with you and the Holy Spirit, one God, now and for ever. Amen."

Here is another from *The Book of Common Prayer*. Notice the elements are slightly rearranged but are all there.

"Be present, O merciful God, and protect us through the hours of this night, so that we who are wearied by the changes and chances of this life may rest in your eternal changelessness; through Jesus Christ our Lord. Amen." [10]

Open the "Holy Story" section of your journal. Write a Collect based on the work you have done in Chapter 1. Use this simple formula:

1. Address God

2. Describe an action or several actions of God

3. Ask God for something

4. Thank God

By composing this simple Collect, you have moved your prayer life from one step to another.

✦

Endnotes

[1] (Society of St. John the Evangelist., 1997, p. xii)

[2] (May & Metzger, 1973, p. 365 NT)

[3] (May & Metzger, 1973, p. 803 OT)

[4] (Thomas, 1994, p. 213)

[5] (Peterson, 2001, p. 124)

[6] (Smith, 1994, p. 52)

[7] (Fjellman, 1992, p. 24)

[8] (Peterson, 2001, p. 270)

[9] (Episcopal Church., 1979, p. 216)

[10] (Episcopal Church., 1979, p. 216)

CREATION } *How Did I Get Here?*

MAIN GATE

In the film *Pinocchio,* the Blue Fairy says to Pinocchio, "Little puppet made of pine, Wake! The gift of life is thine." This is the beginning.

Let's start at the very beginning. I hear it's a very good place to start.

How did I get here?

We ask this question many times during the circumstances of life. I stop. I look around. I see where I am. I wonder what happened. How did I get here?

Most of the time, I don't have an answer. More to the point, I often don't have time to figure out an answer. I keep moving. There is always something else begging for attention. Another task already at hand. There is somewhere else I need to be. Something else due yesterday. When something is completed, twenty new tasks take its place. I move on. There is no reflective moment.

But there was a beginning to where I find myself right now.

How did I get here? Sometimes there may be more than one answer or several possible suggestions.

What role did God play in creation?

The Book of Genesis gives us two stories of creation. The first creation story is six days of work and one day of rest. The second creation story portrays God as a potter, shaping and forming the mud of the earth into a sexless doll, and breathing life into it. That is how it all started according to the Book of Genesis.

Science suggests that there was a big bang. Gas exploded, causing the universe to expand outward into and through space. We are part of the creation of that explosive moment. What Christians hold to be true, even if we disagree on how it happened, is that God created all of it. God created it and called it good. Although not all Christians believe it is good!

Every day, we encounter people judging others, labeling them and declaring that they are unworthy of God's love. We step over people on the streets, turn away from neighbors in need, run away and ignore people who are mistreating others. We live in a world where people are disposable.

We have lost our basic understanding of the creative moment. God says it is good. God said work and rest. We are working ourselves to death.

How did I get here?

What we believe about Creation and God's relationship to us impacts everything that we say and do.

What did God accomplish when God created this world? What was God's hope when God created me? Will I ever be able to see myself the way God sees me? Will I ever be able to see others as God sees them?

This is the work of the creative moment. We are called to separate the chaos. We are to work to create systems built on love and fairness. We build relationships with God and with each other by inviting others into community. Then we rest and worship and reflect.

When we forget who we are and have no idea about how we got here, our life becomes pointless. Pointlessness leads to an existential crisis.

How did I get here?

We need to stop, breathe, take a moment and look around. Without reflective moments, I am vulnerable. Without retreat, I lose perspective. Without community, I am not accountable. Without accountability, there is no direction. Without direction, I lose hope. In times of crisis, I become easily susceptible to the desires and motivations of others.

I need to recall, discover, and claim.

At the Walt Disney Company, it all began with an Imagineer. What is an *Imagineer*? "You won't find it in the dictionary. But any *Imagineer* can tell you the word is both a verb and a noun. To *imagineer.* To be an Imagineer. Like *Supercalifragilisticexpialidocious,* Imagineering has become a purely Disney word. The name combines imagination with engineering to describe both what (each word does) and who (each one is). Creating a name for a group whose only job is to come up with ideas to build on. (Building) those ideas really took some Imagineering. But that is what Walt Disney was all about."[1]

What was God imagining when God created this world? What was God imagining when God created you and me?

The work of this chapter invites us to take a journey to the beginning.

Our Holy Scripture gives us two explanations of how it all began. At the Walt Disney World Resort, we are invited to consider a third telling of creation in *Ellen's Energy Adventure*. Here, in wonderful, graphic detail, we experience first hand the Big Bang theory. The Big Bang asserts that from a singular ball of gas, a massive explosion occurred.

The circumstances we find ourselves in are often the results of several choices combined with beginnings, middles and ends. In order to be good stewards of God's universe, we must act. If we take the time to reflect before making a choice, we are able to live into choices that are our own. When we reflect then choose, when we consider then decide, when we discover the context then take action, we are truly living.

Walt Disney, reflecting on the success of the Walt Disney Company, said, "Let's not forget, this all started with a mouse."

 IN THE QUEUE

St. Teresa of Avila once said, "The present moment is pregnant with God." It is in the present moment where everything that has ever happened to you or to me happens. In the present moment, I am born. In the present moment, I fall in love. In the present moment, I begin a new job. In the present moment, I suffer a loss.

"The present moment is pregnant with God."

As we move in the queue, our minds tend to drift from the present moment. Sometimes the present moment is too much to deal with. We want to be distracted. We want to feel excitement. We want to be somewhere else. But presently, I am in the queue.

Our work while in the queue is about beginnings.

HOLY STORY

Find and claim intentional space. Then open up to the "Holy Story" section of your journal.

Begin by praying the following prayer.

"Holy God, you are the Alpha and the Omega. You are with me at the beginning and you are with me at the end. Help me feel your Spirit's power as I start a new beginning in my life. Help me feel your Spirit's power as I walk through the endings of my life. Comfort me and grant me your peace. All this I ask in your Holy Name. Amen."

Then, consider the beginnings of your life. Birth. Baptism. New schools. New jobs. New loves. New leases on life. New moments of loss.

Take a moment. Take a breath. Then, create a list of beginnings. If you can, write them down. Try to recall the year, the month, the date, the hour. By each beginning, try to recall details and context.

As your list begins to build and take shape, spend some time to reflect on each beginning. What comes to mind as you recall each event? What were your thoughts, feelings, insights? Where did this beginning lead? You may want to create a mini-timeline for each beginning and follow the direction it took or continues to take.

As you reflect on the timelines of your beginning, ask yourself what went well and what went wrong. Consider the surprises you encountered. Claim the disappointments you discovered.

Finally, as you look at the timelines, look for common themes. Were the beginnings full of hope? Were they full of anxiety? Did you choose this beginning or was it a beginning forced upon you?

Write down the common themes. This will help you create a Rule of Life about beginnings.

MY RULE OF LIFE

Open your journal to your "Rule of Life" section. Consider the statement below. When you are ready, begin to enter your beliefs about beginnings, perhaps using the following formula.

BEGINNINGS

"When I begin something new, God is _____. Beginnings are _____. Some of my best beginnings in life were _____. Some of my most difficult beginnings in life have been _____.

When I experience a new beginning, I will _____. I invite God to be with me during the beginnings of my life by _____.

FROM THE BOOK
Genesis 1:1-2:3 and Genesis 2:4-2:24

How did it all start? How did I get here? What happened? Is there someone I can blame for this mess?

The Hebrew Scriptures, which Christians call the Old Testament, begin with the Book of Genesis. Genesis is a complicated and challenging book. In just fifty chapters, Genesis answers these difficult questions and many more. Genesis contains many of the Bible's most well-known and well-loved stories.

Genesis begins with the story of the Creation. We are presented two versions which are both very compelling but very different approaches to God's creation of the world.

The first creation story tells of God making the world in six days, completing a task, declaring it is good, then resting on the seventh day. The second creation story focuses on the making of humankind from a mud doll. Like a potter, God shapes the doll from the mud of the Earth and then blows breath into it, making it come to life.

The two creation stories come from separate traditions. One introduces us to a God who is distant and creates the world by the power of naming or commanding it to happen. The other features a God who gets down and dirty, reaching into the mud, shaping humans from the very sediments of the

Earth God created.

But as soon as everything is made and declared good, shift happens. Adam and Eve live in Paradise, but they want to be like God. They want knowledge, but are not aware of the responsibility that comes with it. They want to make choices. As the story tells it, the first choice was bad! And we've been afraid to make decisions ever since.

As murder and hate infests Paradise, God uncreates, allowing the chaos of the waters to fall from the heavens and spew up from below the Earth's flat surface. The waters rise up, transporting Noah, his family, and pairs of animals of every kind, to a new creation and it all begins again.

Years later, nations appear and people build a Tower of Babel to be closer to God. The Earth becomes populated with people of every kind. God searches for a faithful person and finds Abraham through whom God will build a nation. The foundation for a covenant relationship with God is prepared by the patriarchs and matriarchs of the Book of Genesis. But that relationship will be broken over and over and over again. The relationship will have to be re-established over and over and over again.

If only we all could have a new beginning, a slate wiped clean, the possibilities are new and exciting: to the beginner, many possibilities, and to the expert, few choices.

GENESIS 1:1-2:3
THE FIRST CREATION STORY

In the beginning when God created the heavens and the earth, the earth was a formless void and darkness covered the face of the deep, while a wind from God swept over the face of the waters. Then God said, "Let there be light;" and there was light. And God saw that the light was good; and God separated the light from the darkness. God called the light Day, and the darkness he called Night. And there was evening and there was morning, the first day.

And God said, "Let there be a dome in the midst of the waters, and let it separate the waters from the waters." So God made the dome and separated the waters that were under the dome from the waters that were above the dome. And it was so. God called the dome Sky. And there was evening and there was morning, the second day.

And God said, "Let the waters under the sky be gathered together into one place, and let the dry land appear." And it was so. God called the dry land Earth, and the waters that were gathered together he called Seas. And God saw that it was good. Then God said, "Let the earth put forth vegetation: plants yielding seed, and fruit trees of every kind on earth that bear fruit with the seed in it." And it was so. The earth brought forth vegetation: plants yielding seed of every kind, and trees of every kind bearing fruit with the seed in it. And God saw that it was good. And there was evening and there was morning, the third day.

And God said, "Let there be lights in the dome of the sky to separate the day from the night; and let them be for signs and for seasons and for days and years, and let them be lights in the dome of the sky to give light upon the earth." And it was so. God made the two great lights—the greater light to rule the day and the lesser light to rule the night—and the stars. God set them in the dome of the sky to give light upon the earth, to rule over the day and over the night, and to separate the light from the darkness. And God saw that it was good. And there was evening and there was morning, the fourth day.

And God said, "Let the waters bring forth swarms of living creatures, and let birds fly above the earth across the dome of the sky." So God created the great sea monsters and every living creature that moves, of every kind, with which the waters swarm, and every winged bird of every kind. And God saw that it was good. God blessed them, saying, "Be fruitful and multiply and fill the waters in the seas, and let birds multiply on the earth." And there was evening and there was morning, the fifth day.

And God said, "Let the earth bring forth living creatures of every kind: cattle and creeping things and wild animals of the earth of every kind." And it was so. God made the wild animals of the earth of every kind, and the cattle of every kind, and everything that creeps upon the ground of every kind. And God saw that it was good.

Then God said, "Let us make humankind in our image, according to our likeness; and let them have dominion over the fish of the sea, and over the birds of the air, and over the cattle, and over all the wild animals of the earth, and over every creeping thing that creeps upon the earth."

So God created humankind in his image, in the image of God he created them; male and female he created them.

God blessed them, and God said to them, "Be fruitful and multiply, and fill the earth and subdue it; and have dominion over the fish of the sea and over the birds of the air and over every living thing that moves upon the earth." God said, "See, I have given you every plant yielding seed that is upon the face of all the earth, and every tree with seed in its fruit; you shall have them for food. And to every beast of the earth, and to every bird of the air, and to everything that creeps on the earth, everything that has the breath of life, I have given every green plant for food." And it was so. God saw everything that he had made, and indeed, it was very good. And there was evening and there was morning, the sixth day.

Thus the heavens and the earth were finished, and all their multitude. And on the seventh day God finished the work that he had done, and he rested on the seventh day from all the work that he had done. So God blessed the seventh day and hallowed it, because on it God rested from all the work that he had done in creation. [2]

Genesis 2:4-2:24
The second creation story

A river flows out of Eden to water the garden, and from there it divides and becomes four branches. The name of the first is Pishon; it is the one that flows around the whole land of Havilah, where there is gold; and the gold of that land is good; bdellium and onyx stone are there. The name of the second river is Gihon; it is the one that flows around the whole land of Cush. The name of the third river is Tigris, which flows east of Assyria. And the fourth river is the Euphrates.

The LORD God took the man and put him in the garden of Eden to till it and keep it. And the LORD God commanded the man, "You may freely eat of every tree of the garden; but of the tree of the knowledge of good and evil you shall not eat, for in the day that you eat of it you shall die."

Then the LORD God said, "It is not good that the man should be alone; I will make him a helper as his partner." So out of the ground the LORD God formed every animal of the field and every bird of the air, and brought them to the man to see what he would call them; and whatever the man called every living creature, that was its name. The man gave names to all cattle, and to the birds of the air, and to every animal of the field; but for the man there was not found a helper as his partner. So the LORD God caused a deep sleep to fall upon the man, and he slept; then he took one of his ribs and closed up its place with flesh. And the rib that the LORD God had taken from the man he made into a woman and brought her to the man.

Then the man said,
"This at last is bone of my bones
        and flesh of my flesh;
this one shall be called Woman,
        for out of Man this one was taken."
Therefore a man leaves his father and his mother and clings to his wife, and they become

one flesh.[3]

RIDE THE ATTRACTION
Ellen's Energy Adventure

The Walt Disney World Resort all began with Walt's vision of building an Experimental Prototype Community of Tomorrow. How will we live, work and play side-by-side as population increases and resources decrease? People from around the world would live temporarily in the City of the Future, dreaming and working with innovative corporations, becoming good stewards of the urban landscape. Land was acquired and the company decided to focus on The Magic Kingdom as a draw to the property while plans for EPCOT were developed and built.

Walt Disney died in 1966, five years before the opening of Disney World. When Disney World opened October 1, 1971, it consisted of The Magic Kingdom, four themed hotels and a campground. Just over ten years later, a modified version of Disney's Epcot would open as the second theme park on the property.

Approaching Epcot is exhilarating. The large golf ball, the geodesic sphere, is Spaceship Earth, Epcot's focal point. A monorail journeying from the Ticket and Transportation Center moves past Spaceship Earth, allowing guests onboard to get a 360-degree introduction to Epcot's two sections of pavilions - Future World and World Showcase.

Future World invites guests to dream of the hopes of tomorrow's child, a world where we leave a legacy of imagination coupled with innovation. World Showcase is a permanent World's Fair. Representative countries from around the world invite guests to discover the people, food, culture and dreams of distant shores.

Once the monorail enters Future World and passes Spaceship Earth, the first pavilion that comes into view is The Universe of Energy. Immediately noticeable to guests is an impressive rooftop made up of photovoltaic cells. These cells capture the energy of the sun, which provides 15% of the power needed to operate the attraction. Within the pavilion is an indoor traveling theater hosting *Ellen's Energy Adventure.*

Ellen DeGeneres, the popular talk-show host and comedian, invites time travelers to dream with her through a spectacular journey that traces the history of energy from the evolution of fossil fuels, to our dependence on them, and to what we may need to consider in the future. Ellen's dream suggests that events that happened millions of years ago provide the energy of our known universe today. People who don't believe in dinosaurs, the Big Bang Theory, or the Theory of Evolution may not enjoy the attraction. Although we need fossil fuels to power our world, the ride is a powerful story about how God is working within the universe of energy. "We see how the development of these tremendous sources of energy has shaped our past, and how they will continue to shape our future." [4]

When we enter the Universe of Energy, we move into the pavilion's pre-show theater. We meet Ellen. She is lounging around in her New York apartment preparing to watch her favorite television show *Jeopardy*. Bill Nye the Science Guy, Ellen's neighbor, knocks on her door during the first round. Bill asks Ellen if he could borrow some aluminum foil, a clothespin and a candle.

"Another hot date, huh?" Ellen replies.

"Actually, I'm working on an experiment," Bill replies.

"Take whatever you need. I don't want to miss any of the game," Ellen responds.

Ellen is shocked to discover that "Stupid Judy," Judy Peterson, her annoying college classmate, is one of the contestants on today's episode of *Jeopardy*. Judy is doing quite well, outscoring the other contestants. One happens to be Albert Einstein, a true barrel of energy.

Ellen is annoyed with Judy's success. Bill tries to convince Ellen that energy is interesting but Ellen is having none of it. He leaves. She falls asleep and as we enter, Ellen begins to dream. Suddenly, she is a contestant on *Jeopardy*, standing next to Albert Einstein and Stupid Judy Peterson. The game is just starting.

Alex Trebek begins the round by introducing the categories.

"Here are the categories for the first round of play: Solar Energy. Wind Power. Energy from Water. Fossil Fuels. Fusion. And finally ... Gas. Ellen, since this is your dream, we'll let you make the first selection."

Ellen's dream is becoming an energy nightmare as she realizes she is unprepared to compete. But the dream shifts, leaving the present round of *Jeopardy*, moving backward in time millions upon millions of years in the past.

We leave Ellen's dream for a moment as guests leave the pre-show and board a traveling theater where we will travel together with Ellen for the next forty minutes.

In the first theater, Ellen and Bill Nye are surrounded by darkness. A small, insignificant, flashlight size ball of gas will explode, creating the world as we know it.

Bill prepares Ellen for what she is about to witness, saying, "See that single point of very hot, very dense matter? It contains all the energy of the universe, that's about to expand. At an astonishing rate! It's ... the Big Bang! What you're about to witness took place over billions of years. We better take cover!"

We then witness through beautiful graphics and amazing surround sound the third story of creation, the creation story that is not in the book of Genesis. It is a beginning of the universe that leaves behind the power of myth and moves into the world of science. For those of us who believe that God is always working and creating in this universe in mysterious and miraculous ways, we get an incredible introduction to how energy is infused within everything we know or can imagine.

After the Big Bang, Ellen and Bill find that they have traveled through time to the time of dinosaurs. But Ellen has missed something.

"Where's the energy?" Ellen asks.

"Oh, it's all around you," Bill Nye the Science Guy replies. "You see, these plants and animals are soaking up energy from the sun. When they die and get buried, time, pressure, and heat will cook them into the fossil fuels we rely on today. Like coal, natural gas, and oil."

Ellen's dream then takes us through the world of dinosaurs and through the rest of recorded time within a matter of minutes. Younger guests will find this part of the ride the most exciting. Dinosaurs eat and fight and spit and move and we are right in the middle of it all. The journey back in time moves into the pavilion's second theater where we are invited to ponder what energy solutions need to be worked through in order to support our current energy consumption. Ellen and Bill discuss the advantages and disadvantages of each energy solution presented. A lot of technical information is quickly presented in an entertaining format.

Ellen's Energy Adventure concludes on *Jeopardy* where Ellen suddenly does remarkably well. Stupid Judy thinks she is cheating because thanks to Ellen's time-traveling journey, she has learned a lot about the universe of energy. It all comes down to Final Jeopardy.

Alex Trebek presents the answer. "Our Final Jeopardy category on today's program is The Future of Energy. Here's the Final Jeopardy answer for you: This is the one source of power that will never run out. Good luck."

In *Ellen's Energy Adventure*, the world as we know it begins with a big bang. We may not know or understand how it started or how long it took but we do know it created a force of energy that sustains the power of the universe.

FOR REFLECTION

How did it all start? How did I get here?

For things to begin, somebody, someone, or something out there has to say "yes." Then things get put into motion. A planet breaks through space. A story steps off the page. A song moves from the earbud into the soul. Once this beginning is put out there, we have to decide whether we will inhabit it or not. All of life is a series of choices.

For an actor, the beginning is often with words on a page. Denys Arcand's powerful film *Jesus of Montreal* follows an acting troop hired to dramatize the story of Jesus' life, passion and resurrection for urban dwellers of Montreal. A local actor named Daniel Coloumbe (Lothaire Bluteau) is contracted by the local Catholic shrine to write and produce a new interpretation of The Passion. The Governing Board finds the traditional text a bit stale. Or at least they think they do. Daniel begins to reach out to artists to collaborate. They will infuse a traditional story of truth with the latest religious scholarship and realities of life.

Daniel immediately hires an actress from the traditional Passion Play not realizing she is having an affair with the priest of the shrine. Another actress is a model using her body to sell cologne. One of the actors Daniel hopes to recruit is currently doing voice-over for a documentary about the beginning of the universe. Daniel, accompanied by two artists who have agreed to be a part of this

religious journey, visit René. They find him in a studio, recording the documentary's narrative tracks. As he reads the text for the audio engineers, dynamic graphics are projected on a huge screen illustrating the creation of the universe.

René reads, "It is impossible to talk about the origin of the universe. The mind can't conceive of time before it all began 15 billion years ago. All matter condensed to nearly nothing at a temperature we cannot imagine. The big bang was an explosion of inconceivable force. A million years later, the heat hasn't abated.

"Stars are born and die. Our sun is one of them. We live on a tiny planet orbiting an ordinary star on the periphery of a typical galaxy among billions of other galaxies. We don't know how many solar systems there are. If most stars have planets it's probable that other forms of life exist by the millions. But since solar systems result from highly exceptional stellar processes we may be alone.

"Five billion years from now, our sun will have burned its nuclear fuel. Earth will revert to the galactic gases that formed it. But we will be long gone. The world began without man and the world will end the same way. When the last soul vanishes from Earth, the universe will bear no trace of man's passing."

As the narrative ends, the universe disappears and the screen goes black. René addresses the documentary's producer, stating the text "leaves a lot unanswered." The producer agrees, answering, "The text is valid today, but in five years, it may change."

All of us on the religious journey experience change. In matters of faith, there is little consistency. Some will argue that God is consistent. Jesus is a rock. The Holy Spirit is a sustainer. Other faithful people will say this hasn't been their experience at all. The only thing consistent was the choice to walk the walk, to engage the creator and to hope to get to

know the Son of God.

In order to understand where we have been and where we are going, it is essential to remember how it all started. Where is my place? How did I get here? The waters of chaos crash and toss into the winds of change. An explosion bursts outward through lightning and rain creating and moving into expansive space. Land and sea collide, creating mud, evolving into dry land and puddles of pond and shore. God scoops up dirt, creates a doll, then breathes life into it. It is good. This is the beginning. But remember you are dust and to dust you shall return.

The writers of Hebrew Scripture were afraid of water. They were nomadic. Most wandered through deserts and plains. Sightings of huge expanses of water were rare. There were rivers here and small lakes there. But primarily they lived and worked and walked through dry land.

Our matriarchs and patriarchs had a terrarium view of the universe. Before the children of Abraham entered into a covenant relationship with God, there was only water. In the beginning, that is all there was. God's power and creative imagination separated the water, forming the dry land. God controlled the waters, pushing them away to the north, to the south, to the east and to the west. Beneath the flat surface of the earth, there was water below the land. There was water above the land just beyond the heavens. The flat earth took its place in the midst of waters.

This is how it all began.

Waters of chaos plummeted beyond the heavens and just below the dry surfaces. The light faded away and darkness covered the land. God hung the lamps of stars on the firmament of heaven. Beyond that heavenly vale was water. God's command held the waters back and the people lived on the land. God's people become restless, wanting to be like God. Boredom, lack of gratitude and the want of something more fill the mind with temptation and want. We want to understand the secrets of the universe. We want to comprehend the magnitude of God. Burton L. Visotzky, Appleman Professor of Midrash and Interreligious Studies at The Jewish Theological Seminary in New York City says this: "If God can fill the universe, how can God create anything? There's no space. So God has to withdraw to create space for the world to exist. But in the Kabala, that gives rise to a terrible flaw because the empty space is then essentially devoid of Divinity. This has cosmic implications. We have to constantly repair that void."[5] We go against God's wishes and pursue our own desires and wishes at the cost of relationship.

God is disappointed. We have disobeyed. God finds Noah and commands him to prepare an ark and to collect a pair of creatures of every kind. Then, God releases the waters. God undoes creation. Chaos covers the earth. It rains and rains and rains some more. Where will we land? When will it end? This is the beginning. It is God's story. It is our story. Where is your place in this story?

In *Jesus of Montreal,* Daniel recruits an agnostic group reading the Gospel in hopes that they can make it meaningful to an audience today. During their quest, the actors have not rejected outright Jesus or the Good News of the Gospel. The message of the Gospel just isn't relevant to them within the daily routine of their busy lives. The text of the Passion is difficult for the actors to relate to. They begin to look for the truth within the text and how it connects to the truth within them.

Where is my voice? Where is God's voice? How did it all begin? How did I get here? It is important for us to take the time to answer these simple questions.

We live in a world that distracts us from finding meaning by keeping us very busy - busy at work, busy at play, busy at night, busy during the day. These distractions make it harder for many of us to go to church or go to the gym, spend time with friends or find time to rest and regroup.

If I can't find the time to take care of myself spiritually and mentally, others can easily control me.

It is never too late to begin again. It is never to late to recreate. God wiped the slate clean and returned to the beginning. Sometimes we should too.

The actors in *Jesus of Montreal* begin to rehearse their version of Jesus' life and ministry. They play his disciples. They play the people he healed. They play the people who followed him. They play the people who betrayed him. They begin to walk in Jesus' footsteps. They begin to incarnate the Gospel message by doing it and then living it.

Even though they are consciously unaware of it, their lives begin to change. They find meaning in their community. They begin to notice how outside influences have influenced their previous choices in dehumanizing ways. They start to find peace within themselves and within the art they are creating. Order in a chaotic world and accountability to an intentional community are established, fostering support for the journey of the faithful.

A right relationship with God and with God's people is essential for a successful beginning. God created a covenant relationship with humankind. We live into that covenant by loving God and loving neighbor. Even though we fail at the covenant, God remembers the beginning and waits for us to return.

The Chinese character for *heaven* is made of three parallel horizontal lines intersected by a single vertical line. The top and bottom parallel lines are the same length, the one parallel line in the middle of the two is shorter. The pictogram illustrates the Chinese belief of right relationship. Everything has its place. The heavens are above. The people are on Earth below. The emperor, the Son of Heaven, works and rules between heaven and earth to keep

relationships in order. When all is in order, right relationship empowers all of us to do the work that God has given us to do.

At Epcot Center at Walt Disney World, directly across from the Universe of Energy, on the opposite side of Future World, is the Journey into Imagination. A character, the Dreamfinder, sings, "One little spark of inspiration is at the heart of all creation. Right at the start of everything that's new one little spark lights up for you."

How did I get here? What was God thinking when God created me? I cannot imagine. What from the moment of creation do I need to discover and claim for my faith journey?

Walt Disney said, "Somehow I can't believe there are many heights that can't be scaled by a man who knows the secret of making dreams come true. This special secret, it seems to me, can be summarized in four C's. They are Curiosity, Confidence, Courage, and Consistency and the greatest of these is Confidence. When you believe a thing, believe it all over, implicitly and unquestioningly." [6]

THE E-TICKET

Roberta Hestness, the International Minister at Large for World Vision shared this with Bill Moyers during the production of his PBS series on Genesis, "James Weldon Johnson wrote a wonderful poem about creation in which God says, 'I'm lonely. I'll make me a man. I found myself asking, 'Was God lonely? Is God lonely? Does God need humans? Is the creation of man and woman a response to some need inside of God?' After wrestling with the text over a number of years my own answer is 'no.' I believe the creation is an outflowing of the fullness of God. It is a gift, and a demonstration of the richness and wonder of God. He creates and lets that creation have a separate identity. He doesn't grasp it and hold it and control it in some narrow, constricting way. The relationship between man and woman expresses something of the community within God and the relationship that exists externally with God." [7]

The great Zen master, Shunryu Suzuki, says this about beginnings, "To the beginner, many possibilities. To the expert, few opportunities."

The blank page is full of potential. What we write or draw or doodle on it is limitless. The more I know, the more I limit my creative potential.

HOLY STORY

Reflect on the two creation stories encountered in the Book of Genesis - Genesis 1:1-2:3. Compare and contrast the two stories. How are they similar? How are they different? What do they each say about God? What do they say about you?

Recall creation as presented in Theater 1 of *Ellen's Energy Adventure* in The Universe of Energy. How is Ellen's story similar to the Genesis stories? How is it different? What does it say about God? What does it say about you?

Which creation stories, choosing from the two recorded in the Book of Genesis or the one presented in *Ellen's Energy Adventure* in The Universe of Energy, speaks to you the most? Why? What does it say about your relationship with God?

Spend some time in silence. Then reflect upon how you believe God is working in your life, in the people that surround you and in the world. Write down your reflections.

Then record the following responses.
During Creation, God _____ .
The Church teaches me that in Creation _____ .

A movie or book or television show that I think reflects my beliefs about Creation is _____ .
I believe Creation is _____ .

RULE

We have many beginnings. We are born. Some are baptized. We fall in love. We fall out of love. We meet new friends. Other friends move away and live in our memory. We begin a new school, a new job, a new project, a new hobby, a new endeavor.

Think about the many beginnings in your life, the creative moments when something new moved you in a new direction.

Turn to the "Rule of Life" section of your journal. Write down a rule about a way you pray to handle the beginnings in your life.

Begin with:

CREATION

God created the world and God said it was good. I believe humankind is created …
Continue from there.

 # THE COLLECT

The prayer book for the Episcopal Church, *The Book of Common Prayer*, has a beautiful Collect about creation.

"O heavenly God, who hast filled the world with beauty: Open our eyes to behold thy gracious hand in all thy works; that, rejoicing in thy whole creation, we may learn to serve thee with gladness; for the sake of him all things were made, thy Son Jesus Christ our Lord. Amen." [8]

It is your turn to write a Collect based on your work in this section.

We have reflected on beginnings and life decisions and how they relate to creation. You may want to pray a Collect of Thanksgiving for Creation similar to the Collect above from *The Book of Common Prayer.* You may want to pray about a beginning that has changed your life drastically. You might want to write about something coming up, a new beginning, a new creative act, or a new approach to beginnings.

Write a Collect.

Take your time.

Begin by praying the Collect above.

Remember the parts of a Collect.

1. Address God

2. Describe an action or several actions of God

3. Ask God for something

4. Thank God

Record your new Collect in the "Holy Story" section of your journal.

✝

ENDNOTES

1 (Imagineers (Group) & Walt Disney Company, 1996, p. 11)
2 (May & Metzger, 1973, pp. 2 - 3 OT)
3 (May & Metzger, 1973, pp. 3 - 4 OT)
4 (Wright, Imagineers (Group), & Walt Disney Company, 2010, p. 42)
5 (Moyers, 1996, p. 6)
6 (Smith, 1994, p. 43)
7 (Moyers, 1996, p. 10)
8 (Episcopal Church., 1979, p. 814)

A WORLD OF RITUALS

This collection of artifacts, mainly from the Serks Zong region, reflects the extreme importance of the Yeti in local tradition.

Prayer Wheel - Used in the Buddhist and Bon traditions. (Bon is the ancient religion of Tibet) Each time the wheel is spun, a prayer is generated.

Chorten - monuments in the Buddhist tradition. A chorten can be no more than two feet tall or large enough to walk through.

Prayer Wheel - within each wheel is a dense coil of written prayers.

(The ancient religion of Tibet) These stones accumulate along roadways, eventually forming walls.

Serks Zong, the Yeti plays such an important part in local Buddhist culture its image is found everywhere.

A Yeti stamp issued by the Kingdom of Bhutan.

The ancient practice of animal sacrifice to placate the spirits, has been replaced in recent centuries by symbol-images of animals. This represents the influence of the compassionate beliefs of Himalayan philosophies and their respect for all living creatures.

The Yeti is a popular image in local folk art.

A souvenir Yeti stamp issued in Halville Islands (Sri Lanka) in 1992

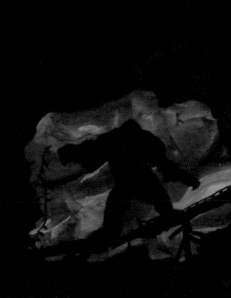

MYTH } *How Does Story Help Me Understand God?*

MAIN GATE

Tigger says to Winnie the Pooh, "That's the story of you and me. From the beginning, we were meant to be."

This is a joyful proclamation! It is a wonderful statement about love and friendship. It illustrates an understanding that the journey through this life is part of a story contained within a larger story. "We were meant to be" is a delightfully naive exhortation of predestination. I'm pretty sure that's not what Tigger had in mind. It's just a part of the story.

Where are you in the story? How do you know what you know? What is your place within the larger story?

For many of us, we first get to know God through holy story, the sacred scripture, the Holy Bible. We hear stories of Noah and the Ark, Deborah and her mighty army, David and Goliath, and Mary and her son. For those of us who attend church, these stories are preached within the context of Church tradition.

As we move into our faith, we begin to act. We pray before bedtime. We give thanks before a meal. We sing praises for receiving a blessing. As we mature in our faith, we act to bring about justice. We confront the powers that derail the people of God. We move onto the streets to speak in the public square, becoming good citizens and stewards of all that has been given to us.

Through the teachings of the Church and through our actions and experiences, we begin to create a belief system around how God works in this world and how we are called to respond.

We desire to express our experiences so we create movies and songs, magazines and books, all sorts of expressions that contribute to the popular culture and inform our belief system.

Then, we endlessly and repeatedly cycle through Church, Tradition, Culture and Action over and over and over again until it all integrates into a seamless dance.

How do I know what I know?

We read and study the Hebrew Scriptures, discovering a God yearning to be in covenant relationship with us. We read the letters of Paul hoping to understand through grace what the death and resurrection of Christ have to do with the community where we worship, live and work. We read the Gospels discovering more about God through God's incarnational presence with us in Jesus Christ.

What is the story? Where is my place in the story?

The inspirational singer Kate Bush suggests that we step off of the page and into the sensual world. Something that once was known primarily through the Word in now standing in front of us in the Flesh.

It is difficult to comprehend a life without skin and bones, a world without inhabited bodies walking around it. When I see the incredible diversity of peoples who inhabit this Spaceship Earth, I learn something about the incredible creative, and imaginative capacity of God.

What is the story? How do we enter the story? How do we find our place? What is my personal story? What is our shared story? Where did it all begin?

The story lines, the narrative structures, the plot points, the conflicts, the climaxes and the resolutions are all a part of our ongoing story. Our choices are limitless. The stories are numerous. But the primary story, the truth that is informing all of the other characters and subplots, is ongoing, shifting and evolving. It comes from the power of God.

We step off the page and into the sensual world. What was once drawn on the page and then projected onto a screen is standing next to us and walking around at Disney parks. Walt Disney's animated characters come to life, sign our autograph books, pose for pictures and even parade down Main Street for all to see.

We read about Snow White in a book by the Brothers Grimm. We see the animated classic film by Walt Disney. We meet Snow White, the Seven Dwarfs and the Wicked Queen in person as we roam around eating Mickey Mouse-eared ice cream—from word to story, from the page to standing in front of me.

We understand our lives through story. We write stories to understand the context of our lives. We make sense of our lives through claiming contextualization.

It started with the Word that, through the mystery of faith, became flesh and lived among us. "We interpret the world and understand ourselves via images and stories. When the faculty to imagine gets wounded or diseased, we find ourselves caught in destructive fantasies from which there is no escape. Fear of the unknown or unfamiliar takes over with destructive and malevolent results. To make matters worse, the culture bombards us with ready-made images falsely promising fulfillment

and happiness. It is no wonder so many of us are depressed. The basic image of our culture is that we are simply consumers. The basic image of the great religious traditions is that we are related - connected to each other, to the world, and to God." [1]

We want to be connected. We want to experience what we've read about. We want to ride what we've seen on the big screen. We want to engage with family and coworkers, with neighbors and enemies, with friends and strangers. In the digital age, it is easy for us to create images of things that were once words that so many find difficult to relate to.

We look to the Bible to understand God, to understand God's people and to find our space in the story.

What am I supposed to do?

In essence, the Bible is not a book. It is a library. It is a collection of books and gospels and letters that contain nearly 3000 years of history. In reality, this is a span of time that is difficult for us to get our minds around. We mush and squash, mix and match, pick and choose, at the cost of context and meaning.

God is mysterious and complicated and cannot be reduced to a sound bite.

We walk into the pages of the Bible seeking understanding. Who is God and does this really matter to me, today, right now, in the midst of all this?

How does story help you understand God?

 IN THE QUEUE

As we move through the queue together, we notice different things. Our personal experiences become a part of our spirit, soul and body. What happens to us is written on our faces. What hurts or heals us melts into the chambers of our hearts.

Experiences develop and stimulate our senses, inviting us to look over here, taste that over there, listen to this sound and completely miss another sound altogether. What does and doesn't appeal to me tells me something about my entry point into God's story.

In order to embrace my walk through God's story and in order to know my place within it, I need to begin to discover and to be aware of how I know what I know.

It is a complex puzzle to solve. It is a difficult question to answer. But this awareness is key to deepening my relationship with God. It is necessary that I give meaning to and reflect upon my everyday decisions so that I may live life like Jesus Christ. If I spend time reflecting on the story, I will be empowered to move through the world with my actions being in line with the power of the spirit.

We sprint. We slip. We tumble. We fall. But if we carve out space for the work of story, it becomes easier, in most cases, to find our way back to faith.

In order to understand God's story, in order to find meaning in my story, I must be willing to embrace and participate fully in it. Everything I say or do matters. Compartmentalizing is dangerous. Compartmentalizing fragments us and makes us inconsistent. For many of us, it is a survival skill. But it is a very detrimental one. We must integrate the moments in our lives, for these moments are a part of our soul, our being. Like the slogan for the powerful David Simon HBO series *The Wire* states, "All the pieces matter."

The story of the people of God recorded and collected together in the Bible is a complex library of different literary genres. We encounter recorded history next to hymns about God. We read letters to gathered communities next to gospels proclaiming the ministry of Jesus Christ. We enjoy literature telling the chaotic adventures of people just like you and me alongside prophetic proclamations calling on us to get our act together! Remember that we are people of God so we need to live and love and act that way.

Easier said than done.

Some of the collected books in the Bible speak to us. Others do not. Scholarship suggests that within chapters of the Bible, several narrative sources have been combined in order to preserve the history and move the narrative forward. Biblical editors weren't concerned about contractions. Their biggest concern was preservation, preserving everything they had experienced about God through their history.

For the religious, holy story influences how we take on the reality of our faith experience.

Which holy story speaks to me? For the Jewish, it is the Books of Moses and the Hebrew Scriptures. For Christians, we look at the Gospels, the Hebrew Scriptures and an assortment of letters stapled together in the New Testament. For Hindus, the stories of the Mahabharata or the Ramayana tell how God has been made manifest. For Muslims, the Holy Koran as revealed to the prophet Mohammed is the starting point of religious understanding.

These holy stories were created to help us understand the truth of our humanity and how that truth impacts our relationship with our creator. These holy stories help us to consider answers to questions such as "How did I get here?" One could suggest that the Holy Bible relates a myth about God and the Hebrew people.

The Biblical narrative was told orally for generations. Then, as the people of God became separated due to circumstances, such as exile or diaspora, the traditions were written down and several stories and sources edited together in order to be preserved for wherever the people or tribe settled. Jewish followers of Christ wrote all the Gospels, pastoral letters and the apocalyptic text of the Revelation to John. Therefore, we can say that the Holy Bible is a myth about the Hebrew people and the God they are in covenantal relationship with. Like the Bible, we are a collection of tales that contribute to and make up who we are as persons of God.

As people created by God, we are bound together by that common beginning. We live within this created reality. But, because of who, what and where we have lived, we start to hear the story differently. Because of the religious beliefs, sacred stories and ritualistic traditions we have been exposed to, we may worship differently than our neighbors or friends or even family members. Because of the books we have read, the films we have watched, and the television shows and music that speak to our individual experiences, we become a people with an incredible variety of beliefs.

Scripture, tradition and cultural forces shape our actions and beliefs. Faith is often created within the gaps. "Faith is a central force which grounds all human culture and knowledge. There is no human life without beliefs, orientations and expectations. Faith precedes knowledge, providing a structure or a context or a paradigm within which we experience or imagine the world."[2]

How does story help us to understand God? How do we know what we know?

It is time to begin the work "In the Queue."

Scholars at the School of Theology at the University of the South at Sewanee have been teaching a disciplined approach to understand sacred story for many years. During the 1970s, they developed a program called Education for Ministry (EfM) to help all people everywhere develop, deepen and maintain a commitment to God in Christ. As a way of helping us understand why we believe what we believe, they developed a theological reflection method based on Four Sources—the Four Source Model.

The Four Sources are Action, Tradition, Culture and Position.

The first source is Action. Action is what we do and what we experience. Action is made up of lived experiences and through the thoughts and feelings associated with them. We identify thoughts and feelings in hopes of understanding what influences our choices most. We try to examine a microscopic moment in time so we can shake it up a bit and unclog the arteries. Actions are what we do.

The second source is Tradition. Tradition references our religious upbringing and practices. For a Christian, Tradition is made up of scripture, Church teachings, worshipping styles, music and hymnody—anything that finds its origin in organized religious experience. Traditions are stated in creeds, resolutions, canons and sacramental beliefs.

The third source is Culture. Culture is the world around us, captured in literature, film and music. It takes a look at art, architecture and messages from the mass media. Culture examines how created messages impact our relationship to the circumstances we find ourselves in.

The fourth source is Position. Position is where we apply meaning to life experiences. Position encompasses opinions, attitudes and beliefs. It is dangerous to hold positions and not understand the truth behind the steps and circumstances that have created them.

As we move through the world, as we encounter God, as we relate to God's people, we enter the conversation, we enter the experience, we enter the relationships through one of these sources. Sometimes, it could be a combination of two or three or all of them at the same time. But after some reflection, we will see this model as a good way to begin a conversation with family and friends and other sojourners about the journey of the faithful.

How do I know what I know? Is this a message from Culture? How do I know what I know? Is something that I learned in church? How do I know what I know? Do I believe this because of a circumstance or an experience I had?

Find a place to sit. Get comfortable. Claim the space. Invite God to be with you. Open your journal to the "Holy Story" section.

Write down your reflections on these questions that will move you quickly through the Four Source model.

Reflect upon and write down an event within the last few months that stands out in your life. What were your thoughts and feelings? How did the experience end?

Reflect and write about a piece of Scripture, a prayer or a teaching of the Church that has been significant for you during the last few months. Why is it important today? How did you encounter this part of Tradition?

Reflect and write about a song, book, movie, magazine story or news item that has impacted you lately. Why? What about this particular aspect of Culture has grabbed your attention? What aspect of Culture do you relate to the most?

Write down a Position, something for which you recently took a stand. Begin your position statement by writing "I believe …"

Now examine your responses to the Four Sources. Does one of the Four Sources speak to you more than the others? If so, which one? Why? If not, where are you most comfortable?

How do you know what you know?

FROM THE BOOK
John 1:1 – 2:4 a

The Gospel of John is a beautiful collection of conversations, relationships and images to help the reader become a believer. Jesus is the one sent from heaven so that all will have life in Christ's name. Jesus' conversations with the Woman at the Well and night crawler Nicodemus are some of the most beloved in the Gospels. Scholarship suggests that the Gospel was written by an exiled community, Jewish congregants who were tossed out of the synagogue because of their belief that Jesus was the Messiah. John uses this opening prologue to immediately remind and help the Jewish community to remember their context within God's covenant with the people repeatedly told in Hebrew Scripture.

John 1:1-2:4a
The Word Became Flesh

In the beginning was the Word, and the Word was with God, and the Word was God. He was in the beginning with God. All things came into being through him, and without him not one thing came into being. What has come into being in him was life, and the life was the light of all people. The light shines in the darkness, and the darkness did not overcome it.

There was a man sent from God, whose name was John. He came as a witness to testify to the light, so that all might believe through him. He himself was not the light, but he came to testify to the light. The true light, which enlightens everyone, was coming into the world.

He was in the world, and the world came into being through him; yet the world did not know him. He came to what was his own, and his own people did not accept him. But to all who received him, who believed in his name, he gave power to become children of God, who were born, not of blood or of the will of the flesh or of the will of man, but of God.

And the Word became flesh and lived among us, and we have seen his glory, the glory as of a father's only son, full of grace and truth. (John testified to him and cried out, "This was he of whom I said, 'He who comes after me ranks ahead of me because he was before me.'") From his fullness we have all received, grace upon grace. The law indeed was given through Moses; grace and truth came through Jesus Christ. No one has ever seen God. It is God the only Son, who is close to the Father's heart, who has made him known.[3]

RIDE THE ATTRACTION
Expedition Everest

At Disney's Animal Kingdom, an inviting mountain range in Asia beckons us to come closer, board a train, have trust in the tracks and climb up towards the heavens and explore the hidden peaks of Forbidden Mountain. This is *Expedition Everest*, a roller-coaster experience like no other at the Walt Disney World Resort. Its steam trains cross bridges, travail high mountain peaks and drop over the mountainside into hidden valleys providing adventurers with incredible thrills. It is the most expensive coaster ever built; the final price tag was close to $100 million. Like *Splash Mountain* at The Magic Kingdom, it displays all that is right and good with Disney's Imagineers. It immerses guests in a good story, creates a sense of place and character and travels to places unexpected, hidden by the ride's design.

As we approach the attraction, everything we encounter reveals secret after secret to a mysterious story. We have to connect the dots to understand and occupy our place and part in the story, tempting our fate within this mountain adventure. By the time we are brave enough to board the train taking us skyward, we are totally aware of what was, is and is to come.

At the base of the mountain we move into the office of "Himalayan Escapes." This makeshift travel agency is hoping to be our guide, to be hired to accompany us up the mountain. As we look at the snow-covered crevices of Forbidden Mountain, we are drawn to move forward and conquer the secrets of the mountaintops. We want to climb and explore and risk it all just to say we made it to the top and lived.

As we leave the world we are familiar with behind, we feel closer to heaven, changed, transfigured, possessing an increased awareness. At the top of the roof of the world, we see a bigger picture, discover a sense of expansiveness and gain a new perspective on our place in the world.

We move through the offices of "Himalayan Escapes" into a village temple. In this sacred space we contemplate our belief in God or gods. What is God's place in my life and in this adventure? Are we tempting fate by leaving the safety of the village? Can the gods protect us from the spirits of the mountain? Temple bells ring out from all around, calling me back into the reality of the present moment and what lies ahead.

Just beyond the temple is an equipment storage area. We learn about all of the equipment necessary for a successful climb. What kind of food should we bring? What type of clothing is needed for protection? What sort of hiking boots ensure a safe and successful climb?

From there, we move into the Yeti Museum where our willingness to take the journey is challenged by the reality of what has happened to those who have gone before. Previous expeditions have traversed the Forbidden Mountain to find themselves face to face with a mythical beast that resides within the hidden caves above. In the museum, there are casts of Yeti prints and tales of Yeti woe. We discover that one particular expedition team took the journey that we are preparing for and never returned. No one knows what really happened to them except that a camera was recovered from the team's campsite. Once the film was processed, it appears that they were attacked by an animal of some sort. The pictures are out-of-focus and hard to decipher. What is clear is that something went terribly wrong. And that they never returned.

As we move into the train station, we have a decision to make. Do I dare board the train or do I escape through a final exit door conveniently placed for guests who have changed their minds?

In the queue, what have I discovered? What story has been told? What ahead is exciting and what scares me?

We board the train. The village of Serka Zong is our port-of-entry to Forbidden Mountain. Why is the mountain forbidden? Because the region's protector lives there. "Legend holds… from Nepal to India to China… that high in the mountains lives a creature that haunts the remote forests and fiercely guards this land, long considered sacred… and forbidden. Belief in this protector has kept thousands of acres of land pristine. The region around Mount Everest is such a place."[4] Our train moves through the village and the mystery of it all beckons us to journey onward. As we approach the base of the mountain, we are at the point of no return.

The train moves quickly through a temple and up a mountain bridge. We go higher and higher and higher and higher. Serka Zong and the people living and studying and working there become smaller and smaller and smaller. What am I doing here?

The tracks twist and turn and stop suddenly at what appears to be broken track. There is only one way out, but something is behind us, chasing us, wondering what we are doing up there. There is no way forward or we will certainly plunge to our death.

At the top of Forbidden Mountain, one encounters the oldest gods in the world. In Sanskrit, *Himalayas* means "home of the gods." "In Hindu mythology, here was the home of Shiva, one of the supreme triad and the lord of animals. Also here,

in Hindu and Buddhist mythology, was Mount Meru, the center of the earth, inhabited by gods, particularly Kubera, lord of the treasures of the earth and king of the yakshas (supernatural beings) who watched over the fertility of the land."[5]

Has my lack of respect to the gods or to the legend of Forbidden Mountain gotten me in a load of trouble? Ahead only broken track and sky. Behind the noise of something scary and unfamiliar. Could we end up like the previous expedition teams whose photographs were on display in the Yeti Museum? Who believes in the Yeti anyway?

"The legend of the Yeti is a common component of the mythologies passed down from generation to generation within many cultures that live in the shadow of the Himalayas. These stories have traveled through Tibet, Nepal, India, and southwestern China, always with certain core elements that are consistent over all these miles and over all these years. These people believe that the Yeti is a real creature, capable of eating a yak from your field when you're not paying attention, but also existing in a mythical realm in which it carries out its protective duties."[6]

Have I entered sacred ground? Many of us take for granted the sacred all around us. Familiarity seduces us into forgetting the miracle behind it all. As I sit on those broken tracks, I feel as if I have taken it all for granted. Remove your sandals for you are standing on sacred ground. Really? How would I know? "The Sacred Lands program run by Conservation International seeks to legally recognize and guard these ancient sites, many consider *beyuls* - a word describing secret and protected places, traditionally protected by the Yeti."[7]

The train tracks shake. The engine begins to move. But where are we going? I am no longer in control.

I am on sacred ground. What do I need to do to recognize and remember that?

FOR REFLECTION

It is written on a collection of stele plates. It is found within a forest of history. Most of the story is carved directly on the stele. Some of the narrative is cut directly in the rock that holds up the stele.

The rock is jagged and is cold to the touch. The stele structures tower above, with the wisdom of the past written all over them.

It is a forest of stele. Several thousand stone bases holding up thousands more stele tablets creating this forest of monuments.

The Forest of Stele is on display in several rooms of a Confucian temple.

Thousands of Chinese characters cover the stele's surface. Some are traditional Chinese characters. Others are so ancient they are not recognizable, are untranslatable, and completely unreadable. If you run your fingers across the plate, you are traveling across thousands of years of history.

In this forest of stele, on one of the plates, believed to have been written around 750 AD, the following is written, "The True Lord of the Primordial Word, in absolute stillness and constant naturalness, crafted and nourished all things. He raised the earth and established the sky. He took on human form and his compassion was limitless. The sun rises, darkness is banished, and we are witnesses to the true wonder." [8]

This is what is written in this forest of stele.

The Gospel of John opens with a beautiful, complex prologue. Some say this incredible opening was written by a school of theologians. Others say this prologue was adopted from popular poems or hymns that were being circulated at that time.

Some say the Gospel of John was written about 90 years after the death of Jesus Christ. Others say it was written nearly 125 years later. Dating the Gospel is difficult. Opinions vary. But most scholars lean toward the former.

The Gospels of Mark, Matthew and Luke proclaim the miraculous life, deeds and teachings of Jesus Christ. In the Gospel of John, we encounter writings of another kind. John wants us to understand Christ's unique relationship with God and Christ's unique relationship to us, so that you and I may believe. It is a relationship built on the coming together of our mortal coil and the kingdom of heaven.

We are called to discover how the sphere of the eternal world of God, the cosmic world, relates to the sphere of the temporal world of God, our world, where we encounter each other. According to the Gospel of John, Jesus Christ is the bridge between these two spheres.

"In the beginning was the Word, and the Word was with God, and the Word was God." – the sphere of God, the sphere of the eternal world.

"There was a man sent from God, whose name was John. He came as a witness to testify to the light, so that all might believe through him." – the sphere of humanity, the sphere of the temporal world, our world.

"And the Word became flesh and lived among us, and we have seen his glory." – the sphere of Jesus Christ, where both the eternal and the temporal come together and redeem us.

For many, this beautiful prologue is all that is necessary for us to understand how the entire world changed once Jesus Christ came into the world as a baby. John's gospel prologue is a powerful theological statement that has challenged Christians throughout time. John's prologue, and a summary of what it means, made its way to a forest, a forest of stele, and this stone has been an inspiration to many Christians in the world's most populous nation.

The ancient walled city of Xi'an is located in the center of The People's Republic of China.

Xi'an sits at the end of the ancient Silk Road. It has served as the capital of 14 dynasties. Within Xi'an's city gates are a mosque, a Christian church, and a Buddhist temple. Xi'an is a city of bell towers that were used to warn people of attacks from hostile enemies. Xi'an is a city of pagodas that reminded holy people that the sacred realm surrounded them. Xi'an is a city of Confucian temples that called people to notice how they were related to the world and how they were related to each other.

Just outside the Southern city gate entrance is one of those Confucian temples. It was established during the Song Dynasty, around 1000 AD. It was a place where scholars from all around China came to study.

Inside this Confucian center of learning is the Forest of Stele. In this scholar's forest, you find a large collection of the Chinese classics on filial piety. You can find the official history of three powerful dynasties, the Song, Han and Qing dynasties. In this Forest of Stele, you can find the only recorded history of Christianity's introduction to The People's Republic of China.

According to the stele tablet, it happened around 612 AD.

The history preserved on the stone says, "In the beginning, the whole universe was in an absolute silence: the earth was formless and empty; while the Spirit of God was hovering over, it began uttering words. By the magic power in these words, everything in the world was created... At this moment, our merciful Trinity God gave up his power over the world and became flesh. He came to earth to lead people to find their way back to God... By trusting God and being obedient, they could come to perfection. If they would ask earnestly and praise him loudly, people could hear his voice speaking to them, and if they were able to do what they heard, the way to glory would be stored up for them." [9]

The prologue of John proclaims that the word became flesh and lived among us. The earth and the heavens met in the person of Jesus Christ. God comes to us as a baby and says journey with me through life. Look toward me to learn how to fully live. Love like me so that all are free to love and to laugh and to be. Grow up with me and be a teacher and counselor to all. Walk beside me and be a healer in our broken world. Be inspired by me and become a leader to the nations. If we are able to do this, the kingdoms of heaven and earth will meet within hearts, and the world as we know it will truly be transformed.

The stone in the Forest of Stele, in the ancient capital city of Xi'an, calls on Chinese Christians and all of us to act. Because the two spheres met in Jesus Christ, we must respond in several ways. We must "penetrate the mysteries, bless with good conscience, be great and yet empty, return to stillness and be forgiven, be compassionate and deliver all people, do good deeds and help all people reach the other shore." [10]

The stone stele says that when we stare with awe and wonder at the two spheres coming together in Jesus Christ, there is a spiritual stirring in our heart and soul.

Transformation has the power "to calm people in stormy times, helps us to understand the nature of things, enables us to maintain purity, nourishing all things, respecting life, responding to the needs of those whose beliefs come from the heart. These are services that the religion of the son can offer." [11]

Calm. Help. Nourish. Respect. Respond. Transform.

John's prologue is a beautiful prayer for us. In a few short poetic phrases, John dares us to examine our relationship with Christ. This is the true work of the Christmas moment.

Do I have a relationship with Jesus?

In John's prologue, Jesus is there at the

moment of creation, sitting at the right hand of God, a part of the essence of all that was and is and is to come.

Who is Jesus to me, anyway?

In moments of despair and anxiety, Jesus is light and life, bursting through the dark crevices of my heart, calling me out of myself, inviting me into the realm of God.

Am I brave enough to believe it?

Jesus is in the world, and though the world was made through Him, the world didn't and doesn't recognize him.

What will it take for me to recognize Christ in the world and in my life?

John proclaims with boldness and confidence, the word is made flesh and lives among us. This is written so that I might believe.

God help me in my unbelief.

THE E-TICKET

Our story picks up where The Book of Acts ends. The next scroll is ours to write, inhabit, incarnate and move out into the world. How does story help us to understand God?

Turn to the "Holy Story" section of your journal.

Open it so that you have a blank page on the left side of the fold and a blank page on the right side of the fold. At the top, centered across these two pages, write "Four Source Influences."

You are going to create a four-quadrant chart. From the top of the page to the bottom of the page, just past the binding on the right, draw a vertical line from the top of the page to the bottom of the page. In the center of the spread, going from the left page to the right page, draw a horizontal line. We have created four quadrants in the shape of

the cross.

Next, you want to identify the four sources. Label the top left quadrant "Action." Label the top right quadrant "Tradition." Label the bottom left quadrant "Culture." Label the bottom right quadrant "Position."

We will now create a list within each quadrant of the Four Sources.

In the "Action" quadrant, list significant events that occurred throughout your lifetime that have become a very part of your being and influence who you are today. List as many as you like. Take your time. If you run out of space, turn to the next page past your "Four Sources Influences" page. Label the next page "Action" and continue the list there. Once you have finished the "Action" quadrant, move to the "Tradition" quadrant.

In the "Tradition" quadrant, list significant scripture passages, holy stories, church music and teachings that speak to you in significant ways. List as many as you like. Take your time. If you run out of space, turn to the next page past your "Four Sources Influences" page. Label the next available page "Tradition" and continue the list there. Once you have finished the "Tradition" quadrant, move to the "Culture" quadrant.

In the "Culture" quadrant, list several books, films, television shows, music, and pieces of art that speak to who you are. Try to recall cultural influences from when you were younger and other cultural influences in years past. What is really speaking to you today? Take your time. If you run out of space, turn to the next available page past your "Four Sources Influences" page. Label it "Culture" and continue the list there. Once you have finished the "Culture" quadrant, move to the final quadrant, the "Position" quadrant.

In the "Position" quadrant, write several statements of belief. Begin each statement with "I believe…" Take your time. If you run out of space, turn to the next available page past your "Four Sources Influences" page. Label it "Position" and continue the list there.

Once you have finished the "Position" quadrant, take a break. Breathe. Get a drink of water. If you are at the Walt Disney World Resort, ride another ride and then come back to the list.

Look at the four quadrants. Which quadrant was easiest for you to fill? Which quadrant was the most difficult? Which is the quadrant that you are most comfortable living within? Which quadrant has the most room for growth?

Before you work on your "Rule of Life," list the quadrants in order, beginning with your favorite quadrant and finishing with your least favorite.

Once you have done this, turn to the "Rule of Life" section.

Use the following pattern to compose your Rule:

HOLY STORY

I believe God speaks to me most through _____ .

Personal experiences _____ .

Holy Scripture is _____ .

The Church is _____ .

Popular Culture is _____ .

I believe _____ .

I am most comfortable in the _____ quadrant.

I am least comfortable in the _____ quadrant.

I want to grow in the _____ quadrant.

 # THE COLLECT

We have looked at aspects of the story- God's story, your story, stories expressed by God's people, and personal beliefs based on your experiences through all of it.

Take some time to write a Collect based on your work up to this point. If you would like, you can use the following guidelines.

God, I thank you for all that was and is and is to come.

In your story, _____ .

In my story, _____ .

I get lost in _____ .

I am found in _____ .

Be with me and let me inhabit your story. All this I ask in your Holy Name. Amen.

ENDNOTES

[1] (Jones, 2005, p. 151)

[2] (Lynch, 1973, pp. 9-10)

[3] (May & Metzger, 1973, p. NT 125)

[4] (Revenson, 2006, p. 2)

[5] (Revenson, 2006, p. 6)

[6] (Wright, Imagineers (Group), & Walt Disney Company., 2007, p. 98)

[7] (Revenson, 2006, p. 5)

[8] (Palmer & Wong, 2001, p. 230)

[9] (Palmer & Wong, 2001, p. 223)

[10] (Palmer & Wong, 2001, p. 229)

[11] (Palmer & Wong, 2001, p. 223)

Which do you enjoy mo

The journey

The destination

HISTORY } *How Do I Find My Place in the Story?*

MAIN GATE

"There's a great big hunk of world down there with no fence around it," says Tramp in *The Lady and the Tramp.*

Walt Disney needed more space to create. He had transformed an orange grove in Anaheim, California, into Disneyland. The park's unprecedented success invited other entrepreneurs to gobble up the land that surrounded it. What was once an attractive orange grove was now a popular theme park, surrounded by the good, the bad and the ugly.

Walt wanted enough property to create the city of tomorrow. He envisioned EPCOT, an Experimental Prototype Community of Tomorrow. It was to be a place where corporations, individuals and technology innovators would temporarily reside, side-by-side, imagining and creating sustainable solutions from the Earth's limited resources. Disney shared, "What is needed in addition to the creative ability is courage - courage to try new things, to satisfy the endless curiosity of people for information about the world around them." [1]

Epcot, the second theme park built at the Walt Disney World Resort, is a response to that vision. The park is divided into two distinct but related areas. When guests enter, they pass under *Spaceship Earth* into Future World. Several pavilions are arranged in a circle that challenge us to use our imaginations to live into the hope of the future. The pavilions include Communication, Energy, Body, Space, Transportation, Imagination, Land and Sea.

Carl Walker, chairman and chief executive, said Epcot had four primary objectives. "First, we want Epcot to be a *'demonstration and proving ground for prototype concepts'*... constantly testing and demonstrating practical applications of new concepts, ideas, and emerging technology from creative centers around the world. Second, we want Epcot to provide an *'ongoing forum of the future'* where with the best creative thinking of the industry, government, and academia is exchanged regarding practical solutions to the real needs of mankind. A third important objective we have established is for Epcot to be a *'communicator to the world,'* utilizing the growing spectrum of information transfer to bring new knowledge in the most effective ways to the world community. Last and possibly most important of all, we want Epcot to be *'a permanent international people-to-people exchange'*... advancing the cause of world understanding among its citizens." [2]

The Communications pavilion in the middle of Future World is called *Spaceship Earth,* a term coined by futurist Buckminster Fuller. "He first used the term in his seminal 1969 work *Operating Manual for Spaceship Earth,* in which he put forth a vision of the people of this planet as crew members on a cosmic voyage, bound by our shared destiny, moving toward our common future. He generated some of the earliest concepts of sustainable living, of responsible use of resources, and design with an eye towards its long-term implications." [3] Buckminster's *Operating Manual for Spaceship Earth* is the ever-evolving blueprint for Epcot.

Beyond Future World, surrounding World Showcase Lagoon, is Epcot's permanent World's Fair. Host countries inhabit culturally themed pavilions promoting tradition, tourism and trade. "World Showcase presents the people, places and cultures that make our world special. (Guests) sample the food, admire the architecture, and learn the legends that make each step along the way unique. It's this vision of unity that leads us all into a shared future." [4] If you are working through the spiritual exercises in this book while visiting the Walt Disney World Resort, Epcot is a good park to sit and breathe and write and observe.

The pavilions for Mexico and Norway feature boat ride attractions similar to *It's a Small World* in The Magic Kingdom. The pavilions for The Peoples Republic of China, Canada and France feature beautiful films introducing guests to the scenic sights and music of the hosting country. The pavilions for Germany, Japan, Italy and Great Britain are primarily food and shopping experiences. Morocco is the most beautiful pavilion with every nook and cranny providing a breathtaking peek into eternity. The United States, at the center of World Showcase Lagoon, is the host pavilion. It features a dynamic multimedia presentation called "The American Adventure," hosted by Ben Franklin and Mark Twain.

A walk around World Showcase Lagoon is often relaxing, educational and entertaining. Artists from the host countries regularly gather to entertain guests with present cultural artistic programs

that inform and engage the senses. Restaurants, both upscale and quick service, allow a taste of international cuisine.

Every night, on World Showcase Lagoon, Epcot hosts a unique fireworks show called "IllumiNations: Reflections of Earth." Because of the park's circular design and vast, open spaces of water and land, it is a truly unifying experience. The narration begins, "We've gathered here tonight around the fire, as people of all lands have gathered for thousands and thousands of years before us, to share the light and to share a story— an amazing story, as old as time itself, but still being written. And though each of us has our own individual stories to tell, a true adventure emerges when we bring them all together as one. We hope you enjoy our story tonight: Reflections of Earth."

The show begins with the explosive creation of the known universe. Our Spaceship Earth appears out of the chaos and we witness across time and space, the evolution of communication and culture. The pavilions take their place in the story with laser lights and musical interjections and together we go on into the promise of the future.

A voice sings out to us, "With the stillness of the night there comes a time to understand, to reach out and touch tomorrow, take the future in our hand. We can see a new horizon built on all that we have done and our dreams begin another thousand circles 'round the sun. We go on through the joy and through the tears. We go on to discover new frontiers. Moving on with the current of the years, we go on moving forward now as one. Moving on in the spirit born to run. We go on with each rising sun to a new day. We go on."

On many nights, this firework spectacular closes Epcot for the evening. The country pavilions stand proudly illuminated in the darkness of the sky. Guests and hosts move about finishing a meal or concluding a celebration as others continue to do the work of the moment. Spaceship Earth, the illuminated sphere at the Epcot's entrance, guides all of us to the pathway home and into the future.

A voice invites us to go in peace and work together to create a better future. She sings, "Every evening brings an ending. Every day becomes a legacy. Every sunset leads to morning with the promise of opportunity. We can reach for the stars we find along the way, dreaming as we learn to love every day. Promise you will take my hand as tomorrow comes. We'll go on growing closer through the years, moving on through the good times and the tears. Ever on, another thousand circles 'round the sun, we'll go on. There is music, if you listen, in the rhythm of each breath we take, destinations undiscovered, revelations from every choice we make. And I know there are diamonds dancing in the sky. All we have to do is open our eyes. Promise we'll walk side by side as a new day dawns; we'll go on. We'll go on growing closer through the years moving on through the good times and the tears, ever on another thousand circles round the sun. And we live to keep the promise – we'll go on."

 IN THE QUEUE

"Life's not a spectator sport," quips Laverne from Disney's version of *The Hunchback of Notre Dame*.

Are you a participant or a spectator? For many of us, it depends on the day! There are days when we wake up, full of energy, jump into the shower and are ready to go. Then, there are other days when it takes every bit of strength in our being and every ounce of faith in our heart to open up our eyes in the morning, open the door and walk out into the world.

Due to circumstances and situations, we often forget that we are one of God's beloved. The vision given to each and every one of us through the power of God is almost too good to believe. So we believe other voices that reinforce our personal demons. If we have a vision of where we are headed and of what we want to do, we can quickly remember the person God created. If the vision isn't true to our spirit, we might be headed for trouble.

It is difficult to live into God's vision for us, not because of God, but because of everything that besets us during the course of a day. As most of the sciences have proven, negative energy creates more negative energy. And once we are trapped in it, it is difficult to move past it.

We live in a world of stories. We write them. We tell them. We see them at the movie theater. We sing about them at the music venue. Often, stories of others inspire us to do something on the days when life seems extremely difficult. On the other days when we are feeling most blessed, our story touches someone else and they gain the ability to open their eyes, walk out the door and live into a grace-filled vision of themselves.

If we are trying to find our place in the story, we must have vision. One way to begin is to broaden our perspective. We need to zoom out and look at the connections and disconnections of our life. Where do I find meaning in what I do? Where is meaning lacking? Where do I feel connected with others? Where do I feel lost and alone and lonely?

Our work for Holy Story is examining what scholars and theologians are currently calling relational neighborhoods. Their relational neighborhoods are those we work with, play with, worship with, study with or hang with. Using the street name, we ask you, "What gang or gangs do you belong to?"

Each and every one of us is in a gang. We all have gang affiliation. During biblical times, gangs were called the tribes of Israel – like-minded people who gathered together for power, protection and a place to belong. Popular gangs today include political parties, religious denominations, such as the Episcopal or Catholic or Lutheran or Baptist Church. Other common gangs are fraternities and sororities, alumni organizations, country clubs and even Girl and Boy Scouts. Which gang are you affiliated with?

If we are too afraid to call these groups by a negative media slur such as *gang*, we can call them "relational neighborhoods."

Move into the "Holy Story" section of your journal. Open it to the next available spread, where there is a blank page on the left and a blank page on the right.

In the center of the spread, write your name and draw a circle around it.

We are going to map your "relational neighborhoods." Give yourself space to work. If you are a social person, you may have a lot of neighborhoods so feel free to use space on the pages following.

List the relational neighborhoods in your life. Begin by naming the group. An example would be "family," "friends," "work," "book club," "church," or "gym," to name a few. Take your time. Think about all of your affinity groups, the people you hang out with for a common purpose or for the living out of a vision.

After you have identified the "neighborhoods" of your life, spend some time writing out the names of the people who are there in those neighborhoods that you engage with on a regular basis. You don't have to name everyone in the group. Near the name of the relational neighborhood, list the people you engage with the most.

Take your time. Do your best to create an exhaustive list.

After some time, consider the following:

Which relational neighborhoods are effortless, full of joy, easy to move to, through and into? Put a heart by those.

Which relational neighborhoods take some effort, full of people you care for, but you cannot always be yourself in? Put a check by those.

Which relational neighborhoods would you like to move out of because they drain your spirit and leave you tired and exhausted? Put an arrow by those.

Finally, are there any neighborhoods that you used to be in that have shut down due to time, space and distance? List those neighborhoods and put a circle by those.

Look at the neighborhoods. Is there one that really excites you and provides meaning to your life? Take a moment. Go to a new page in "Holy Story" and label the page "The Story of (name of neighborhood)."

Tell the history of that neighborhood. Some guiding questions might be: What brings the neighborhood together? Who is in it? Why does this neighborhood mean this much to me? Tell the story.

FROM THE BOOK
1 Corinthians 12:4 – 13:13

Corinth was a cosmopolitan town. Its location, just south-southwest of Athens, made it a destination city for the trader and the traveler. Caesar had populated the city by ordering emigrants from other parts of the Empire to move there. He encouraged upwardly mobile freepersons to settle there and transported others just released from prison to the city's outskirts.

This colorful cast of characters quickly helped Corinth to become known as "Sin City." People seeking adventure made their way to

Corinth to purchase products from its artisans, or to participate in the city's more risqué entertainment enterprises. Downtown, next to the market, just beyond the theater, was a Christian basilica, sharing the block with the Fountain of Poseidon and the Temple of Aphrodite. Modern archaeologists have found evidence supporting the existence of more than two dozen temples, several altars and shrines, including a huge gathering space believed to be a temple for all Gods.

Paul became upset with the Christian community he founded at Corinth because he observed that they no longer seemed concerned for their fellow citizens.

Early Christians, fearful of being persecuted by the empire, once met in secret, gathering in homes for a simple meal shared by all, followed by a prayerful remembrance of Christ's love for them, exemplified by his sacrifice of body and blood. But now in Corinth, as Christians gathered, the rich ate the finest meats and the poor gathered up the crumbs that were left under the table. This division of "rich" and "poor" upset Paul.

His letters call on the followers of Christ to take care of all the members, not just the ones who look or think, dress or act like you. True followers of Christ, whether living in the 1% or in the other 99% are charged by Jesus to take care of all people. Paul believed that our love of God is best shown through our love and care for each other.

The people of Corinth were forgetting this.

1 Corinthians 12:4 - 13:13

Now there are varieties of gifts, but the same Spirit; and there are varieties of services, but the same Lord; and there are varieties of activities, but it is the same God who activates all of them in everyone. To each is given the manifestation of the Spirit for the common good. To one is given through the Spirit the utterance of wisdom, and to another the utterance of knowledge according to the same Spirit, to another faith by the same Spirit, to another gifts of healing by the one Spirit, to another the working of miracles, to another prophecy, to another the discernment of spirits, to another various kinds of tongues, to another the interpretation of tongues. All these are activated by one and the same Spirit, who allots to each one individually just as the Spirit chooses.

One Body with Many Members

For just as the body is one and has many members, and all the members of the body, though many, are one body, so it is with Christ. For in the one Spirit we were all baptized into one body—Jews or Greeks, slaves or free—and we were all made to drink of one Spirit.

Indeed, the body does not consist of one member but of many. If the foot would say, "Because I am not a hand, I do not belong to the body," that would not make it any less a part of the body. And if the ear would say, "Because I am not an eye, I do not belong to the body," that would not make it any less a part of the body. If the whole body were an eye, where would the hearing be? If the whole body were hearing, where would the sense of smell be? But as it is, God arranged the members in the body, each one of them, as he chose. If all were a single member, where would the body be? As it is, there are many members, yet one body. The eye cannot say to the hand, "I have no need of you," nor again the head to the feet, "I have no need of you."

On the contrary, the members of the body that seem to be weaker are indispensable, and those members of the body that we think less honorable we clothe with greater honor, and our less respectable members are treated with greater respect; whereas our more respectable members do not need this. But God has so arranged the body, giving the greater honor to the inferior member, that there may be no dissension within the body, but the members may have the same care for one another. If one member suffers, all suffer together with it; if one member is honored, all rejoice together with it.

Now you are the body of Christ and individually members of it. And God has appointed in the church first apostles, second prophets, third teachers; then deeds of power, then gifts of healing, forms of assistance, forms of leadership, and various kinds of tongues. Are all apostles? Are all prophets? Are all teachers? Do all work miracles? Do all possess gifts of healing? Do all speak in tongues? Do all interpret? But strive for the greater gifts. And I will show you a still more excellent way.

The Gift of Love

If I speak in the tongues of mortals and of angels, but do not have love, I am a noisy gong or a clanging cymbal. And if I have prophetic powers, and understand all mysteries and all knowledge, and if I have all faith, so as to remove mountains, but do not have love, I am nothing. If I give away all my possessions, and if I hand over my body so that I may boast, but do not have love, I gain nothing.

Love is patient; love is kind; love is not envious or boastful or arrogant or rude. It does not insist on its own way; it is not irritable or resentful; it does not rejoice in wrongdoing, but rejoices in the truth. It bears all things, believes all things, hopes all things, endures all things.

Love never ends. But as for prophecies, they will come to an end; as for tongues, they will cease; as for knowledge, it will come to an end. For we know only in part, and we prophesy only in part: but when the complete comes, the partial will come to an end. When I was a child, I spoke like a child, I thought like a child, I reasoned like a child; when I became an adult, I put an end to childish ways. For now we see in a mirror, dimly, but then we will see face to face. Now I know only in part; then I will know fully, even as I have been fully known. And now faith, hope, and love abide, these three; and the greatest of these is love. [5]

RIDE THE ATTRACTION
Spaceship Earth

When I was younger, seeing Cinderella's Castle, or hearing the train pull into Main Street Station, or being able to spot and identify the unique thatched rooftop of *The Enchanted Tiki Room*, always gave me chills of excitement. As I have gotten older, I get the same feeling when I get my first glance of Spaceship Earth. The giant geodesic sphere looms large and welcomes all guests to Epcot.

Just after entering the park and passing through Legacy Plaza, guests pass directly under it. Wherever you may find yourself in Epcot, Spaceship Earth is visible, a marker during your journey through Future World or World Showcase.

Spaceship Earth is currently in its fourth incarnation but the theme of the rides has remained constant since its opening, the history of communication. "The show presents the evolution of man's ability to communicate. For earliest man, it was a distinct advantage to assuring his survival. From a relatively elementary means of handing down lessons learned to generations yet unborn, communication developed into an increasingly sophisticated tool for sharing information over an increasingly large area, and for the transmission of history, culture, ideas. Finally, it has become an incredibly complex network through which information speeds, enabling mankind to share its accumulated knowledge for the common good, to maximize its potential for making wise and informed decisions for the future." [6]

Once entering Spaceship Earth, guests are invited to board their Time Machine Vehicles. The doors close and we immediately begin to ascend, virtually moving backwards in time.

Judi Dench, the current narrator of Spaceship Earth, sets the scene, saying, "Like a grand and miraculous spaceship, our planet has sailed through the universe of time. And for a brief moment, we have been among its passengers. But where are we going? And what kind of future will we discover there? Surprisingly, the answers lie in our past. Since the dawn of recorded history, we have been inventing the future one step at a time."

Our Time Machine Vehicles level off and round a corner. We find ourselves in prehistoric times where Neanderthals fight for survival. Projections on curbed surfaces remind us that we are actually traveling within the geodesic sphere. Ms. Dench continues, "Here in this hostile world is where our story begins. We are alone, struggling to survive, until we learn to communicate with one another."

Our Time Machine Vehicles pass by what is suggested to be the earliest form of communication, cave drawings. But there was one problem. "When we moved, the recorded knowledge stayed behind."

As we round the corner, time travelers discover that the problem is about to be solved. An unknown Egyptian pounds reeds flat, inventing papyrus. Papyrus can record the Egyptian Pharaoh's commands and, unlike a cave drawing, it is portable.

Just beyond the Pharaoh, we discover that we are in a seaport. As sea trade increases, merchants begin to spread language because Phoenicians were able to "create a simple, common alphabet adaptable to most languages."

As we begin to communicate facts and figures and historically significant events, we begin to desire to communicate thoughts and feelings. We move through a performance of "Oedipus Rex" at the Pantheon. Ms. Dench continues, "The ancient Greeks were great inventors of the future. First, they established public schools, and then began teaching an intriguing new subject called mathematics. With math comes mechanical technology and the birth of the high tech life we enjoy today."

Just across the way, time travelers encounter the creation of Roman infrastructure. Roads and canals and aquaducts begin to connect citizens near and far. "With lessons learned from the Greeks, the Romans create a powerful empire. To move their armies around, they built a system of roads all over the known world. Rome built the first World Wide Web, and it's leading us to the future."

Connectedness also leads to vulnerability and Rome falls in 476 AD. The Library at Alexandria in Egypt is burned, but we learn that Arabic and Jewish scholars had been preserving a lot of the texts that were in the library. "Call it the first back-up system. The books are saved, and, in them, our dreams of the future."

As time travelers pass monks who are painstakingly copying manuscripts so that they can be passed on and shared, we are about to witness another revelatory communications game-changer: the invention of the movable type printing press by Johannes Gutenberg. This sharing of information and ideas fueled the Renaissance, which our Time Travel Vehicles move through next.

Time travelers witness a woman sitting for a portrait. Then we pass under an intricate scaffolding set-up built for Michelangelo for the painting of the Sistine Chapel.

With the advent of machinery, we begin to move rapidly into the modern era. We witness the evolution of the telegraph, radio, telephony and movies. Ms. Dench addresses us: "Communication technology races headlong into the future, and soon people all over the world are sharing life's most important moments faster than ever. By now we're all communicating from anywhere on Earth." Within a few feet, we witness the televised broadcast of the Apollo 11 moon landing, the invention of the mainframe computer, culminating with our Time Machines passing through binary code.

We emerge from the tunnel and find ourselves moving through the vastness of Space. From this out-of-this-world vantage point we see Spaceship Earth from a distance. Ms. Dench concludes this part of our journey, saying, "After 30,000 years of time travel, here we are, a truly global community networked online poised to shape the future of this, our Spaceship Earth."

Since we have traveled from the dawn of recorded time to the present moment, it is time for time travelers to find their place in the story. As the ride descends, Ms. Dench gathers information, helping guests identify their passions, interests and hopes for the future.

As we return from our adventure through time, we are invited to imagine what kind of future we want to dream about and create.

FOR REFLECTION

The Book of Acts opens with, "In the first book, Theophilus..."

Theophilus means "God-lover." We do not believe Theophilus is an actual person but is all of us. The Book of Acts addresses all of us who call ourselves lovers of God.

Dear God-lover, . . .

Our hope, our prayer, our shared reality is that our story is a part of God's story. What will it take for me to remember that I live under God? God is the common thread to everything in my discombobulated life. Most times, I stay discombobulated instead of remembering the one common thread.

In the Book of Acts, there is a lot of history,

a lot to speculate about as we read between the lines. The Book of Acts informs our understanding of the beginnings of the early Church and what it means to be a church today. The Book of Acts introduces us to the first disciples of Christ, those who are charged with the mission of spreading the Good News and what it means to be a people of Good News today.

The primary theme of the Book of Acts comes together in a fiery moment where all the faithful are transformed into the resurrected body of Christ. In the moment of Pentecost, we are called to feed, to heal, to serve and to proclaim that all are God's people and that all are beloved by God. This is a hard message to proclaim. We live in a world that does not want to believe that all are equal in God's eyes.

We live a discombobulated life because we forget that God is with everyone, everywhere. We label. We dismiss. We put on a pedestal. We put in the gutter. We fragment our existence so we can act one way over here and another way over there. We forget the truth and get lost in the story, stuck on a footnote that does not add much to the thread.

After Pentecost and after the Book of Acts ends, we are called to find our place in the story. The Book of Acts finishes abruptly, but the story it is writing is not over. We are to turn the page and vision and write and live the continuation of God's salvation story. The theme is quite simple. Love God. Love my neighbor. The rest is lagniappe. What is your place in God's ongoing story of love and salvation?

Power comes from inequality. We want to label, to condemn, to divide and conquer, so that we can believe that the inequalities of this world are ordained by God. I am often puzzled when people say to me, and priests hear this a lot, "I don't like organized religion." I usually respond by saying, "What's the alternative, unorganized religion?"

To respond to the Gospel call, we must be organized. We must be held accountable. We must be in relationship with God and with God's people. We must have others to remind us of who we are when we seem to have forgotten. This is what the Church does. This is what community does.

Community helps us answer where we have been, where we are and where we are going. The truth is, we do not like to be held accountable to anyone, not even to God.

In the Book of Acts, Jesus' twelve disciples became apostles. In the beginning, they were working together in Jerusalem. But as differences in faith-teachings emerged, many left, traveling to far away lands, spreading the message of new life.

Then questions began to shape the mission. Who should be allowed to do this work? The elect? The special? The newly ordained? Certainly not everybody! Right?

Throughout the Book of Acts and buried within all of Paul's letters is the basic question of who is in and who is out. Can people without Jewish heritage really be admitted into this fellowship of faith? Paul's answer was yes. Like Paul who had a thorn in his side, none of us are perfect. Paul reminded us of that! But also Paul reminded us that by God's grace, we can create community and live out the mission of loving God and loving each other with much success.

Jewish authorities in Jerusalem were not pleased with Paul's missions to the Gentiles, to the outlying churches. They did seem happy to see him when he was bringing the tithe he was collecting for the Temple in Jerusalem, however.

When we read the Book of Acts, we discover that their story is our story.

We ask the same questions.

How do I respond to God?

What must I give?

Who is in and who is out?

Is it possible to suffer and to remain faithful to Christ?

What do the crucifixion and resurrection of Jesus Christ mean and what do they have to do with me anyway?

In a noisy world, the seasons of the Church help us learn and live and respond to the narrative journey. The seasons are markers so that we may participate.

At the beginning of the Church year, usually early December, during the Season of Advent, we celebrate hope and expectation. We pray to discover God's hope for us. We pray to hear God's call to us. "Stir up your power, O Lord, and with great might come among us; and because we are sorely hindered by our sins, let your bountiful grace and mercy speedily help and deliver us!" [7]

During Christmas, we celebrate birth and new life. We stare at the crèche and ponder the mystery of God with us in Jesus Christ. We have cleared the space. We have seen the angels. We have heard the shepherds yelling out that we all must journey and sit in the mystery. "God, you make us glad by the yearly festival of the birth of your only Son Jesus Christ: Grant that we, who joyfully receive him as our Redeemer, may with sure confidence behold him when he comes to be our Judge." [8]

After the birth of Christ, we begin the journey of faith. We look to the stars to get us back on track when we stray from the path. We look to the faith of others to comfort us and to heal us when we are sick with despair. We find the path. We lose the path. We find the path. We lose the path. "God, by the leading of a star you manifested your only Son to the Peoples of the earth: Lead us, who know you now by faith, to your presence, where we may see your glory face to face." [9]

Lent invites us to examine our lives, to see where we are and to regroup. It is a time for prayer. It is a time for forgiveness. It is not a time to beat ourselves up. We have the world to do that. It is a time to ask God to find us in the desert and to heal what needs to be healed. As a healthy, happy person, we can joyfully proclaim the love of the Gospel. "God, whose blessed Son was led by the Spirit to be tempted by Satan; Come quickly to help us who are assaulted by many temptations; and, as you know the weaknesses of each of us, let each one find you might to save." [10]

As we begin to find our place in the story, we move into Holy Week. As we walk with Jesus during his last week in Jerusalem, we look at where we are so that we can claim it as holy, so that we learn to walk with confidence the way of the cross, so that we might incarnate, to take on, the ministry and actions of Jesus. "God, mercifully grant that we may walk in the way of his suffering, and also share in His resurrection." [11] We wash feet, we pray for the world at the foot of the cross, we see death and the tomb, then as the morning breaks, a new dawn comes and new life is the gift of God.

We move through the Book of Acts where we learn about the history and foundation of the Church so that we can discover together what it means to be people of God.

Our Easter journey ends at Pentecost, with the gift of the Holy Spirit, the beginning of our mission, where we pick up the rest of the story.

What is the theme of the story? What is the mission of God? How do I find my place in the story? Remember the seasons.

"For everything there is a season, and a time for every matter under heaven: a time to be born, and a time to die; a time to plant, and a time to pluck up what is planted; a time to kill, and a time to heal; a time to break down, and a time to build up; a time to weep, and a time to laugh; a time to mourn, and a time to dance; a time to throw away stones, and a time to gather stones together; a time to embrace, and a time to refrain from embracing; a time to seek, and a time to lose; a time to keep, and a time to throw away; a time to tear, and a time to sew;

a time to keep silence, and a time to speak; a time to love, and a time to hate; a time for war, and a time for peace." [12]

This is my story. This is your story. This is God's story. May we find the faith to live into all of God's hopes and dreams when God created the world and the people inhabiting it.

THE E-TICKET

Walt Disney once said, "The way to get started is to quit talking and start doing." [13]

Return to the "Holy Story - Relational Neighborhoods" section of your journal.

Look at your relational neighborhoods. Our task at hand is to identify the role of God through you in each of these neighborhoods. Generally, does God's spirit guide your thoughts, actions and relational motivations in each neighborhood?

In each neighborhood, ask the following questions: What gifts do I bring to this neighborhood? What do I give to this neighborhood? What do I take? Where is God in this neighborhood? Is God present or is God absent? If God is present, how does God impact the decisions you make while in this neighborhood? If God is absent, why? What would it take from you to make God present in this neighborhood. Identify thoughts and feelings about each neighborhood.

Once you have moved through the neighborhoods, where is God totally absent? Where is God totally present? Are there inconsistencies among neighborhoods? If there are, why? Review the thoughts and feelings and look for disconnects.

Our challenge in God's story is to make everything we say and do somehow connected with God. Where there are disconnects in our thoughts and feelings, there is trouble.

Ask yourself: How do I make God the common thread in all of these neighborhoods, in all of my life, so everything I do is directed by God? Because everything we do matters.

Rule of Life

For this Rule, look over the gifts you bring to your relational neighborhoods. Move to the "Rule of Life" section of your journal. Write the word *Story*. If you know your place in God's story, begin your rule with "My place in God's story is…" If you are searching for a place, begin your rule with, "I do not know my place in the story but…"

Story

My place in God's story is _____.
or
I do not know my place in the story but …

Then list the gifts you bring to the story. Finish your rule by saying how you can use these gifts in everyday life.

 # THE COLLECT

You will write a Collect that encompasses meaningful aspects of your life. What you have done or what you have left undone is all a part of the story.

Begin your Collect by addressing God. Next, proclaim an aspect of God that you have been thinking about as you moved through the work of this section. Next, compose a line stating whether today you feel like a participant or a spectator. Claim it. Name it. Describe it. Give thanks for your relational neighborhoods. Name them. Next, give thanks for the gifts you bring. Name them. Then, ask God to help you develop other gifts. Where do you want to grow? Conclude the Collect.

+

Endnotes

1. (Gordon & Kurtti, 2008, p. 163)
2. (Beard & Disney, 1982, p. 29)
3. (Wright et al., 2010, p. 34)
4. (Wright et al., 2010, p. 75)
5. (May & Metzger, 1973, p. NT 242-244)
6. (Beard & Disney, 1982, p. 40)
7. (Episcopal Church., 1979, p. 212)
8. (Episcopal Church., 1979, p. 212)
9. (Episcopal Church., 1979, p. 214)
10. (Episcopal Church., 1979, p. 218)
11. (Episcopal Church., 1979, p. 219)
12. (May & Metzger, 1973, p. 212)
13. (Smith, 1994, p. ix)

THE OTHER } *How Do I Know My Neighbor?*

 MAIN GATE

"If you walk the footsteps of a stranger, you'll learn things you never knew you never knew," sings Pocahontas in Disney's version of her life story.

People are different. Our only commonality is that God created all of us. But that simple fact is easy to forget as differences divide us.

Division runs deep. There is me. There is us. Then, there is THEM.

We have created labels to help us quickly identify THEM, to help us quickly identify differences - name, race, gender, sexuality, religion, birthdate, country of origin, "this" or "that" or "other." What happens if you check "other"?

The list of identifiers goes on and on. At many times during our lives, we have had to write out or circle in with a # 2 pencil. What identifies me as "me" quickly separates me from the "other." As we identify ourselves against the "other," our differences are reinforced and build our identities and self-worth as "me" and against "them."

If we can easily identify differences, we can easily develop prejudices.

Once done, it is hard to undo.

As a citizen of the United States, it is easy to believe that there are people who want me dead. As a creature of God, how do I forget my fear and love my neighbor as self? As a creature of God, I am compelled to believe that God created this world and called it good. How can I look through the prejudice and hate and see the overwhelming majority of humanity living into loving neighbor as self?

Our scripture is full of comparisons to the other. They are "this." We are "that." They do "this." We do "that." Within the Biblical context, this pointing out of differences is simply a call to be faithful. As people who are drawn to wallow and get stuck in our own sins, it is easier to stick to and point out the differences that lead to the development of a "holier than thou" attitude. This attitude is keeping the younger generations from walking into the doors of churches and temples and synagogues and mosques all over the world.

Is it possible to stop the labels and move beyond the prejudices? A clergy friend of mine who has done a lot of anti-racism work does not think so. He said to me once, "I believe we are just wired this way. It's in our DNA."

I don't know if I believe that. But when I look around the world, the evidence suggests that there may be some truth in his statement. If it is true, it challenges some of my basic beliefs about God. I rarely agree with my friend's statements, but he is one of the smartest and most mystical people I know, so his belief gives me much pause.

The world is getting smaller. We communicate with each other, with people all around the world, in an instant. Thanks to advancements in communications technology, we talk through culture, language and social barriers with ease. Young people think it is quite normal to speak to and see someone in Japan or China with the click of a button on any smart device.

Because of the glow of technology's light, are the differences disappearing? Even though we are not the same, can we see through all of this and recognize our common humanity under God?

From time immemorial, we have put all our hopes and dreams on the next generation. Unfortunately, we have also passed on our fears and prejudices. But, as young people say, "I know such-and-such from Syria" or "so-and-so is my friend and he is gay," are differences recognized but no longer leading to prejudicial thinking? Can we celebrate the promise of the future through the children of the world?

At the Walt Disney World Resort, differences are pointed out and celebrated. World Showcase at Epcot is a shopping mall of cultural differences that people admire and charge to their credit cards to take home. At Disney's Animal Kingdom, we travel from continent to continent encountering different cultures, ecosystems, and animal wildlife and understand a new way to be citizens of the world. Most guests do not appear to be alarmed by the differences even if they do not know how to interact with some of the attraction hosts from different countries. A loud laugh or a deafening guffaw is often heard as people step out of their comfort zone and engage with the other.

In Fantasyland, at The Magic Kingdom, *It's a Small World* is an attraction you either love or hate. There doesn't appear to be any middle-ground here. I love it. I know people who hate it.

I have to ride *It's a Small World* every time I visit The Magic Kingdom. It just doesn't feel like a trip to Disney World without this traditional boat ride. I know people who won't even be seen near the ride except that *Peter Pan's Flight* is right across the way.

There is something about *It's a Small World* that irks a lot of people. Perhaps it is the repetitive song. Perhaps it is just too happy for some. Perhaps it is a fear of dancing dolls. Maybe we are just too cynical to enjoy the message that is being shared with us.

What is the message?

I think the ride is filled with messages. Some are consistent. Some are not. Does the ride prepare us to want to know and celebrate our neighbor? Or does the ride easily fall into the label category where we can enjoy a boat ride and say "I am this, but I am definitely not that."

As life lets us down, we begin to blame our differences for our inability to communicate with the "other." We put others in their place, so we can lay claim to where we stand.

At *It's a Small World,* the children of the world invite us on the happiest cruise on Earth. Can I accept their invitation and dare to dream of a place where we are different, but a place where God as creator unites us by a common thread?

We like to ignore or overlook differences. We want to eliminate the differences. We want to say we are all alike. We are not. The God we created is so vast and expansive that a wonderful and inspirational aspect of God incarnate plays out in the differences of each and every one of us.

What are we to do? Love God. Love neighbor. Is it really that simple? Probably.

Walt Disney said, "We have created characters and animated them in the dimension of depth, revealing through them to our perturbed world that the things we have in common far outnumber and outweigh those that divide us." [1]

IN THE QUEUE

Love God. Love your neighbor as yourself.

Jesus sums all of God's commandments, in the Old and New Testament and Gospels combined, in a summary response.

Perhaps this is too simple.

Is this it a trick? I don't think so.

Just imagine the world if we could love our neighbors and if we could love ourselves. What a transformation would occur.

To love, we must respond. Love is not passive. It is active. Love requires work, care, and nourishment, or it dies, and possibly turns into hate.

Our level of fear corresponds with our ability to love. Jesus knew this, which is why Jesus challenges us with this summary commandment. Love God. Love your neighbor. Love yourself.

If we really love God, we must love the other. Just as God created me, God created the other. There are no exceptions to this. People who are different from me came from the same place I did ——God.

In the Disney animated classic, *Beauty and the Beast,* a jealous hunter stirs up the village people to get rid of a beast that lives in a castle at the top of a hill. As the overzealous crowd marches toward the castle bearing knives and cudgels, they sing, "We don't like what we don't understand and, in fact, it scares us, and this monster is mysterious at least. Bring your guns, bring your knives, save your children and your wives, so save our village and our lives! Let's kill the beast!"

And so off they go, intending to do just that. "We don't like what we don't understand, in fact it scares us."

When we belittle the other, when we refuse to love, we crucify. Crucifixion is happening all around us all the time in our dismissiveness of the other. It may not be as bloody as Jesus' crucifixion but it much more dangerous and deadly. It is dangerous because we don't see it. We must take notice of all who are being crucified so that we can pray and be inspired by the spirit to act.

Open your journal to the "Holy Story" section. At the top of the next available page, write "The Other."

Take a moment to consider who is "other" to you. Take some time. If it is a person you know, write down the name. If it a particular group of people, write down the label.

Next, list the places where you have traveled. Begin with your native country. Then move to the borders beyond. What places did you enjoy; what places made you feel uncomfortable; what places made you scared? List the places and answer the questions.

Then consider this: How do you know what you know? Who are your neighbors? Are they in the same neighborhood? City? State? Country? How do you get information about your neighbors? List the neighbors you hear about most often. What do you know about them? What is the source of your information? Write it down.

Spend some time considering movies or books or newspapers you have read recently. Conclude this section by listing countries you want to visit and list why. List countries you would be afraid to visit and list why.

Who is your neighbor?

FROM THE BOOK
Luke 10: 25-37

Tradition asserts that the Gospel of Luke was written by a physician, a person who knew Paul and occasionally accompanied him. In spite of the fact that he was a Gentile, an outsider to Jewish customs and traditions, he was very knowledgeable of the law. The Gospel of Luke and the Acts of the Apostles were written by the same person. The Gospel concludes with a preview of the first chapters of Acts while Acts opens with a summary of the conclusion of the Gospel. Luke focuses on the life and ministry of Jesus while Acts presents the story of early discipleship and the beginnings of Christian communities, the early gatherings that evolved into the Church of today. It appears the Gospel was written after the fall of Jerusalem, dating it around 85 to 90 AD. Scholarship suggests that Luke relied heavily on the Gospel of Mark as a source. It also appears that Luke conducted extensive interviews with witnesses "so that you may know the truth concerning the things about which you have been instructed." [2]

Being an outsider, Luke is particularly driven to proclaim that the Gospel message of Jesus is for all people everywhere. Luke also believed that Jesus' life, death and resurrection played out in history calling for a 180-degree societal shift in response to the poor and oppressed. This is beautifully illustrated in Mary's "yes" to bear the Christ Child through her proclamation of the Magnificat. Luke calls on the followers of Christ to trust the power of the Holy Spirit when working with the other in ministry, in the seeking of justice and when standing side-by-side in the public square.

LUKE 10:25-37

"Teacher," he said, "what must I do to inherit eternal life?" He said to him, "What is written in the law? What do you read there?" He answered, "You shall love the Lord your God with all your heart, and with all your soul, and with all your strength, and with all your mind; and your neighbor as yourself." And he said to him, "You have given the right answer; do this, and you will live."

But wanting to justify himself, he asked Jesus, "And who is my neighbor?" Jesus replied, "A man was going down from Jerusalem to Jericho, and fell into the hands of robbers, who stripped him, beat him, and went away, leaving him half dead. Now by chance a priest was going down that road; and when he saw him, he passed by on the other side. So likewise a Levite, when he came to the place and saw him, passed by on the other side. But a Samaritan while traveling came near him; and when he saw him, he was moved with pity. He went to him and bandaged his wounds, having poured oil and wine on them. Then he put him on his own animal, brought him to an inn, and took care of him. The next day he took out two denarii, gave them to the innkeeper, and said, 'Take care of him; and when I come back, I will repay you whatever more you spend.' Which of these three, do you think, was a neighbor to the man who fell into the hands of the robbers?" He said, "The one who showed him mercy." Jesus said to him, "Go and do likewise." [3]

RIDE THE ATTRACTION

It's a Small World

It's a Small World is the happiest cruise on Earth. Located in Fantasyland at The Magic Kingdom, the attraction was originally designed as a tribute pavilion for the United Nations Children's Fund (UNICEF), premiering at the 1964 New York World's Fair. Mary Blair, an animator Imagineer, created the attraction's look featuring costumed children in festive settings from all around the world. The traveler is invited to contemplate an existential reality. We are living on a very small planet in an incredibly overwhelming universe. What binds us together? What do we have in common?

The music for *It's a Small World* suggests

that despite our cultural contexts, our shared humanity connects us with each other. Composers Robert and Richard Sherman never imagined the impact that their simple tune would have. "They considered donating their royalties to charity. 'Don't you ever do that!' Disney chided when they told him. 'This song is going to see your kids through college. Make a donation... but don't give away your royalties.'" [4]

Many other of Disney's signature attractions were designed to premier alongside *It's A Small World* at the 1964 World's Fair. Disney had begun to develop a vision for EPCOT, the Experimental Prototype Community of Tomorrow. He was hoping to establish relationships with companies working with cutting edge technologies. If the World's Fair partnerships were successful, Walt hoped they would come on board and help vision and build the EPCOT. Center project. In addition to UNICEF and Pepsi Cola sponsoring *It's a Small World*, "Ford agreed to a Magic Skyway exhibit that would carry people through the dinosaur and Stone Age diorama. General Electric was also eager to work with Disney, especially with the hopes of improving its tarnished reputation after a price-fixing scandal: Disney proposed a rotating Audio-Animatronics household that would highlight the benefits of electricity... (T)he State of Illinois cast its support behind a lifelike orating model of President Lincoln." [5]

At the conclusion of the fair, these rides found a new home at Disneyland. The Stone Age diorama became a part of a tunnel attraction along the route of the Disneyland Railroad. *The Carousel of Progress* became part of the renovated Tomorrowland. The encounter with President Lincoln would find a new home on Main Street but it would eventually inspire the creation of the Hall of the Presidents, a celebration of the history and leadership of the United States of America.

The entrance to *It's a Small World* is just across from *Peter Pan's Flight*. You can't miss it. You might trip on a stroller. The majestic Tower of the Four Winds, which invited the rider to the attraction's boat dock in Disneyland, had to be downscaled to fit into an interior queue of *It's a Small World* because of Florida's dramatically different weather conditions.

Once onboard, we sail past Pinocchio's Village Haus, and travel under a sign that says, "Welcome to the happiest cruise that ever sailed."

As we move into the ride's interior, Robert and Richard Sherman's familiar tune takes hold of our senses. The dolls sing, "It's a world of laughter, a world or tears. It's a world of hopes and a world of fears. There's so much that we share that it's time we're aware, it's a small world after all."

We sail through Scandinavia and the British Isles while ice skaters and the Royal Navy move and perform to the theme song. Just around the bend, we see kicking can-can girls (these are children after all) gathered together under the Eiffel Tower in Paris. Directly across from them, children sing from the moon suspensed just above Big Ben and the Tower Bridge.

"It's a small, small world."

We glide by Ireland and search for a pot of gold at the foot of a rainbow. Then we sail past a gondola parked in Venice's St. Mark's Square. Wooden shoes, cuckoo clocks and the windmills of Don Quixote move us through Western Europe and into the Middle East.

Flying carpets glide just over the heads of belly dancers who give way to Indonesian dancers. India's Taj Mahal is flanked with dancing children; Temple Hosts greet passers-by with *namaste* saying thank you for visiting Asia.

As we prepare to jump continents, the children of the world continue to entertain us, singing, "There is just one moon and one golden sun. And a smile means friendship to everyone. Though the mountains divide and the oceans are wide, it's a small, small world."

Our boat moves through Africa where dense jungles, playful animals and various tribal peoples join in on the song. We head south past the dancing penguins of Antarctica into the warmer climates of Central and South America. Mariachis, street vendors and tropical rain forests invite us to ponder the dramatic climate shifts within this part of the world.

The beauty of the Islands of the South Pacific call us forward. Young hula women, brave fire dancers and giant rocking kangaroos welcome us to our final destination, the Grand Finale.

It appears that the children of the world have assembled to celebrate at an amusement park. There is a roller coaster, a Ferris wheel, several air acrobats and hot air balloons. The beauty of native costumes has been stripped away and everyone is wearing white. The message here is as beautiful as it is disturbing. We celebrate our common humanity, but at the cost of recognizing our differences. Is this a subtle nod towards gentrification? I sincerely doubt this is what the creators of the ride had in mind. But like all created and packaged messages, we bring our experiences and interpretations into the mix.

As we approach the dock, we see *good-bye* written in several different languages and then disembark at the foot of the Tower of Four Winds.

"It's a small world after all. It's a small world after all. It's a small world after all. It's a small, small world."

FOR REFLECTION

"Speak, for your servant is listening."

Have you ever done battle with God in the middle of the night?

It has been one of those days where everything has gone wrong. You can't sleep. Nothing makes sense. Events of the day are replayed over and over and over again. The voices in your mind are loud and they silence the reality around you. All you hear is the negativity dragging you into an abyss of isolation.

"Speak, for your servant is listening."

I want God to speak, but I haven't prepared the space in my heart, in my mind, in my room, in my life. How can I listen when I am not prepared?

We have to prepare a space. We have to keep the candles lit. We have to clear the area so that on nights like these, we can sit in the presence of God and listen.

This takes practice. Sitting in silence. Waiting. Wondering. Then listening some more.

If we don't practice silence, we cannot possibly recognize the voice of God in the midst of the other voice of the mind.

A slight whisper. A pondering. What was that? Did I hear correctly?

Silence. Listening. Waiting some more.

A voice cries out.

It says, "I have a dream that one day, this nation will rise up and live out the true meaning of its creed: 'We hold these truths to be self-evident that all men are created equal.'... I have a dream that my four little children will one day live in a nation where they will not be judged by the color of their skin but by the content of their character. I have a dream today." [6]

Dr. Martin Luther King, Junior, proclaimed those famous words in 1963, a time when our nation was still struggling with who was in and who was out, struggling with who was entitled to equality and who was not, a time when we were dividing into separate camps, camps of us against them.

Today, so many years later, King's words are still hauntingly applicable; we still hear strong opposition to equal rights for all of God's people.

Not everyone is entitled to the American dream.

Not everyone is entitled to food, health and healing.

Not everyone is entitled to dignity, respect, freedom and the chance to live into the person that God created when God created us.

That was then.

This is now.

"Speak, for your servant is listening."

Eight hundred years before the birth of Christ, a time not too different from our own, the people of Israel settled in the Promised Land but the tribes are scattered all about. Foreigners have moved into the land, and with them, their traditions.

These foreigners are different. Scary. They do not look like me. They do not think like us. Where did they come from? Who or what created them?

The twelve tribes of Israel are guided by military Judges. The foreign people encroach upon the Hebrews. The Judges organize the people. The Hebrews attack and push back the foreigners in God's name.

In thanksgiving for victory, the Judges call on the people to be faithful to God and to be faithful to each other.

The people are faithful for a brief time. But some of the traditions of the foreigners remain and start to change how the people think of God and how the people respond to each other. "There are people out there, different from us."

The nations that surround the Hebrew tribes have kings, some of whom even claim to be divine!

The Hebrew people are impatient with God. They want a king. They want a powerful ruler like the pagans surrounding them have.

"Speak, for your servant is listening."

The word of the LORD was rare in those days; visions were not widespread. At the temple of the people of Israel, Eli is an old priest, going blind, but is faithful to God. Eli's sons, who are charged with taking care of the people's relationship with God, abuse their status as priests of the people, satisfying their own desires.

Eli is distressed with his sons' betrayal. Eli knows God will seek justice. He works diligently in the Tent of Meeting, mentoring the young boy Samuel. Because of his sons' bad behavior, Eli knows it will be more and more difficult for him to hear the voice of God.

What does God want from Eli?

What will God do because of Eli's sons' lack of faith?

His sons consume the precious fat of the sacrifices and abuse the women who have come to worship the Lord at the tent of meeting.

First, Eli acknowledges and claims the dire reality of the situation.

Next, Eli remembers who he is as a person of God.

Then, Eli remembers God and the covenants that God has made.

Eli has taken a moment to look honestly at what is going on.

Space has been made.

Eli prays that God will be just. Eli prays that God will remember his faithfulness.

"Speak, for your servant is listening."

Sometimes, it is hard to hear. We live in a noisy world. Often, the noisiness of our surroundings contributes to the noisiness inside our heads.

We have voices that tell us to do something. We hear voices that want to change the way we act. We hear voices that cause us to doubt who we are.

We hear voices that cause confusion in our souls. The noise is loud.

God seems so far away.

How can I silence the voices so that I can hear what is truly being said?

Martin Luther King says this: "Darkness cannot drive out darkness; only light can do that. Hate cannot drive out hate; only love can do that. Hate multiplies hate, violence multiplies violence, and toughness multiplies toughness in a descending spiral of destruction... The chain reaction of evil- hate begetting hate, wars producing more wars - must be broken, or we shall be plunged into the dark abyss of annihilation." [7]

God steps in to break the chain of hate. But in order for God to act, we must have a relationship with God. We must clear a space. We must sit in silence. We must invite God to be a part of our lives.

Pharaoh abuses the people. God steps in, delivering the people from slavery.

Privilege creates suspicion and oppression. A nation divides. People go to war. God steps in and lets the people go.

The birth of a savior, the gospel of feeding and healing, a call to free all people in the name of Christ. We kill Jesus, God steps in, and through the power of resurrection, we are promised new life.

"Speak, for your servant is listening."

Eli, whose eyesight has begun to grow dim so that he cannot see, was lying down in his room. The lamp of God had not yet gone out, and Samuel was lying down in the temple of the LORD, with the ark of God.

A call from God comes to Samuel. But Samuel thinks it is Eli. So Samuel goes in to Eli who responds that he has not called. Eli dismisses Samuel so Samuel goes back to sleep.

But God is restless. The darkness is heavy. The stars illuminate the night sky.

God calls Samuel again.

Samuel, once again, goes in to Eli. But Eli is groggy from sleep. Once again, he sends the boy away.

Waiting. Wondering. Listening some more. A slight whisper. A pondering.

What was that?

Did I hear correctly?

Once again, Samuel wakes Eli, thinking that Eli has summoned him. Suddenly, Eli realizes that God is doing something new through Samuel. Eli instructs Samuel to go and sit and wait and listen.

When God calls, Eli tells Samuel to respond saying "Speak, for your servant is listening."

Eli is a faithful man. He knows that his family will no longer be the priests of God's people. His sons have failed. Eli loves God and waits to hear from Samuel about what God is up to.

"Samuel, my son."

Samuel says, "Here I am."

Eli asks, "What was it that God told you? Do not hide it from me. May God do so to you and more also, if you hide anything from me of all that he told you."

So Samuel told Eli everything and hid nothing from him.

Then Eli said, "It is the LORD; let him do what seems good to him."

Martin Luther King says this: "I have decided to love. If you are seeking the highest good, I think you can find it through love. And the beautiful thing is that we are moving against wrong when we do it, because John was right, God is love. He who hates does not know God, but he who has love has the key that unlocks the door to the meaning of ultimate reality." [8]

As God calls on Samuel to remind God's people of the covenant, Martin Luther King still calls on us to remember that all people are created equal.

But we don't treat all people as if we truly believe in that equality.

When the voices of prejudice, oppression, discrimination and injustice are loud, prophetic voices have to break through the noise, hopefully finding us sitting in the silence of prayer so that we can hear what needs to be done. May we have the patience, and the love, and the strength and the faith to listen.

Martin Luther King says this: "Injustice anywhere is a threat to justice everywhere. We are caught in an inescapable network of mutuality tied in a single garment of destiny. Whatever affects one directly, affects all indirectly." [9]

"Speak, for your servant is listening."

THE E-TICKET

Charles Dickens shares in his tale of otherness, community and woe, the classic *A Tale of Two Cities,* "A wonderful fact to reflect upon, that every human creature is constituted to be that profound secret and mystery to every other."

An entryway into the heart of the other begins with an examination of our own hearts in prayer. According to Jesus' command, if I love self, I will love the other.

Three disciplines follow. One is a discipline of Silence. One is a discipline of Praying with Music. One is a Guided Meditation.

You may choose to try one, two, three or none of these prayer practices. If you choose to do all three, do not do them all in one sitting.

Be open. Like different types of food or different styles of music, we were not created to all pray the same way. But we are called to be in a relationship to God. Perhaps one of these disciplines will help you on your journey of faith.

All three of these prayer practices begin the same way:

Claim space. It could be in a chair. It could be on the floor. It could be on a chair in the park. It could be on a bench in Epcot at Walt Disney World. We begin by claiming space. Look around. Be aware of where you are. Sit.

SILENCE

Read these instructions before beginning.

Silence invites us to quiet the mind and sit in the presence of God. That is all we have to do. We have to claim space. Sit. Be mindful of sitting. You may wish to bow prior to sitting or prior to starting your meditation or both.

Some clear the mind. Others count the breath. Some say a phrase or mantra. Others create an image and stare.

Whatever you choose to do, set a timer. If this is your first time sitting in silence, set the timer for five minutes. If sitting in silence is a prayer practice that appeals to you, increase your time as you move into practicing the discipline on a regular basis.

Wherever you choose to sit, your knees should be below your navel, your spine should be straight, and your eyes should be gently closed or barely open, staring at a fixed spot. Your arms should be resting on your legs, hands open facing upward. There are several more positions for the hands suggested by the practice of yoga or zazen.

If you must shift your body during the allotted time, you should create a gesture of respect that you do just prior to adjusting your body. This keeps you mindful.

When the timer rings, do a slight bow, and walk around a bit to connect your prayerful state of mind with the reality of the world we are living in.

MUSIC

Read these instructions before beginning.

Listening to music is a stimulating way to

pray. Music stimulates the senses and it encourages our minds to be aware of messages being sent to it through the mass media.

Select a piece of music that speaks to you. The music can be a pop tune, a piece of classical music, be Led Zeppelin, or Bach or Beethoven – whatever speaks to you.

Get a notebook and a piece of paper. Have it handy for when you finish praying the song.

Claim space using the technique above. You may wish to establish a ritual like the steps suggested above for silence to prepare yourself for listening to the music.

Claim space. Sit. Play the music.

When the music has finished, sit in silence for two minutes.

Then record your answers to the following questions: Why do you like this piece of music? What do you believe the artist was thinking when creating it? What are your thoughts and feelings when listening to it? Does the music stir up an image? If so, what is it?

If you were going to associate a piece of scripture with the music just played, what would it be? Grab the scripture. Find the passage. Read it. What are your thoughts and feelings about the passage? See if they are the same or different from the thoughts and feelings you associated with the piece of music.

Then write something you believe about the piece of music or the scripture passage. Begin by writing, "I believe…"

Guided Meditation

Read these instructions before beginning.

It is best to have someone with you to lead you through the guided meditation.

Claim space using the technique above.

Then ask your friend to lead you through the following set of questions, pausing between each for at least two minutes. Do not respond out loud. Just listen and see what comes to mind.

Who is the "other" in your world? Why are they the "other"? When did you first notice differences between you and the "other"? How old were you when this happened? How are you different from the "other"? How are you the same?

Who are you afraid of today? Why? How can you overcome that fear?

Love God. Love self. Love neighbor.

When you are finished, consider your thoughts and feelings during this practice.

Move to the "Rule of Life" section of your journal. Use the following formula to compose a Rule.

Neighbor

Who is my neighbor?

My neighbor is _____ .

I love God by _____ .

I love self by _____ .

I love neighbor by _____ .

THE COLLECT

Write a prayer for the "other".

Begin by naming God. Then name a quality of God. Next, write a general statement about the "other" based on everything we have reflected upon in this section. "Pray for the others" you are comfortable with. List them. Pray for the "others" you are uncomfortable with. List them. Ask God for something as you reflect on the first part of this Collect. Ask in God's name.

✛

Endnotes

[1] (Smith, 1994, p. 17)

[2] (May & Metzger, 1973, p. NT 77)

[3] (May & Metzger, 1973, p. NT 97-98)

[4] (Peterson, 2001, p. 97)

[5] (Peterson, 2001, p. 292)

[6] (King & Washington, 1991, p. 219)

[7] (King & Washington, 1991, p. 594)

[8] (King & Washington, 1991, p. 250)

[9] (King & Washington, 1991, p. 290)

NEIGHBORS } *How Do We Live Together?*

MAIN GATE

Lilo, of *Lilo and Stitch*, explains, '*Ohana* means family. And family means nobody gets left behind or forgotten.'

Lilo's simple insight is loaded with meaning. It invites us to consider family. What is family? Who is my family? Is what culture holds up as family what Holy Scripture says is family? What did Jesus say about family? What am I supposed to do?

We are born into family. We move into family. We extend it and create family. We redefine family. When we are lost, we rely on family, although it may not be the family we were born into. Family can be biological. More often, it is not. Family are people we rely on to create a safe space called home. Home may be a physical place of windows, doors and walls. Home may be a place in the heart of belonging, safety or comfort.

We define "family" through a system of values. We understand "home" through a collage of experiences. Jesus lived to challenge our traditional definitions and understandings. According to Jesus, all of our neighbors, wherever they are and whatever country, culture or tradition they were born into, are our family.

Is it possible for us to live into that Gospel definition?

In Luke's Gospel, Jesus' mother and his brothers "came to see him, but they could not reach him because of the crowd. And he was told, 'Your mother and your brothers are standing outside, wanting to see you.' But he said to them, 'My mother and my brothers are those who hear the word of God and do it.'" [1] Jesus suggests that whoever aligns their life under God is family. Jesus' definition extends beyond institution, culture, color or creed.

We forget our common thread is God. God commanded. The world was created. God calls us into relationship. We respond or we do not. God lives with us in Jesus to show us how to love God and neighbor. We reject this Gospel imperative so Christ is killed. God sends the spirit to help us continue the work of Jesus, even when we do not know what we are doing. Jesus is the beginning and the end, the Alpha and Omega who, in eternity, looks at the human family as judge.

What will Jesus be judging?

As judge, Jesus will look at how we have loved God, how we have loved self and how we have loved neighbor.

Did we live into being a family of God?

It is easy to become obsessed with the sin of the individual. These sins are easy to judge, control and manipulate. Corporate sin, the sins of all as a group, is more difficult to discern and to comprehend. But our corporate life concerns God. God called a group of tribes together in the Hebrew Scriptures. Jesus created a new family from a group of people who, in the Gospel narrative, left their "traditional" families behind. Paul writes in his letters to the churches of a gathered community and calls them to love one another through the grace of God so that they can live together as family. We are called to live out the sacred life of God in community.

The Protestant mistake is emphasis on the individual: individual calling, individual testimony, individual sin, and individual redemption. These narrow our focus into a narcissistic reality. Our culture, our media, our society, particularly for those of us born in the United States, supports this overblown focus on self and self-reliance. In the end, our accountability to God's family and even our reliance on God is cut out - eliminated.

Scripture supports another reality. God calls individuals to gather together as family in order to be faithful to God. God doesn't save individuals. God saves all of us. This is God's work.

It has been said, "It takes a village." This popular phrase is losing its meaning. As we live into a global neighborhood, we might need to simply say, "It takes each and every one of us." This is more difficult to accomplish than just a village. It means that everything, each and every one of us does matters to everyone.

Villages are clusters of people who look alike, think alike, act alike, and share social customs and norms. Villages are rural and keep people separate and in their place. People move to rural areas often to avoid people who are different than they are.

City life is made up of clusters of villages combined. Difficulties arise when a new urban identity is needed to benefit all who live together. This is not easily accomplished. We are often suspicious of those who are different from us.

In a culture that preaches scarcity, we often ignore our urban identity and return to village mentality in order to preserve self and others who

we believe to think as we do. But Jesus calls us to move beyond our walls into the global family, living and working and playing amongst all people who live together on this Spaceship Earth.

At the Walt Disney World Resort, we are constantly challenged to seek a wider understanding beyond our individual limited scope. We are to dream, create and imagine together so that we can confidently walk into the future hand-in-hand.

Every day, 365 days of the year, a temporary community gathers throughout the Disney World. How will we behave as a gathered community together under God? Will we look around and notice the other and realize we are all participating in this theme park adventure together? Will we revert to tribalism, taking care of self and the family unit to get what we need out of the theme park experience by sacrificing the community? Will we notice the incredible diversity of humankind that gathers here to seek connection through a communal experience? Will we be trying to manipulate reality so hard to have fun that we push and move others out of the way, not seeing neighbor but only seeing self? These situations are twofold. Some are Godly-living manifested in behavior. Others are selfish living manifested by a culture of consumerism. We travel through both. We need to keenly be aware of the path we are on.

Lilo explains, "*Ohana* means 'family.' And family means nobody gets left behind or forgotten."

When we experience a spark of delight at the prospect of someone being left behind, we are no longer living Jesus' commandment to love God and love neighbor. We have stepped into tribalism, survival of the fittest. I need to get mine before they get it. I have paid for it so I deserve it. I worked hard for it so I am entitled to it. These are not Gospel realities. These are cultural truisms that stand between us and God and God's people.

Love wins. No one is left behind. God created all and God will redeem all. It pleases God

to see us live and love and take care of the other like we truly believe this. Do you believe it? What are you called to do about it?

In the Gospel of John, Jesus prays that we all may be one. "Sanctify them in the truth; your word is truth. As you have sent me into the world, so I have sent them into the world. And for their sakes I sanctify myself, so that they also may be sanctified in truth.

"I ask not only on behalf of these, but also on behalf of those who will believe in me through their word, that they may all be one. As you, Father, are in me and I am in you, may they also be in us, so that the world may believe that you have sent me. The glory that you have given me I have given them, so that they may be one, as we are one, I in them and you in me, that they may become completely one, so that the world may know that you have sent me and have loved them even as you have loved me." [2]

This isn't a prayer for all to be Catholic, or all Baptist, or all Episcopalian, or all Evangelical. God is not an institution. This is a prayer for all people to be God's people. This vision of unity starts with the heart, spirit and motivation of the individual, an individual who seeks out all people to proclaim the love of God. And although I firmly believe we need organized religion to accomplish the work of the kingdom and hold us accountable, I do not believe we have to be in the same institution. For those of us who participate in organized religion, our biggest challenge is to see beyond our institutional walls and live with all of the family of God.

 IN THE QUEUE

In order to love neighbor and to love self, we must be able to see the world as God sees the world.

Theologian Roberta C. Bondi has written a book called *To Love as God Loves: Conversations with the Early Church.* Her prayer to live into the Gospel call to love God, neighbor, and self is addressed in an honest and accessible manner.

According to Bondi, the challenge of living into our Christian identity is to see the world as God sees the world. If we pray and strive to do this, we can incarnate the love of God into everything we say and everything we do. This is a constant challenge. It is an ongoing process. But, this simple discipline empowers us to live into Jesus' commandment to love God, to love neighbor and to love self.

Bondi dialogues with the mothers and fathers from early Christianity who lived in desert caves, creating intentional space, in hopes of discovering how to love deeply and completely. These remarkable people believed that, "in spite of society's pressures, …love is the goal of the Christian life and humility is what it takes to bring us toward it." [3] This type of love is not perfect. It does not mean we are more pious than the next. It simply means that we are ordering our life under God through love. Bondi asserts, "Only as we learn to love God and others do we gain real freedom and autonomy in a society in which most people live in a state of slavery to their own needs and desires." [4]

We will use some of Bondi's insights to do our work while we move through the queue.

Open to the next available page of the "Holy Story" section of your journal. Create two columns. Label one "Easy to love." Label the other "Difficult to love." Create a list in each column. In one, place people, things, and circumstances that are easy to love. In the other, place people, things, and circumstances that are difficult to love. The list does not need to be exhaustive. You can always come back and add more to it!

On the next available pages, work through both lists. For each item on the list, answer the following questions:

I see _____ .

God sees _____ .

What I cannot see _____ .

What I hope to see _____ .

Once you have completed that, reflect on the list. Where are you OK with your position? Put a check by that. Where do you have a long way to go? Put an arrow by that. Where are you unwilling to go? Put an X by that. Take inventory of how many checks, arrows and X's you have.

On the next available page in "Holy Story", place a dot in the center. Next, using as much of the page of you can, draw a perfect circle surrounding that dot. Once you have drawn the circle, recall the number of arrows you have. Place those arrows sporadically around the circle. Do the same with the arrows and X's. You should end up with a circle full of random checks, arrows and X's.

Bondi looks to sixth-century monastic leader Dorotheos of Gaza to understand how we are related to God through our love for each other. "In one homily he exhorts the brothers not to judge or condemn each other, but remember that the love of God and of other people are so closely related that it is impossible to love God and have contempt for the sins and weaknesses of other people at the same time." [5]

Bondi quotes Dorotheos: "Suppose we were to take a compass and insert the point and draw the outline of a circle. The center point is the same distance from any point on the circumference… Let us suppose that this circle is the world and that God himself is the center: the straight lines drawn from the circumference to the center are the lives of human beings… Let us assume for the sake of the analogy that to move toward God, then, human beings move from the circumference along the various radii of the circle to the center. But at the same time, the closer they are to God, the closer they become to one another; and the closer they are to one another, the closer they become to God." [6]

Take a moment and look at your circle. What are the implications? What comforts you? What frightens you? What concerns you?

Is it possible for you to love as God loves? Do you want to love like God loves? Why or why not?

Bondi defines humility as a "world-transforming attitude of the heart,… the living-out of the conviction that all human beings, every man, woman, and child are beloved creatures of God." [7]

FROM THE BOOK
Luke 9:28-36

The writer of Luke was interested in examining and overturning societal arrangements that prevented people from being accepted and loved as persons of God. Being a Gentile, Luke was keenly aware of who was in and who was out. Luke's primary concern was that all people would come to know God through Jesus Christ, would accept their neighbor, whoever they were as partner and missioner, then go out and change the world in God's name. Our prejudices and convictions and traditional beliefs often get in the way. Our circumstances and experiences often prevent us from seeing things as they really are. The Gospel of Luke hopes that all will have a direct experience of God through Jesus Christ and the people of God so that we can see things as they really are.

LUKE 9:28-36
THE TRANSFIGURATION

Now about eight days after these sayings Jesus took with him Peter and John and James, and went up on the mountain to pray. And while he was praying, the appearance of his face changed, and his clothes became dazzling white.

Suddenly they saw two men, Moses and

Elijah, talking to him. They appeared in glory and were speaking of his departure, which he was about to accomplish at Jerusalem. Now Peter and his companions were weighed down with sleep; but since they had stayed awake, they saw his glory and the two men who stood with him.

Just as they were leaving him, Peter said to Jesus, "Master, it is good for us to be here; let us make three dwellings, one for you, one for Moses, and one for Elijah"—not knowing what he said. While he was saying this, a cloud came and overshadowed them; and they were terrified as they entered the cloud. Then from the cloud came a voice that said, "This is my Son, my Chosen; listen to him!"

When the voice had spoken, Jesus was found alone. And they kept silent and in those days told no one any of the things they had seen." [8]

RIDE THE ATTRACTION

Festival of the Lion King

At Disney's Animal Kingdom, in the continent of Africa, guests are invited to participate in *The Festival of the Lion King*. A troop of singers, acrobats, and creatures of every kind perform one of the most lively and entertaining shows at the Walt Disney World Resort. The festival seems to take place after Simba has become the Lion King, for the show does not rehash the story but presents highlights of the film's popular musical numbers.

As guests enter the theater in the round, they are separated into four different sections: Lions, Giraffes, Warthogs and Elephants. A talented acting troop comes center stage to prepare the gathered community for the festival. Immediately, differences are pointed out by sound and shape. People in each section are called upon to act out the animal's section they are seated in.

Once the crowd has settled in, the troop begins by performing "Circle of Life." This beautiful anthem suggests that there is rhythm and rhyme to life. It becomes our life's work to figure it out so that we grow into what God created us to be. The troop sings out, "The Circle of Life moves us all through despair and hope, through faith and love until we find our place on the path unwinding in the circle—the circle of life."

We are restless and do not want to follow the rhythm of life. We want it now so we ignore what reality is telling us. We become impatient, bored and we just want to get on with it. Often, the journey of faith is learning and practicing the rhythm of life. We will not live into our true selves until we find the current and ride it out.

The festival moves into celebration of Simba's journey, recalling his feelings of impatience during his journey, performing, "I Just Can't Wait to Be King." Timon enters first, followed by Pumbaa, who joyfully announces that he is sitting in the Warthog section. The elephant enters, then Simba joins the festival, remembering, "I'm gonna be the mane event like no king was before. I'm brushing up on looking down. I'm working on my roar." Streamers circle the air, stilt walkers fill the space in between and the festival gets into full swing as all of the popular characters of *The Lion King* take their places in the auditorium.

Gymnastic rings drop from the sky and the Tumble Monkeys begin to move about the stage. Timon is not happy because he is trying to be the center of attention. The monkeys crawl about and eat fleas off of each other while Timon commiserates with Pumbaa.

All leaders must be ready to make decisions and take on responsibilities. They hold out a vision and move towards it. Can one lead with a "Hakuna Matata" philosophy? The monkeys tumble, flying through the air with the greatest of ease. Timon sings, "Hakuna Matata! What a wonderful phrase.

Hakuna Matata! Ain't no passing craze. It means no worries for the rest of your days. It's our problem-free philosophy. Hakuna Matata!" Timon concludes, saying, "That's our motto!" Pumbaa asks, "What's a motto?" Timon responds, "I don't know! What's the motto with you?" The monkeys go into hysterics. We all want a carefree life, but the Gospel life calls us to work and respond. "Yes, we have no bananas."

Suddenly, the mood shifts slightly from festive to dark and mysterious. A crush of thunder and a flash of lightning call out a fire dancer who takes center stage. He twists and turns a stick of fire igniting the floor of the stage with bravado. The dancer balances fire on the souls of his feet, concluding his dance by putting out the fire with his mouth. The lead singer of the human singing troop shares, "So prepare for the coup of the century. Be prepared for the murkiest scam. Meticulous planning. Tenacity spanning. Decades of denial is simply why I'll be king undisputed, respected, saluted and seen for the wonder I am. My teeth and ambitions are bared. Be prepared!"

After the dance of danger, the troop moves into a dance of love. The lighting changes and we are dwarfed in the shadows of a forest midday. Bird dancer acrobats draw our attention to the stage and the air. Tension between the younger members of the singing troop lend melody to "Can You Feel the Love Tonight?" Part of the rhythm of life is self-care. We need work and rest and love and peace to renew and to continue. "Can You Feel the Love Tonight? The peace the evening brings? The world for once in perfect harmony with all its living things."

Once again, the lighting shifts and the head of the singing troop states, "The world in perfect harmony with all its living things - that, my friends, is a time for joyous celebration. For when all things exist in balance, it is then when all of us are connected in the great Circle of Life." We are now moving into the Grand Finale. We hear "Circle of Life," all of the performers return to the stage, and Simba is thrilled with the celebration.

He lets out a mighty roar. "And now everybody, it is time for you to join in on the fun as we kick off our celebration finale! The natives are getting restless. Let's have a party!"

Timon returns to center stage, leading a wonderful version of "The Lion Sleeps Tonight." With incredible energy, we are treated to a quick summary of everything that has come before, followed by the concluding version of "Circle of Life."

FOR REFLECTION

Once a year, the city of New Orleans celebrates the mystery of life during the festival of Mardi Gras. The Mardi Gras parties and parades transform the streets into an endless sea of diverse humanity, finding joy in the mystery and in the absurdity we face every day in this thing called life.

In a typical Mardi Gras parade, bands play popular marches to get the crowd moving, dance clubs perform to tap into the crowd's spirit. Kings and queens and jesters pass by to remind us of the privilege and responsibility of leading others. Decorated floats full of members of the krewe toss out trinkets and beads and even coconuts to thank the crowd for coming out to celebrate.

Wherever you are, and on whatever corner you find yourself on, you hear the constant question being yelled out, "Where you at, dawlin'?"

"Where you at, dawlin'?"

"Where you at, dawlin'?" is a courtesy question, a common greeting, asking, Are you seeing what you really need to see? Are you doing what you really need to do? If not, where do you need to be to see things as they really are?

Where do you need to be to see things as they really are?

"Where you at, dawlin'?"

We are invited by Jesus to journey to the mountaintop, accompanied by Peter and John and James,

Luke's account of the transfiguration, the story of a revealing moment on the top of a mountain, is all about where you are at. Are you seeing what you truly need to see?

We often hear, "the honeymoon is over." We all have images and ideas about what the honeymoon being over means.

I believe when we say the honeymoon is over, we are quickly moving into the "now I begin to take everything for granted" period of our lives.

I forget the miracle of the moment.

I take for granted and take advantage of what is right in front of me. Am I truly seeing what I truly need to see? How do I regain my vision? Where do you need to be to see things as they really are?

Some of us go to the mountaintop. Others dive into the pages of book. Some of us go on retreat. Others of us go to a ball game. Some of us travel to Walt Disney World. Others cook up a meal and serve it to people who are hungry.

The cautionary warning embedded in Luke's telling of the transfiguration is that if we are not intentional, if we are not awake, if we are not in tune with the reality of our lives, it does not matter where we are, we are going to miss the point. We are going to miss the transfiguration and get stuck in the mundane. There is nothing mundane about being in relationship with God and God's people through Jesus Christ.

According to Luke's telling of the transfiguration, it is a sleepless night. Jesus is about to move into a new and critical moment in his ministry. He needs some space. He needs to prepare. He needs to pray. He needs time apart.

Jesus' friends are tired. Their work of feeding and healing and moving about from town to town is preventing them from seeing things as they really are. They are a little off their game. They have forgotten just how important their work is. Although Jesus has told them that he will suffer, be rejected, be killed and raised on the third day, it appears as if they have not heard or seemed to understand the magnitude of what is ahead.

Jesus takes Peter and John and James up the mountain to pray. While Jesus is praying, the appearance of his face changes. His clothes become dazzling white.

Suddenly, standing and talking with him, are Moses and Elijah.

Peter is enamored with the vision and wants to build three dwellings. One for Jesus, one for Moses and one for Elijah - a mountaintop university, per se. A place where people could come to the mountaintop, sit around and imagine how life should and could be, talking and dreaming about it instead of living it out, instead of doing something.

We have all been there. I know when I believe I am experiencing a profound experience of the holy, I want to preserve the moment, grab onto the facts, somehow capture the reality so it is with me always.

But it is already gone. Unless I do something about it.

A cloud overtakes them. For a brief moment, they lose sight of each other.

Out of the cloud, penetrating through the fog, a command is heard, "This is my son, listen to him."

Jesus, probably just a little bit amused with Peter's enthusiasm, tells him and the others not to say anything.

What has just happened?

What is the point?

Am I seeing things as they really are?

Do I need to go to the mountaintop to

understand what just happened?

Maybe. Maybe not.

"Where you at, dawlin'?"

Teresa of Avila did not go to a mountaintop to see things as they really are. She made an interior journey of prayer determined to encounter God through Christ.

St. Teresa of Avila, a sixteenth century Carmelite nun and mystic, wrestled with the reality of God all of her life. She loved God. She hated God. She argued with God. Teresa of Avila once said that, "The present moment is pregnant with God."

"The present moment is pregnant with God."

According to Teresa, in the present moment, God is moving within us, transfiguring us, reconciling us, calling us to God, and to each other.

Teresa was fearful of living in delusion. She was terrified that if she became distracted with memories of the past or fearful of things to come in the future, she would miss out on an intimate relationship with God, played out in the present moment, right here and right now.

"The present moment is pregnant with God."

The present moment is scary. We cannot control the present moment.

In the present moment, God is with us. In the present moment, the past is gone, truly gone forever, and the future is yet to arrive. We miss the reality of our lives because are not living in the present moment.

Why do we live in the past?

We live in the past because we can nurture and control regret. We live in the past because we can manipulate the truth, the reality, of what has happened. We can change the facts. We can rearrange and relive the emotions. We can place events into compartments and create the delusion of meaning.

Why do we live in the future?

We live in the future because we can manipulate and predict how we will feel. We can

live in the fear of things that have not yet happened to us. We can create excitement when we are so very uncomfortable sitting in the present.

But everything that has ever been done to you and to me has been done in the present moment. This is where transfiguration occurs. This is where we have to place our awareness. This is where we have to invest our energy. This is where God is calling to us.

"Where you at, dawlin'?"

In Thomas Mann's *The Magic Mountain* we learn from another type of mountaintop experience.

In the city of Hamburg, Germany, along the banks of the Elbe River, we encounter Hans Castorp, a young man who is prepared to begin his career as a shipbuilder. But, before beginning his new job, Hans decides to visit his sick cousin Joachim Ziemssen.

Joachim lives apart in a sanatorium, in Davos, Switzerland. He is hoping to be cured of tuberculosis.

The world is about to enter its First World War. Factions are organizing into influential power groups preparing for battle.

Hans leaves the flatlands of Hamburg, venturing to the mountaintop to visit his sick cousin.

The mountain air is thin and crisp. The sanatorium is in an idyllic setting, right in the middle of the Alps. And the people living in the sanatorium with his cousin are equally fascinating to Hans. They are an eclectic mix of people representing the social political scene of pre-World War I Europe.

Hans begins to fall in love. He is falling in love with the mountaintop surroundings, and he is falling in love with the people who are held up there too, seeking a cure for tuberculosis.

Hans begins to feel at home in the sanatorium. He forgets about the world he came from. He forgets about his plans for the future.

Hans' reality begins to shift. Just the thought of returning home, leaving the mountaintop sanatorium, makes him sick. He is lost in the seduction of a community of ideas and emotions, a community that is isolated, inward thinking, focused on group survival, a community that is not getting well. And before Hans realizes it, seven years have passed.

The mountaintop life seems perfect to him, but he doesn't seem to realize just how sick he has become. He is no longer seeing things as they are. He is in control, but the cost is that he has lost sight of the world of reality.

Suddenly, on a mountaintop...

Suddenly, in a moment in time, Peter and James and John have a direct experience of reality.

Suddenly, they see a future that is out of their control, a reality where seeking justice and fairness and equality has a cost, a reality where the only barrier between them and God is a true, deep understanding of who Jesus Christ is.

"This is my son. My chosen. Listen to him."

Like Peter, James and John, we often forget to listen, we fail to see things as they really are. We get caught up in the parade. We get lost at the carnival ball. We take all of the spectacle for granted so it looses its power and loses its meaning.

We all must find a place to listen– a mountaintop, a park bench, a ball game, a church or chapel or meditation hall – a place where we can listen and remember and wake up so that we see things as they really are.

The present moment is pregnant with God. "Where you at, dawlin'?"

THE E-TICKET

Images and stories impact and shape what we believe to be true about our neighbors. In the past, government regulations administered through the Federal Communications Commission (FCC) ensured a variety of voices to be represented in mainstream media. Today, in the United Stares, all media channels are primarily owned by six corporations. They control almost everything we read, see or hear. Those companies are Time Warner, The Walt Disney Company, Viacom, Rupert Murdoch's News Corp., CBS Corporation and NBC Universal.

In a consumer-driven economy, messages are created and tailored to get me to act, primarily to get me to buy something. If I buy something, perhaps I will feel better about myself.

In a Gospel-driven economy, messages are created and tailored to motivate me to act, primarily to see the world as God sees it. What is incongruent, I may be called upon to change. If I change it, I, with God's help, will bring about the kingdom of heaven.

What do I know about my neighbor through popular media channels?

Take some time. Gather together popular magazines, newspapers, journals and company reports. Look through popular images with heavy traffic hosted on the internet.

Turn to the "Holy Story" section of your journal. Label the next available page "Reports on my Neighbor." Create a collage of what popular media channels are saying and showing about your neighbor.

Next, on the next available page, label it "God Sees My Neighbor." Collect images that you feel illustrate the way God sees the world around you. Try to find images that support your belief about how God sees your neighbor as they appear on the "Reports" page.

Look at both collages. What are the similarities? What are the differences? What have you identified in both collages?

Take a moment to write a belief statement

about both collages.

At the bottom of the each collage, write, "I believe …"

Finish your thoughts.

Then move to the "Rule of Life" section of your journal. Perhaps you would like to use the following formula to create your rule about neighbors.

Neighbors

A neighbor is _____ .

My neighbors are _____ .

Neighbors I love _____ .

Neighbors that frighten me _____ .

To love my neighbor as God loves my neighbor, I _____ .

 THE COLLECT

The Book of Common Prayer from the Episcopal tradition has this beautiful Collect about the peoples of the world. "O God, you have made of one blood all the peoples of the earth, and sent your blessed Son to preach peace to those who are far off and to those who are near: Grant that people everywhere may seek after you and find you; bring the nations into your fold; pour out your Spirit upon all flesh, and hasten the coming of your kingdom, through Jesus Christ our Lord. Amen." [9]

Identify the parts of the Collect that correspond to the formula we have learned. Write a Collect about neighbors. Pray for knowledge about how we can live together.

Endnotes

[1] (May & Metzger, 1973, p. NT 92)
[2] (May & Metzger, 1973, p. NT 152)
[3] (Bondi, 1987, p. 10)
[4] (Bondi, 1987, p. 10)
[5] (Bondi, 1987, p. 25)
[6] (Dorotheus & Wheeler, 1977, pp. 138-139)
[7] (Bondi, 1987, p. 42)
[8] (May & Metzger, 1973, p. NT 95)
[9] (Episcopal Church., 1979, p. 100)

HUNGER } *How Do I Feed Myself and My Neighbor?*

MAIN GATE

"Fate is kind. She brings to those who love, the sweet fulfillment of their secret longing," says Jiminy Cricket in *Pinocchio*.

Our secret longings make us hungry.

What are your hungry for? Is it love, power, a fulfilling job or possibly children? Do you desire fame, meaning to life, financial security or financial wealth?

We hunger because God hungers. God hungered for relationship so God created this world. God hungered for justice so God called us into covenant. God hungered for love so God lived among us as Jesus Christ. God hungered for reconciliation so God empowers us to act through the Holy Spirit.

Hunger fuels our survival. Hunger can impede our ability to act rationally. It can inspire us to do good and it can fuel cruel motivations to live at the cost of another's dignity. We see hunger everywhere.

What are you hungry for?

There are several types of hunger. Our hearts hunger when we desire love, change, or happiness. Our bodies hunger when we do not have access to food or when we fail to take care of ourselves even when nourishment is accessible. Our spirits hunger when we long to know God or when we pray to believe that God will act.

Hunger is closely related to desire. Desire is directly connected to action. When we desire, we suffer. We may choose to do something about our desire or we may just continue to suffer. C3PO, the beloved golden robot in the popular film series *Star Wars*, while lost and wandering around in the desert, said to his friend R2-D2, "It seems I was born to suffer."

As a Christian hoping to live the Gospel life, I desire justice and fairness and equal access for all. Circumstances and situations vary, but the hope of my desire remains. When I witness suffering in the name of love, I desire enough faith to continue the journey in order to discover fulfillment of promises made. It is in these moments of doubt that the root of our hunger is often made manifest. While the majority of the people in this world hunger for shelter, food and water, those of us living in consumer-driven culture suffer because we desire things. I want a car. I want a house. I want a new television. I want to stay at the Grand Floridian. Without a reflective moment, I become a non-reflective consumer. I hear messages and then respond based on how others want me to act.

Walt Disney World is a vacation destination holding out, for all of us to see, the best and worst of consumer-driven culture. I am a big fan of Disney World, the Walt Disney Company and, as a shareholder, I thank each of you for your support. That being said, there are a few things for us to consider as we contemplate how hunger plays out in the world. Since we are on a theme park adventure together, we will examine how Walt Disney World operates within a consumer-driven culture.

Consumer-driven culture brings out the best and worst kind of hunger in each of us.

Consumer-driven culture does not provide equal access. You pay, you play. I earned it. It's mine. Now go and get yours. The good aspect is philanthropists rise up and give in hopes of striking a balance. Unfortunately, even the most generous are riding the wave way behind the rising tide. At Disney Theme Parks, the cost is prohibitive for many who have been exposed to their invitation to come to the place where dreams come true. But, in spite of what Blondie says, dreams are expensive.

Consumer-driven culture breeds entitlement. I have done this and I have done that so the least this moment can do is give me this and give me that. Entitlement is a human trait. Each and every one of us, no matter who or where we are in the spectrum of life, feels we are entitled to something. If you take a moment, you can probably come up with a few things you believe you are entitled to. For me, fairness and equality are just the start! As we move around the happiest place on Earth, cries of entitlement rear their ugly heads everywhere. Sometimes we feed entitlement just to get someone to shut up! I'm entitled to peace and quiet so I will buy you a laser-light twirling thing-a-ma-jimmy that causes others to go into seizures. I try to measure my feelings of entitlement with the stories of faithful people I have met throughout my journey through life. Sometimes this helps me make a better decision. Sometimes it does not.

Consumer-driven cultures suggests meaning with no context. Results are reported without the necessary steps taken along the way. Often, the steps were skipped so there are no check points to validate the outcome. There are no logical steps to conclusions that are reported as facts. The popular entertainment-posing-as-news show *Inside Edition* is a good example of this lack of context.

Listening to the logic of reporters, I'm not sure "C" is the logical conclusion of "A + B." None of it adds up. Yet the truth has been declared. We need context. At Epcot, inside Future World, the newest attraction is *Mission: Space*, the one ride I have vouched never to ride again. Once was enough. As expensive as the ride was to develop, I am unclear as to how this thrill ride inspires me to imagine a better tomorrow. The context and meaning of Future World is clear. *Mission: Space's* place in it, is not. The pavilion is conclusion with no context. Thrill with no meaning. A ride with no outcome.

Consumer-driven culture gives the illusion of abundance while actually sending out a message of scarcity. There is enough to go around. But if we actually lived with enough, demand would decrease, perhaps causing an economic crisis. So, everything is available. I cannot afford it. So it is thrown away. People go without. Our contexts prevent us from seeing the reality of the larger world. I go to bed every night full. How can people on this planet be starving and dying of hunger? I walk into a hospital and because of privilege, I am treated. I take this for granted. How can people really not have access to health care? At the Walt Disney World Resort, the parks are designed to handle large groups of people. And yet, people push and shove to move into immense auditoriums just to get a seat. Aren't there enough seats? And no, I don't want to go all the way to the end of the aisle. I want the center seat! I'm entitled to it.

Consumer-driven culture empowers institutions to survive at the cost of the individual. In the United States, money means power. Corporations and institutions have more rights than individuals. As my hunger for power overshadows my ability to see things as they really are, I am giving away my rights as I gobble down my unlimited bread sticks and salad at Olive Garden. The Walt Disney Company is one of six corporations controlling everything I hear, see or learn about how the world works. Their agendas are packaged into messages, creating desires and making me hungry for more. I desire this but is it my own desire or is it someone else's?

At the Walt Disney World Resort, we are exposed to hundreds of thousands of messages. Some appeal to my imagination. Others appeal to my longing for something else. As a company in the business of entertainment, some of the messages of the resort are extremely satisfying because they are tailored to my need to get away from it all. As a company in the business of making money, some messages are designed to get me to buy something. The parks are designed to make me vulnerable by appealing to what I hunger for.

What do you hunger for?

I hunger for a better world. I read the Scripture and listen to the teaching of Jesus Christ and I hope we can build a world in which God's love is accessible and available to everyone. But I have surrendered a lot of my principles in order to joyfully partake in a consumer-driven culture.

I hunger for a world where everyone's story is heard and labeled sacred. At Disney World, we move into and through a lot of stories. The stories speak to our common humanity. Evil is confronted. Good wins. In a world littered with cynicism and doubt, we need to remember that love wins so that we can live like we believe it.

God said the world is good. We are hungry. Since we hunger, we desire. What are you hungry for?

 IN THE QUEUE

Two priests, one Catholic and one Protestant, are on an upside-down cruise ship. It is just barely New Year's Day. The final voyage of the S.S. Poseidon has just turned terribly tragic.

The movie *The Poseidon Adventure* was originally brought to the big screen by disaster film guru Irwin Allen. It premiered in 1971 to rave reviews. It was nominated for eight Academy Awards and won a special Oscar for visual effects. Primarily fate, disaster and doom play out before our eyes. Things explode. People fall into light fixtures. Christmas trees are turned into ladders out of hell. In the midst of this, two priests, one Catholic and one Protestant, debate about the nature of things. Actor Arthur O'Connell portrays the Catholic priest, Father John. Actor Gene Hackman portrays the Protestant pastor, Pastor Frank Scott. These two spiritual characters represent the theological debate of faith versus works.

On New Year's Ever, prior to the Poseidon's capsizing, Gene Hackman's character, Pastor Frank Scott, delivers a sermon on the deck of the ship. He proclaims to the people that you "could wear off your knees praying to God for heat in February. And icicles would grow from your upraised palms. If you're freezing," says the Pastor Scott, "you burn the furniture. You get up off of your knees." The sermon continues, "Therefore, don't pray to God to solve your problems. Pray to that part of God within you to have the guts to fight for yourself. God wants brave souls. He wants winners, not quitters. If you cannot win at least try to win. God loves people who try. Resolve to let God know that you have the guts to do it alone! Resolve to fight for yourselves and for others and for those you love. That part of God within you will be fighting with you all the way."

After the sermon, the Catholic priest, Father John, challenges Pastor Scott, calling the sermon somewhat unorthodox.

"But realistic," Pastor Scott replies, adding that, "the church is for more than prayer."

After the boat has been hit by the forty-foot tidal wave and turned completely upside down, the passengers who survived the capsize try to discern what to do next. Should they wait in the ballroom for help to arrive or should they start to make their way upward, above the water's surface, through the bowels of the ship?

Should I sit in hell, having faith in God, waiting for God to act, to rescue me? Or do I work my way out of hell, struggling with others, finding our own paths, carrying ourselves up into the heavenly presence?

Pastor Scott talks to Father John. "Maybe by climbing up we can save ourselves."

Father John responds, "In your sermon, you spoke only for the strong."

Pastor Scott replies, "I'm asking you to be strong. Come with us."

Father John says, "I can't leave these people. I know l can't save them. I suspect we'll die, but I can't leave them. They don't want to go."

Pastor Scott, a little impatient with Father John's response says, "They've chosen to stay. Why should you? What good's your life then? What's it all been for?"

Father John replies, "I have no other choice."

But does he? Does your hunger, your desire, motivate you to act? Or are you waiting for God to mightily snatch you up your feet?

Open your journal to the "Holy Story" section. We are going to create desire timelines. Sounds fun, right? On the next available spread, create three vertical lines, crossing the center and continuing onto the next page. Label one "Emotional." Label another "Physical." Label the final one "Spiritual."

At the top of the page or on one of the timelines, indicate years in 1 to 5 or 10 year intervals. On the timelines, indicate your emotional, physical and past and present spiritual hungers and desires. Identify events and experiences that correspond with

these hungers. Did you respond to the hunger? Did you ignore it? Did you act? Or did you wait?

The next practice will take some time, perhaps a week. You can choose to start it now. You may want to try it later. If you are at the Walt Disney World Resort creating intentional space and time, it might be constructive to do it during your time there. And then create it again once you return home.

On the next available page, we are going to create an incident list. You can take as much space as you need for this.

As you move about, listen and look for hunger and desire. Listen. Watch. Observe. When you hear a hunger stated by someone, write it down. What was the context? What was the person or people's expression a hunger for? In your opinion, will the person or people be able to feed that desire or will it have to come from an outside source?

Decide on a period of time that you will devote to this practice - 1 day, 1 week - 1 month - 1 year. I suggest 1 week.

At the conclusion of the space in time, list out the hungers and desires you have heard. Are there any commonalities?

Did you hear hunger expressed that is similar to yours? Where could you relate to your neighbor? When did you not?

 FROM THE BOOK
Mark 4:26-32

Scholarship suggests that Mark was the first Gospel written. It is a fast-moving Gospel, stating facts, the response of Jesus and then moving quickly to the event. According to Mark, because Jesus has entered our world, there is a cosmic battle being fought between good and evil. Followers of Christ may not recognize Jesus as the Messiah, but evil spirits and possessive demons identify him right

away, beguiling the reader saying, "We know who you are Jesus… What do you have to do with us Jesus of Nazareth?…" The gripping narrative and simple presentation make it possible to read the entire Gospel in one sitting - just under an hour.

MARK 4:26-32

Jesus said, "The kingdom of God is as if someone would scatter seed on the ground, and would sleep and rise night and day, and the seed would sprout and grow, he does not know how. The earth produces of itself, first the stalk, then the head, then the full grain in the head. But when the grain is ripe, at once he goes in with his sickle, because the harvest has come."

He also said, "With what can we compare the kingdom of God, or what parable will we use for it? It is like a mustard seed, which, when sown upon the ground, is the smallest of all the seeds on earth: yet when it is sown it grows up and becomes the greatest of all shrubs, and puts forth large branches, so that the birds of the air can make nests in its shade." [1]

RIDE THE ATTRACTION
Living with the Land

At Epcot Center, on the west side of Future World, is The Land. The Land is our interaction with this planet and the resources - specifically food - that we utilize in order to survive. The pavilion is home to a food court and several attractions including *Living with the Land* and *Soarin'*. As guests move about the pavilion, they are challenged at every turn to consider our relationship with the land.

Living with the Land transports guests into Epcot's four working greenhouses. Guests board a slow-moving boat ride that moves through an impressive demonstration, production and research facility. We begin by traveling through a forest caught in the middle of a severe thunderstorm. What might be frightfully scary to some is a necessary part of the Earth's natural processes for sustaining life of all sorts. The narrator says, "Welcome to a voyage of discovery and awareness of the richness, the diversity and the often surprising nature of living with the land. Our journey begins as dramatic and sudden changes are sweeping over the land. The approaching storm may seem violent and destructive to us but to nature its a new beginning in the cycle of life."

Just as nature shapes and forms the land through water, fire, wind and other elemental shifts, humankind has been shaping the land to serve our needs and wants. We learn that as we consume the Earth's resources, we must be good stewards of the land so that future generations will be able to survive. We hear, "Beneath the surface of the land, roots trap water from the flowing mud, extracting precious nutrients and minerals. These elements, when combined with sunlight, create the diverse living systems of our planet."

The boat moves into a dark rainforest full of plant and animal life. "One of those living systems is the rainforest, home to the most amazing concentration of life on our planet. These dense and beautiful forests cover only a tiny portion of the Earth's surface but they contain more than half of its plant and animal species. Rainforests are also extremely rich in productive living systems providing us with oxygen, food, medicines and other elements essential to our lives."

We move past a beautiful waterfall and into the American prairie. "In the desert, nature has created a very different but no less beautiful living system. And while this arid landscape may seem lifeless, it is very much alive. The plants and animals that have learned to survive in these harsh conditions make use of what little water they can find and avoid the scorching rays of the relentless sun. The American prairie once appeared as desolate as the desert, but over time rainwater and nutrients gradually penetrated the hard surface of this land. Even the hoofs of the mighty buffalo helped create the grooves of this rich soil that would one day become home to the American farm."

A farmhouse with a welcoming dog is around the corner then we enter a multimedia image gallery of uses of the land. "Of all the forces at work on the land, humans have had one of the most profound effects. The need to produce food for a growing world led to the enormous use and sometimes overuse of the land. In our search for more efficient ways to grow, we often failed to realize the impact of our methods."

After we see how we are altering the natural landscape and take a look at the difficulties of living with the land worldwide, we move into the living laboratories. "Today we are learning to live with the land, discovering better ways to grow food that will ensure both human and environmental well being." These impressive greenhouses graphically illustrate all that we are doing to feed, improve, and sustain life on this planet. "How will we meet tomorrow's growing needs for food production yet still respect the needs of the land? Some of these questions are being discovered just ahead in our unique living greenhouse environments."

The boat leaves the exhibit tunnel and moves into the first greenhouse, representing the Tropics. "In these living laboratories, scientists from Epcot, the U.S. Department of Agriculture, and Nestlé are exploring innovative ways to produce bountiful harvests, now and into the future. Within this first greenhouse, we see the controlled production of bananas, jackfruit, pineapple and papaya. "The tropics are home to the greatest diversity of plants on the planet... Many of these are exceptionally high in vitamins and nutrients. Others are well adapted to growing in less-than-ideal

conditions. The fluted pumpkin with its edible seeds and leaves survives in the poorest conditions in Africa, making it a potential staple for millions of people."

Next, our boat enters the Aqua-cell where we learn about the process of controlled fish farming. "When we mention farming, you probably don't think of fish. But fish farming, or aquaculture, is an innovative way to increase harvests and protect wild fish populations. Tilapia, bass and catfish are three popular crops raised by fish farmers around the world. In Asia, tilapia are often raised in rice paddies where the fish waste provides nutrients for the rice. This integrated growing system improves yields and reduces pollution." We learn how controlled farming also helps in the repropagation of endangered species, such as the white alligator.

We move into our second greenhouse for temperate climates. Here we encounter turnip, sunflower, pumpkin and cassabanana. "This greenhouse is full of some our biggest ideas. Giant pumpkins and winter melons are certainly impressive but their real importance far exceeds their record-setting size. These super-sized crops represent the best efforts of scientist and farmers to improve plant yields. Years of careful selection and cross-breeding results in plants that produce more food, are more resistant to pests, and can even grow in marginal climates."

The String Greenhouse illustrates the growing of crops using some innovative techniques such as *vertical growing* and *nutrient film*. "These plants are definitely on their way up. Vertical growing systems like ours increase airflow through the leaves which helps to reduce disease. Diseases and pests are two of the biggest challenges faced by farmers around the world. Innovative growing techniques are just one way to fight these problems. Using beneficial insects to manage pest problems is another technique. We are also growing plants using our novel nutrient film system. By recycling water and nutrients, the system can save farmers money and help protect the environment."

Our boat rounds the bend and we enter our final greenhouse. Here, creative ideas are being explored to yield more crops on land, in the air and even in outer space. "We grow plants without soil throughout our greenhouses. That technique is called hydroponics. Now we are trying out aeroponics. Water and nutrients are sprayed directly on the roots of the plants as they fly by. In our lab, scientists from the U.S. Department of Agriculture are working to develop dwarf pear trees. The fruit will be normal-sized, but the smaller trees will be easier to grow and harvest."

A sliding door glides upward and we begin to make our way back to the loading dock. "These greenhouses represent just a small fraction of the work being done worldwide to produce bountiful harvest for our growing population. Working together we can continue to find innovative ways to increase food production and protect our precious natural environment. Only then will we truly be living with the land."

As guests depart, they are invited to sign up for a private tour of the greenhouse facility called "Beneath the Seeds."

 FOR REFLECTION

A seed. A fire. A teacher. Two nations.

In the Book of Genesis, we read, "The children struggled together within her; and she said, 'If it is to be this way, why do I live?' So she went to inquire of the LORD. And the LORD said to her, 'Two nations are in your womb, and two peoples born of you shall be divided; the one shall be stronger than the other, the elder shall serve the younger.'[2]

A road. A river. A boat. The tree of life.

There is a tree in Wadakona, resting on the White Nile in the Republic of South Sudan.

At the river's edge, off in the distance, breaking away from the desolate landscape, the tree is huge and recognizable. Its leaves are bright olive-green and the massive and majestic roots of the tree stretch out for yards along the riverbank, while drinking water from the White Nile.

The tree is so out of proportion that it almost doesn't seem real. It looks like the Tree of Life from Animal Kingdom, Walt Disney World, a huge centerpiece to a theme park. There is a patch of grass surrounding the tree, dipping then disappearing into the murky river water.

There is one road that travels from Khartoum, the capital of The Republic of Sudan, to Juba, the capital of The Republic of South Sudan. On this road, Stuckey's are replaced with makeshift structures of straw and boxes, creating the roadside "Coffee stop." "Rest areas" become "Short call" stops that are convenient because they encompass the entire countryside. "Short call" is the polite way of saying, "Let's stop for a bathroom break." "Radar enforced" signs are replaced with "Military checkpoints."

The roads are bumpy, sometimes hard to navigate, even difficult to identify, blending in with the shifting Sudanese landscape. Where the road isn't paved, it is made up of tightly packed red clay. When a car passes over the road, even at slow speeds, red dust is tossed up into the air, creating a trail-blazing cloud behind the traveling vehicle.

After crossing into the Republic of South Sudan, just past the town of Renk, and across the White Nile from the tree in Wadakona, there is the village of Lathbior.

The village of Lathbior is in the Diocese of Renk, the Episcopal Church. Lathbior is part of the newly forming nation of the Republic of South Sudan.

The land surrounding Lathbior is desolate, dead and dry. But the village chief dreams of building an irrigation system from the White Nile so the village can grow crops, develop the land, and feed the people.

The central road between Khartoum and Juba is two miles to the east of Lathbior. But, the people have a vision to one day connect their village to the road so that strangers can stop by, have a drink of fresh water, stay a while, and tell a story.

There is one school in Lathbior. It was built by the Episcopal Church of Sudan. It has 120 students and one teacher. But that teacher dreams of recruiting and inspiring others to come and teach with her. The teacher's name is Rebecca. She stands in an overcrowded classroom addressing the youth of Lathbior.

She speaks of a time of civil war, when people found themselves traveling on a road to nowhere, when children were killed and many others were lost. She is strong in the spirit and she boldly proclaims how the seed of faith encouraged strength during her journey.

As she speaks to her class, Rebecca proclaims in a loud, confident voice, "The spirit is upon me. My faith has called me to be here today in spite of my suffering. The spirit pushes me to tell others about the love of God and how it saves lives.

Since 1955, the Sudanese People's Liberation Army (SPLA) has been fighting the Sudanese government in Khartoum, protecting both Christians and Muslims living in Southern Sudan. During the fifty years of Civil War, power for the Northern government came by destroying communities in the South.

Villages were bombed, destroyed. People were massacred. Tribes decimated. Husbands and wives split apart. Villages put under fire, set ablaze. Eyes burning from the smoke of war. Parents and children losing sight of each other, separated.

Rebecca lost five children, snatched from her arms, recruited into death for death. When the dust settled, all she could feel was the burning of the ground on the soles of her feet. She was walking, drifting, searching, with nowhere to go with hundreds of thousands of others, walking through the dust and destruction, wondering how she got there.

The Lost Boys of Sudan, separated from their families and tribes, hid in the trenches, threatened by wild animals, scared of people with guns. . .

In October 2005, the President of Sudan, Omar al-Bashir, negotiated an end to the Second Sudanese Civil War, one of the longest-running and deadliest wars of the 20th century, by granting limited autonomy to Southern Sudan dominated by the SPLA. The Comprehensive Peace Agreement was signed.

Rebecca found herself in the village of Lathbior. But who else would settle there? How could they forget the hurt? Would she ever be able to extinguish the pain?

As the refugees of Sudan began to rebuild their lives, the Episcopal Church of Sudan moved out into the people healing, holding, building, and organizing.

In the midst of villages being reborn, the Episcopal Church of Sudan built community centers to save a suffering people. The church was central to this village compound. Clinics were built next to the churches. Kitchens were constructed to feed the people. Schools were attached. Teachers were needed. Rebecca heard the call. She lost five children but gained one hundred more.

But memories of war and separation remain. Across the river from the village of Lathbior and south, a tree in Wadakona has a story to tell. Members of the SPLA gather in the shadows and stand in silence.

A General calls out to the gathered crowd saying, "We are standing on sacred ground,"

"Here, where we stand, is the final resting place for some of my Christian brothers and sisters. This is a mass grave site."

The beautiful tree of Wadakona shades an execution sight. For over a half a mile, along the shore of the White Nile, faithful people were lined up, executed, dropped to the ground, and left to rot in the Sudanese sun. The General and his military sisters and brothers gathered to remember the three thousand fallen souls who rested there.

The General used his walking stick to shift the red dirt. As the dust from his stick rises from the ground, as he begins to dig a little deeper into the dirt, bones appear. First a rib cage, mangled with a forearm, then parts of a foot, mangled with another rib cage.

I wonder what my sisters and brothers in Christ thought and felt about God as they were taken away from their homes and brought to the river's edge. Did they feel abandoned, forgotten, lost and alone? Was their God, was our God, and the freedoms promised to us through Christ, worth dying for?

The General's anger becomes more pronounced. "Remember what happened here. We are one body. These bones are your brothers and sisters in Christ. We Southern Sudanese have not forgotten. This is just one of many."

As Sudan lives into being two separate countries, will the dust ever settle, or will the two new nations always be eating each other's dust?

In Lathbior, at a crude schoolhouse near the White Nile, Rebecca reflects on her life and what it means to remain in relationship with God and with God's people.

Rebecca says, "Faith has done a good thing to me and I have found new life through my faith. I lost my five children during the war. But my faith in God kept me hungry and prevented me from desiring revenge because of my loss. I have suffered.

God was with me in my grief. And I am in the church because God's spirit is upon me. I now bring all my children to church so that they can love their own people and their own people can love them. Together, with them, they learn, I learn, we learn how to do the work of God. The work of God is a hunger for truth, a desire to love all people, to build up community and to take care of each other. When I love God's people, I must tell them about God's power. When I share the world of God, I hope the spirit will make them hungry and together we can change the world.

THE E-TICKET

Jesus once said the poor and hungry will be with us always. We often equate this statement with a physical reality, but he probably also meant emotionally and spiritually.

There are so many ways to address hunger. We have to be aware of the hungry among us, then look at the world to see if some sort of injustice is contributing to the hunger. "Handing out free food and clothes was a charitable act. Approaching the powers was a political act. We could give people fish, but we could not ask why they had no fish."[3] System realities contribute to our hunger. Recall work you may have done around hunger. Was it prayer? Was it feeding? Was it situational?

Based on the work and stories shared in this section, write your own personal reflection on your experience on hunger. It can be emotional, physical or spiritual.

Turn to the "Holy Story" section in your journal. Begin your reflection with a brief narrative

Begin your reflection with a brief narrative on hunger. Take your time describing the incident. Recall what you were thinking and how you were feeling. Next, find a piece of scripture that has similar thought and feelings to your personal experience. Examine the scripture. What do you know about the context? What is the scripture about? Why do you feel it is related to your incident of hunger? Bring in a movie, song, book or any piece of art that relates to your story and the scripture you selected. Conclude by sharing your beliefs about hunger. How do you feed your hunger? How can you feed your neighbor's hunger?

Next, write a Rule of Life:

Hunger

I hunger for _____ .
I desire _____ .
I need _____ .
When I am aware of my hunger, I _____ .
When I hear hunger in another's voice or see it in their actions, I _____ .
The world hungers for _____ .

 # THE COLLECT

A Collect is a gathering thought, a prayer to helps us focus our thoughts.

We have reflected on different types of hunger - emotional, spiritual and physical - what causes it and how hunger is sometimes dealt with.

Based on everything we have discussed, compose three Collects about hunger you are experiencing. Then compose three Collects about hunger you are hearing from voices in the world.

Endnotes

[1] (May & Metzger, 1973, p. NT 53)
[2] (May & Metzger, 1973, p. OT 46)
[3] (Taylor, 2000, p. 20)

SIN } *Can I Be Loved in Spite of Myself?*

MAIN GATE

"The world is full of temptations…they're the wrong things that seem right at the time," says Jiminy Cricket in *Pinocchio*.

We live in a world which uses personal inadequacies as a motivator for action. We often start the day from the vantage point of not enough. We wake up with not enough sleep. We move through the world with not enough time. We work hard with not enough praise or recognition. We spend time with spouses or partners and there is not enough love. Each of us experiences not enough, which opens the door to sin as we attempt to get more. Each of us wonders if we can be loved in spite of our feelings and our actions.

At the Walt Disney World Resort, most of our favorite attractions delve into a storyline of sin. At *the Haunted Mansion,* Master Gracey, the owner of the estate, seems either to have hanged himself or to have been murdered by a sadistic bride. On the *Pirates of the Caribbean,* we are treated to a multitude of sins, wrath, greed, sloth, and gluttony! "Yo ho, yo ho, a pirate's life for me." At *Mickey's PhilharMagic,* Donald wants to be someone he is not by havring something that is not his. At Dinosaur in Disney's Animal Kingdom, disobeying the rules could put guests in the line of danger. Sin makes any storyline more intriguing.

I struggle to define sin. What is sin? How am I sinning? Can I change?

Others are happy to tell me what my sins are. People who judge others, the self-proclaimed stewards of God's mind, have no clue about the depths of my sins and are often in denial of their own. Sins defined by sex, drinking, and dance are simply sad distractions for more problematic evils. Our public squares are filled with violence, murder, sickness, and loneliness. All that many of us seem concerned about are sins of a sexual nature. This is lazy judgment. There is real work that needs to be done in our sinful world. One difficulty is that our biggest sins require communal, not individual, cooperation to transform.

Sin breeds more sin. When we vicariously delight in someone else's sin, we take their sin on ourselves. We join them and are sinning.

Sin is alive and well and constantly changing. Most of us know when we have sinned. We are often frustrated when we cannot figure out why we did something wrong in the first place. The sooner I can look at my own sin, the sooner I can move past it and, with God's help and with the help of others, redeem it.

When I see the results of the sins of others, I am intrigued and fascinated and scared. I want to know what decisions led them to the choices they made. Thinking of someone else's sin helps me to understand and reflect upon my own.

Sin hurts God. Sin hurts my neighbor. Sin hurts my self.

An action becomes a sin when someone else is hurt. To be aware of how we sin, we must have an understanding of God's hope for all people. This understanding takes time, prayer, people we trust, and honesty.

Neglecting sin breeds shame, anger, resentment, and depression. This neglect ultimately distorts how we see, act, and respond to God's world around us. Being in relationship with others, working and playing and praying in community, is difficult. When we are in relationship with others, their sins and ours eventually come to the surface. I believe my inability to accept my own sinfulness and my ability to accept the sins and transgressions of others are the downfall of religious institutions. We do not have to live this way. God does not want us to live this way.

Most of us just want to forget about sin because we see how sin and judgment are used by our culture to control and ultimately degrade others. People are judged. Others are called out. Angry Christians protest at funerals or about the latest national tragedies, calling their brothers and sisters in Christ sinners worthy of God's damning judgment. With glee and delight, "holier-than-thous" judge the broken-hearted, the defeated, and the lost. I dare say these "Christians" are why many of us do not attend church at all. The sad thing is that because of these righteous judgments and outrageous pronouncements, many of us just do not take sin seriously.

If we can remove judgment and stand in the shoes of a fellow sinner, we might understand our actions better and receive a glimpse of God's hope for us.

We must take sin seriously. We must grapple with sin. We must acknowledge our own sin. We must, by the grace of God, redeem our sin. Sin is as big a part of the journey of faith as is the act of love. After we acknowledge our sin, we must, with the best of our ability, be honest within ourselves in hopes of making better decisions.

We are called by God into a relationship with God and with God's people. The origin of the word *sin* evolved simply from the breaking of relationships. We do something against God. We have sinned. We have broken the relationship. We do something harmful against our neighbor. We have sinned. We have broken the relationship. We do something against ourselves. We have sinned against God and we have broken a relationship with people who care about us. Sin is an act of individual disobedience.

When we sin, we miss the mark. We have the intention of living a life with God and with God's people. *Chatah* is the Hebrew word for "missing the mark." The archer takes aim and releases the bow. After great effort, the archer misses the bull's eye and misses the mark.

When we sin, we miss the mark. We have the intention of living a life with God and with God's people. After great effort, we mess up. We hurt someone. We hurt ourselves. Like the archer, we can try again. We reach out. We hope to recover. Our intention is reconciliation. If we walk away without trying, the sin continues.

Sin has consequences. If we think it does not, we do not really understand sin. According to the Book of Genesis, Adam and Eve sinned against God and against each other. Eve ate the apple, breaking her relationships with God and with Adam. God asked who was at fault. Adam blamed Eve, breaking his relationships with God and with Eve. Does God's love for Adam and Eve change? No. God clothes them and prepares them for the fact that things are now different, but the bond of the relationship remains.

When we act wrongly, we can begin to turn our lives around with the choice to try to recover the relationship. Even after we reach out with the best intentions, having the relationship as it was is close to impossible. Time and trust are needed to finish the reconciliation.

If we prefer remorse to repentance, we remain in sin. The sin continues. We feel bad. We beat ourselves up. We claim how sinful we are. But nothing changes. As Barbara Brown Taylor points out, "Chronic guilt is the price we are willing to pay in order to avoid chronic change." [1]

To stop the sin, we must be willing to change. Sometimes we do not want to change. Most often, we do not know how to change. This is when we need the help and support of people we love and trust. None of us knows how to change, but others can help us to understand that we move through an incalculable number of changes every day. We just are not aware of them.

Honesty is the key. We sin. We live. We lead. We love. We work. We mess up. All of us do. Claim the sin.

Sometimes by the grace of God, relationships deepen as we move together through repentance.

 # IN THE QUEUE

If you are working your way through this travel guide at the Magic Kingdom, you will be moving into the queue at *Mickey's PhilharMagic*. The ride mimics the experience of going to the opera.

As you wait to enter the theater, you are given a pair of glasses. Minnie Mouse invites you to pick up your "opera glasses" so you can experience the performance to the fullest. These 3D glasses allow the theater-goer to narrow vision, to focus, and to see something from another perspective.

The beginning of forgiveness, our ability to move beyond sin towards redemption, is a process of refocusing our attention. This refocusing reflects our willingness to examine more closely, perhaps from a different angle, in order to shift our perception

of what has happened. Sometimes we can easily identify where we missed the mark. Sometimes we do not feel as if we are in the wrong. Many others times, however, are happy to point out that we are. We must be willing to consider their opinions. This willingness is part of healing and reconciliation. "Sin is our only hope because the recognition that something is wrong is the first step toward setting that something right again." [2]

Because of the voices of culture and often because of the voices in our heads, it is easy for us to become stuck in sin. Some believe that when we become stuck, we could be led down a path of despair, destruction, and death.

We need judgment. We need to ask ourselves the right questions in order to move past the sin and into forgiveness and reconciliation.

We become holy people when we begin to take seriously the nature of sin.

Institutional religion tells us that we are born into sin. For me, being broken and being born into sin are not the same thing. As people of the Judeo-Christian background, we can look at the beginning of our sacred writings to see how those who have come before us understand the nature of sin. These writings offer explanations of why bad things happen in the world.

The Torah is made up of the first five books of what Christians call the Bible. For people of the Jewish tradition, the Torah is the Books of Moses. Reading the Torah, we encounter a powerful narrative calling a group of people to be holy so that those who encounter God's people may come to know the power of God.

The Bible begins with creation. God overpowers the waters of chaos, creating us in the image of God, and then destroying us with a mighty flood.

Ten generations later, Abraham is called by God to leave his home and move into uncharted territory, to become a light to the world, an example to all people of what it means to be one of God's people. We encounter Isaac, then Jacob and Jacob's most well-known son Joseph.

Many of Abraham's descendants settle in Egypt after Pharaoh enlists Joseph as a civil servant. Several hundred years later, a Pharaoh who does not know Joseph considers these alien residents a threat to the status quo. He launches a genocidal campaign against them.

God calls Moses to deliver the people from the oppressive Pharaoh, leading them into a forty-year journey in the wilderness.

At Mount Sinai and throughout the desert journey, Moses has conversations with God. Moses receives the Ten Commandments, detailed instructions of worship and ritual observances and rules to help God's people to be holy in God's eyes and in the eyes of each other.

On the outskirts of the Promised Land, the people of Moses wage several unsuccessful military campaigns. As the people prepare to enter the Promised Land, Moses addresses the people, summarizing all of the laws and God's teaching.

Then Joshua is named as Moses' successor in these Books of Moses, the Torah.

The holiness code is found in the Book of Leviticus, in the middle of the Torah. The Book of Leviticus challenges us to learn how to live and to act as holy people.

In the Book of Leviticus, and throughout the Hebrew Scriptures, what Christians call the Old Testament, God calls us into a covenant relationship. God expects us to act demanding spiritual discipline and living by the law. Some of God's commands are concise and applicable. Others are peculiar, strange, and inaccessible.

If you have ever attempted to read the Bible from cover-to-cover, from beginning to end, you might have found the Book of Leviticus, the third book of the Bible, frustrating and boring. You might stop your reading there, concluding that Jesus nullifies the law.

My personal agenda, guided by my own shortfalls, influences how I interpret these holy and ancient writings. The laws of Leviticus are often used by others as a beating stick. For me, Leviticus graphically illustrates that God works with the contexts and circumstances in the present moment. Sin, laws, judgment, and redemption are guided by the spirit within a cultural context. Nowhere in Leviticus is holiness equated with being free from sinful thoughts or unholy action.

Cathleen Falsani, in an article in the Huffington Post, says this: "The Laws of Leviticus call for impartiality in the administration of justice, fairness in the treatment of the poor, provision for unemployed persons, and scrupulous honesty in all business dealings."

Often, a pushback against the cultural norms is the beginning of communal sin. Disregard for self or others is the beginning of sin against God and God's people.

In order to acknowledge and claim my sin, I must have some understanding of what the sin is. Turn to the next available page in the "Holy Story" section of your journal. Record the following reflections as you move through the queue.

Consider your personal belief statements about sin. Start by saying, "I believe sin is …" You may consider writing one belief statement. You may write down several. Keep writing belief statements about what you believe sin is until you feel you have captured most of your understanding of it.

How does sin work in your life?

Recall your past sins or times when you feel you have sinned.

How did you know that your thought or action was a sin?

Write each sin down. Look at your

thoughts and feelings? Is there something you can identify that triggered the sin? Is there a pattern of sin in your life? Is sin sparked by anger, jealousy, pride, authority? Is sin sparked by an inability to accept your God-given goodness?

Take some time to think about God and sin. What is God's hope for you? What is God's hope for this world? What does God want to do with you and your sin?

Write down your reflections in the "Holy Story" section of your journal.

 # FROM THE BOOK

Psalm 51

The Psalms are a unique part of Scripture because they are prayers to God which have become the Word of God to us. They are addressed to God, from the first person and have continual use in the life of synagogues and churches. The Psalms consist of songs of worship, prayer and praise, laments and murmuring, and petitions and curses. Although tradition asserts that the Psalms were written by King David, scholarship suggests they are a unique collection of ancient hymns that, for the most part, are difficult to attribute. Some suggest that some Psalms are comprehensive liturgies often led by prophets, judges or kings.

For all of us trying to live into our human condition, however we define it, the Psalms invite us to do so with God. We pray. We curse. We cry out in distress. We celebrate with thanksgiving. We move forward with confidence. Whatever state we find ourselves in, the Psalms give us permission to speak with God in honesty and truth.

PSALM 51

Have mercy on me, O God,
according to your steadfast love;
according to your abundant mercy
blot out my transgressions.
Wash me thoroughly from my iniquity,
and cleanse me from my sin.
For I know my transgressions,
and my sin is ever before me.
Against you, you alone, have I sinned,
and done what is evil in your sight,
so that you are justified in your sentence
and blameless when you pass judgment.
Indeed, I was born guilty,
a sinner when my mother conceived me.
You desire truth in the inward being;
therefore teach me wisdom in my secret heart.
Purge me with hyssop, and I shall be clean;
wash me, and I shall be whiter than snow.
Let me hear joy and gladness;
let the bones that you have crushed rejoice.
Hide your face from my sins,
and blot out all my iniquities.
Create in me a clean heart, O God,
and put a new and right spirit within me.
Do not cast me away from your presence,
and do not take your holy spirit from me.
Restore to me the joy of your salvation,
and sustain in me a willing spirit.
Then I will teach transgressors your ways,
and sinners will return to you.
Deliver me from bloodshed, O God,
O God of my salvation,
and my tongue will sing aloud of your
deliverance.
O Lord, open my lips,
and my mouth will declare your praise.
For you have no delight in sacrifice;
if I were to give a burnt offering, you would not be
pleased.
The sacrifice acceptable to God is a broken spirit;
a broken and contrite heart, O God, you will not
despise.

Do good to Zion in your good pleasure;
  rebuild the walls of Jerusalem,
then you will delight in right sacrifices,
  in burnt offerings and whole burnt offerings;
  then bulls will be offered on your altar. ³

RIDE THE ATTRACTION

Mickey's PhilharMagic

For lovers of the Disney music catalogue, *Mickey's PhilharMagic* a delightful 4-D experience into the memorable songs of recent animated classics. Located in Fantasyland in the Magic Kingdom, *Mickey's PhilharMagic* invites guests into a symphonic adventure. Donald Duck disrupts an upcoming performance led by conductor Mickey Mouse at Fantasyland's Concert Hall. Donald's desire to be Mickey brings out the worst in him and theater guests journey with Donald through a madcap adventure of some of Disney's most popular musical sequences.

Upon entering the Concert Hall, guests pick up their "opera glasses" and admire posters from past performances. Goofy welcomes guests and opens the Concert Hall doors for them to find a seat.

Once inside the Hall, Minnie Mouse welcomes the guests. After her brief introduction, she tells Mickey that Donald Duck has gone missing. Goofy, the stage manager of the Hall, raises the curtain, revealing Donald pretending to conduct a nonexistent orchestra. The stage is empty. Mickey finds Donald and panics. The stage needs to be made ready. Mickey asks Donald to unpack the instruments while he goes off to find the performers.

Mickey leaves his Sorcerer's hat, made famous during "The Sorcerer's Apprentice" sequence in 1940's *Fantasia*. After Donald unpacks the instruments, he notices Mickey's hat. Donald

Duck puts it on.

Once Donald puts on the hat, all musical instruments stand at attention. Donald is proud of himself. He is in charge of the show! He taps the conductor's stand and the instruments prepare to perform. Donald tosses an enchanted flute, which puts things into motion.

A thunderous wind, accompanied by the musical instruments gathering and then scattering in the waves of the storm, blows the Sorcerer's hat off Donald's head. He begins to work his way through the storm in hopes of retrieving the Sorcerer's hat.

A comical instrumentation of the familiar "Mickey Mouse Club" tune informs us that we have left the safety of the Club House. Cymbals crash. Instruments fly. A black hole sucks us into the vortex while Donald reaches out to the Concert Hall guests yelling, "Help me! Help me! Help me!" Donald gets sucked into the hole and so does the floating and flipping and flying, but elusive, Sorcerer's hat.

Then the guests are in the dark.

Donald's eyes pierce the darkness and he wonders, "Where's my hat?" A match is struck and a flame appears. Donald is startled.

A voice addresses Donald. "Bonjour. It is with deepest pride and greatest pleasure that we welcome you tonight." Suddenly, Lumiere, from *Beauty and the Beast*, appears.

"And now the Dining Room proudly presents your dinner. Be our guest! Be our guest! Put our service to the test. Tie your napkin around your neck, Cherie, and we provide the rest. Soup du jour, hot hors d'oeuvres. Why? We only live to serve. Try the grey stuff. It's delicious! Don't believe me? Ask the dishes."

Donald is amused with himself. He is proud of the music he is making. Food dances and marches about him when suddenly the Sorcerer's hat appears on top of a bowl of French onion soup. Donald notices and makes chase. He thinks he has retrieved the hat, only to discover he has grabbed hold of a magnificently smelling apple pie. Dancing forks and plates and spoons fill the Concert Hall.

Lumiere appears triumphant, ready for the big finale. "Course by course, one by one until you shout, 'Enough! I'm done!' Then we'll sing you off to sleep as you digest. Tonight you'll prop your feet up but for now just eat up. Be our guest! Be our guest! Be our guest! Please, be our guest!"

As champagne bottles pop and spoons celebrate the big ending, Donald pops up looking for his hat. He seems to have forgotten that it is Mickey's. Lumiere's candles go out and we are left in the dark.

A door opens, letting in light and we catch a glimpse of a broom carrying a bucket of water. As Donald digs through a pile of junk that looks like what is left over from the "Be Our Guest" numbers, brooms continually enter through the door carrying more buckets of water. They start to bury Donald with water. Debris floats about and the hat pops out. A big broom towers over Donald, dumping a huge pail of water on his head. Water is everywhere.

As the water covers everything, a small yellow fish named Flounder swims to welcome us under the sea. He notices all of the people looking at him and finds it "cool." The hat drifts through the water and lands in the hands of Ariel, the little mermaid. She looks at it, admiring its design.

Ariel begins to sing, "Look at this stuff. Isn't it neat? Wouldn't you think my collection's complete? Wouldn't you think I'm the girl who has everything?"

Donald appears in a snorkeling outfit and appears to be smitten with Ariel.

Ariel continues, "I've got gadgets and gizmos a-plenty. I've got whozits and whatzits galore. You want thingamabobs? I've got twenty! But who cares? No big deal. I want more."

Ariel reaches out to the audience with a yearning embrace. She is hoping for something beyond the stuff. Donald forgets about stuff for a minute. Ariel longs to be, "where the people are. I wanna see, wanna see them dancing, walking around on those - what do you call them? - feet!"

Donald holds out his duck feet.

Ariel continues, "When's it my turn? Wouldn't I love, love to explore that shore up above? Watch and you'll see; someday I'll be part of that world."

Ariel entrances Donald and he tries to kiss her, but an electric eel passing by shocks Donald and transports us to a desert edge of a rising sun.

Suddenly, out of collage of animals, Simba from *The Lion King* appears singing, "I'm gonna be the mane event like no king was before. I'm brushing up on looking down. I'm working on my roar." Simba swallows up the screen, leaving us in darkness.

Then, Zazu appears, flapping his wings, adding, "Thus far, a rather uninspiring thing." As giraffes appear, Simba sings out, "Oh, I just can't wait to be king!" The Sorcerer's hat appears on the head of one of the dancing giraffes.

Donald yells out, "That's my hat!" As Donald leaps for the hat, the giraffes look left and the hat goes flying.

Simba continues, "Everybody look left. Everybody look right. Everywhere you look I'm standing in the spotlight!" But Zazu yells in a very strict tone, "Not yet!" plunging us into darkness and then revealing Donald tumbling on the sun shining over the African continent.

An animal chorus continues, "Let every creature go for broke and sing. Let's hear it in the herd and on the wing. It's gonna be King Simba's finest fling."

Donald finds himself in the center of a kaleidoscope of animals as Simba and the chorus

THE
WOLF GANG
TRIO

I PAGLIACCI

performed by

WILLIE
THE
WHALE

proclaim, "Oh! I just can't wait to be king!"

Simba finds himself on the top of a tower of water. It collapses; the Sorcerer's hat zooms by. Tinker Bell appears from a trail of pixie dust. The guests fall with Donald through the clouds and onto the immense clock hands of Big Ben.

The shadow of Peter Pan lands on the big hand. The hat falls next to him. Then Donald lands on the big hand and knocks the hat and all of them into the skies just above London where Peter Pan and Wendy are off to find Never, Never Land.

Peter Pan yells, "Here we go!"

The Neverland chorus sings, "When there's a smile in your heart, there's no better time to start. Think of all the joy you'll find when you leave the world behind. And get your chance to fly. You can fly! You can fly! You can fly! You can fly!"

Peter Pan sprinkles some pixie dust, as Donald continues to chase the Sorcerer's hat. The gusts of wind carry the hat higher into the clouds where it disappears.

A flying carpet suddenly bursts into the sky, carrying Aladdin and Jasmine. Aladdin begins to charm Jasmine, singing, "I can show you the world. Take you wonder by wonder. Over, sideways and under on a magic carpet ride. A whole new world! A new fantastic point of view. No one to tell us no or where to go or say we're only dreaming."

The hat passes through the clouds, but Donald has it all under control, having hitched a ride on a carpet of his own.

Aladdin and Jasmine continue, "A whole new world. That's where we'll be. A thrilling chase. A wondrous place for you and me."

Mickey's sorcerer's hat is sitting comfortably next to Jasmine on the Magic Carpet.

Donald pursues them, yelling out to the hat, "Where are you going? There it is!" Jasmine picks up the hat places it on Donald's head.

Donald waves and yells, "thank you" as Jasmine and Aladdin continue the Magic Carpet journey.

The annoying parrot Iago knocks the hat off Donald's head and it starts to tumble to the ground. Donald goes after it but gets caught in a whirlwind. Instruments pass through the clouds as Donald tumbles out of control.

As the clouds start to clear and the storm starts to settle, we notice Mickey, with the hat on, conducting and taking control of the symphony. Everything falls to its place.

Mickey looks at the exhausted Donald, takes the baton from Donald's hand, and says, "Thank you." The music concludes with a triumphant rendition of "The Mickey Mouse Club" theme.

FOR REFLECTION

"Welcome, sinners!"

I can remember quite clearly the first time I was addressed that way, as a sinner, as a sinner who was - "welcomed."

I was fourteen years old. I was in confirmation class, preparing to make my adult proclamation of faith, really unsure of what that actually meant. Our small, earnest study group was going on a field trip, a spiritual pilgrimage. We left the safety of our home parish, All Saints River Ridge, a beautiful little church of about 300 people nestled right on the levee of the Mississippi River.

My confirmation class traveled together, about six miles, to Uptown New Orleans, to the city, to the Cathedral, Christ Church Cathedral, on Saint Charles Avenue, just blocks away from the French Quarter.

I had a feeling, call it divine intuition, that it would be much easier for me to make an adult proclamation of faith from the very center of Bourbon Street. Quite frankly, I was more interested in visiting the French Quarter than the Cathedral.

Our confirmation class, with our faithful confirmation teachers, arrived at Christ Church Cathedral. We walked in. The place was huge. Everybody was in a suit or in a fancy dress. The place was pretty quiet. As we entered, everyone in the pews turned around to see who we were.

It was quite intimidating.

A man in a collar was near the entrance to the Cathedral, standing near the baptismal font. As our suburban eyes adjusted to the darkness of the place, a voice yelled out from out there somewhere, "Welcome, sinners!"

"Welcome, sinners!"?

What kind of greeting was this?

And who did that man think he was talking to?

Me?

A sinner?

What did he know that I did not know? Or, an even more frightening possibility, what did he know? It turned out he was the Dean of the Cathedral. I did not know what a Dean was and I did not much care.

"Welcome, sinners!"?

Whoever had not turned around before to check us out was now definitely turning around to see who or what had just walked through the door.

I was a little taken aback, to say the least and it takes a lot to shock me.

We awkwardly made our way to the reserved pews, the pews up front, reserved for guests, reserved for confirmation classes coming to town from all around the diocese.

After that greeting, I really did not want to stay. But we had to stay. We had no choice. We were there to worship in the Cathedral and meet our Bishop. We were there to prepare for the time when the Bishop would lay hands upon us, an adult proclamation of faith, committing our lives to God in Christ.

"Welcome, sinners!"

I certainly did not like being addressed as a sinner.

Had I sinned? Most definitely.

Did I want people to know I was a sinner? Most definitely not.

Is everyone a sinner? I will leave that up to you to answer.

The teachings and traditions of the Church have an answer. The answer is "yes." We are all sinners. However, I am not personally comfortable with the Church's assumption.

Every time the word *sin* is mentioned, whenever it is brought up, I have to struggle with what it means exactly, in that moment in time.

What is sin?

Where and when have I sinned?

And, what does sin have to do with my relationship with God?

I guess I know sin when I see it. Especially in someone else!

I have met with people who truly believe that God cannot, and will not, and does not want to redeem them from their sin. I have even heard pastors and priests who are comfortable damning people to hell because of their sins.

What is that about really?

For me, they are trapped in the world of no forgiveness, no redemption, no relationship and, ultimately, no hope.

If I truly believe that I am totally beyond redemption, then nothing I do matters. My relationship with God does not matter.

But, if I believe that God can redeem every one and every thing, then everything, and I mean everything I do, matters.

"Welcome, sinners."

John the Baptist called out to the people of

God in similar fashion.

Gospel writers tell us that as people approached John to be baptized, he yelled out to them, saying, "You brood of vipers! Who warned you to flee from the wrath to come? Bear fruits worthy of repentance."

"Welcome, sinners."

"You are my Son, the Beloved; with you I am well pleased."

"A brood of vipers…"

The mixed messages of faith.

Am I sinner? Am I a viper?

Am I redeemable? Am I beloved?

The multitude of the answers makes it difficult to know how to be truly honest with myself on this journey of faith, this journey with Christ, this journey towards God, a journey where I turn away from sin, whatever that may be, and look towards God, praying that God can open a door, or crack a window, or make a path straight, and show me the way.

"Welcome, sinners."

How can I discover my true self, my God-given identity, which is hard enough to understand, to claim and to recognize, when I am swimming in my own pool of sin?

The people came to John. Like me, I imagine they did not know the answers. But what they did know was that there was and there is something out there, bigger than our sins, much larger than our egos, more powerful than our fears and anxieties and doubts, that knows each of us and loves each of us, even when we do not have a clue about what is going on in our lives or in the world.

"Welcome, sinners."

When people approached John the Baptist, when people were looking at how they had missed the mark, "the people were filled with expectation." What are you expecting from God?

As I walked into that Cathedral as a messed-up fourteen-year-old boy, I desperately wanted to know that I was worthy of being loved and that I was capable of giving love.

Perhaps sin is the inability to love anyone or anything.

You are my daughters. You are my sons. You are my beloved. With you I am well pleased.

In a noisy world, it is extremely difficult for us to remember our limitless capacity to love. It is so much easier to hear and to claim everything that is wrong with ourselves. If there is evil, it is exactly that, a power within us that prevents us from loving.

John the Baptist was a radical. At the river's edge he appeared. Leave behind what keeps us separated from God. "Prepare the way of the Lord." He was mad at the middleman. Temple-goers had to pay the priest, the middleman, a toll to come before the presence of God. The toll included a ritual bath, a temple sacrifice for bodily purification. The ritual was to be performed daily and was an expensive ritual for those who took God seriously.

John proclaimed one wash, one baptism, one moment, for the forgiveness of sins; a moment where every trace of sin within each of us, where everything that stands between each of us and God is washed away forever.

"Do not fear, for I have redeemed you; I have called you by name, you are mine. When you pass through the waters, I will be with you; and through the rivers, they shall not overwhelm you; when you walk through fire you shall not be burned, and the flame shall not consume you. For I am the Lord your God, the Holy One of Israel, your Savior."

According to *The Book of Common Prayer*, "Sin is the seeking of our own will instead of the will of God, thus distorting our relationship with God, with people, and with all creation."

When I am lost in my sin, I forget who I am.

When I am stuck in my sin, I forget who God's people are.

When I claim my sin, I am given power by God to leave it behind, to seek forgiveness, to come to the water's edge and to be with others who are on the same journey.

"Welcome, sinners."

Jesus is with us at work and at play, in the midst of love and in the midst of sadness, during moments of celebration, alienation and anxiety, and at the times when we sin or when we are stuck in it.

Jesus stands with us in the River Jordan, splitting the heavens open reminding us that we are God's people, we are beloved, and that God is well pleased.

"We are sealed by the Holy Spirit in Baptism and marked as Christ's own forever."

Forever.

Forever means forever.

"For I am convinced that neither death, nor life, nor angels, nor rulers, nor things present, nor things to come, nor powers, nor height, nor depth, nor anything else in all creation, will be able to separate us from the love of God in Christ Jesus our Lord." [4]

Welcome, sinners.

THE E-TICKET

Are there times when you have turned away, missed the mark, struggled within a sinful condition that you still have not been forgiven by someone else or haven't forgiven yourself for?

In the Episcopal *Book of Common Prayer*, an intentional conversation between two people is part of the process of moving beyond sin. Prayers are said. The nature of sin is given some context. Then the person seeking reconciliation states the sin in order to claim it. At the end of the conversation, the priest says, "Go in peace, and pray for me, a sinner."[5]

Sometimes, we do not want to have these conversations with others. But externalizing the sin can help. Before we write a Rule about sin, let us do a little more work in the "Holy Story" section of our journal.

Think of something you are seeking forgiveness for. Think of a title for this event. Place it at the top of the page.

In a paragraph or two, write the action of the event. Identify the thoughts and feelings of the event. Look for Biblical passages where there were similar thoughts and feeling associated with the event.

As you look at the scripture passages that recall your event, answer the following questions and record the answers:

- How were others hurt because of the action?
- Where is God in the action?
- What does God need to do to redeem the action?
- What does the person in the Scripture need to do to redeem the action?
- Recall your event. What do you need to do?

Recall something from popular culture that describes your event. Think of a popular movie, song, book, poem or magazine article that brings to mind what you are experiencing.

Conclude by writing a belief statement about this incident and how it still impacts your life. Use the following formula.

I believe sin in this incident is _____ . I missed the mark by _____ . In order to move forward, I must _____ . God wants me to _____ . An action I am willing to take is _____ .

You may complete this exercise for as many "sins" as you feel the need to. If you have someone you trust, encourage that person to do this exercise with you and then discuss how you both may move forward.

When you are ready, write a Rule of Life about sin. Follow the pattern below.

Sin

Sin is _____ .

I recognize my sin by _____ .

I address my sins by _____ .

I forgive others sins by _____ .

 THE COLLECT

Some of us confess our sins regularly. Confession may have been part of our religious tradition as we were growing up. Some may have heard about the confession of sin, rejected the practice and dismissed organized religion. Prayer and acknowledgment of sin changes our hearts and actions. Praying shapes believing.

We are going to write three Collects: one addressing sin, one addressing God, and one addressing self. We will modify the formula a bit.

Formula for Collect addressing sin
1. Address sin
2. Define sin as you see it
3. Identify causes of sin
4. State how to move away from this type of sin
5. Name what you are willing to do about it
6. Name who you need to help you

Formula for Collect addressing God about sin
1. Address God
2. Define God's relationship to sin
3. State what God thinks of sin
4. Name what God does with sin
5. Name what you need from God regarding sin
6. Conclude the Collect

Formula for Collect addressing self
1. Address self
2. Address God's relationship to self
3. State a sin concern
4. Claim why it is bothering self
5. What do you need God to do
6. Conclude the Collect

✠

Endnotes

1 (Taylor, 2000, p. 66)
2 (Taylor, 2000, p. 59)
3 (May & Metzger, 1973, p. OT 717)
4 (May & Metzger, 2010, p. 1098)
5 (Episcopal Church., 1979, p. 448)

SUFFERING } *Why Do I Suffer?*

MAIN GATE

"Listen to me. The human world is a mess," says Sebastian to Ariel in *The Little Mermaid*. Ariel, tired of life with a fin, desires to be up there, where the people are. Sebastian, a delightful little lobster, tries to convince Ariel that the world under the sea is enough because everything she could ever want is right in front of her. She just does not see it. She desires more. Her life seems incomplete.

Desire is a powerful motivator. It impacts our decisions and influences everything we do. It moves us forward. Desire drags us down. It clouds our vision. It manipulates us to wish everything to be different from what it really is. Ultimately, when we desire, we suffer. Desiring something other than the reality surrounding us causes us to create a world of delusion. We forget what is real and we live into the delusion of what we desire. Living in a world of personal desire, it becomes difficult of us to connect with and to care for others. Desire is of God, who desired a world, separated the waters, and set out dry land. The second creation story tells us that humankind was formed from the mud of the earth. A sexless mud doll receives the breath of God and we are born.

Desire is part of our DNA and we suffer for it. We desire to be like God so we do exactly what God tells us not to do. We feel estranged from God, but God continuously reaches out to us. God transcended time and space and sought to teach us how to live and love through the ministry and the teaching of Jesus Christ. Some believe Christ's experience of suffering on the cross reconciles us to God. According to Christian belief, God suffers with us to free us from our sins. God understands suffering and through grace is able to forgive us when we sin. The fact that God is present during our suffering provides comfort to some, but we want more.

The empty tomb and the resurrection of Christ is a graphic and tangible reality of God's hope for all of us – that we die to all that is holding us back and that we live into a new life.

In spite of the life, death, and resurrection of Jesus Christ, we still suffer. When we suffer, most explanations of our suffering are not satisfying.

Why do I suffer? Why do others suffer?

Suffering changes our perspective of things. It causes us to question our status and our worth. It challenges our faith beliefs, sometimes causing us to seek a deeper understanding of exactly how God is working in the world.

Does God want me to suffer? Does God care when I am suffering? Is suffering caused by a twist of fate, a roll of the die, a spin of the wheel? We want to know why we suffer in hopes of giving our challenges context, meaning, and ultimately, redemption.

Some of us are able to move through suffering with confidence. Others of us move through suffering waiting for the final straw to snap and drop us down into the abyss of no return forever.

The Walt Disney World Resort is the perfect playground for the suffering and desiring. When we suffer, we want to escape. When we desire, we want to fulfill it. If we can dream it, we can do it.

We live in a culture that says if I have enough, I will not suffer. Advertising supports our desire to change, to be different, to be fulfilled, to be self-actualized. "A group of writers condemns Walt Disney World's consumerist contrivances, complaining that guests cannot separate the pleasure of the rides from the pleasure of the gift shops… (suggesting that) Disney audiences (are) passive consumers of entertainment for whom rides and commodities, and hence fantasy and reality, are one and the same." [1] If we can experience it or buy it, we will not suffer at the place where dreams come true. Disney tells stories and makes memories to get our money. Walt Disney World is a business. We live in a consumerist culture and must understand why we suffer, what God hopes for us, and what we are willing or not willing do about it.

In 1937, *Snow White* was adapted into Walt Disney's first full-length animated feature film. The classic Grimm fairy tale follows the adventures of a beautiful 14-year-old princess who escapes the murderous intentions of her evil stepmother, the wicked queen. The queen is threatened by the young maiden's innocence and beauty so she orders Snow White to be killed. The stepmother is suffering because she wants to be something different. She wants to be the fairest of them all. She believes she will be if Snow White is killed.

Snow White is portrayed as a beautiful, but amusingly, naive youngster, living in a secluded cottage in the woods inhabited by seven dwarfs. "I'm Wishing" and "Whistle While You Work" are popular Disney classics about love, longing,

and finding contentment in mundane, everyday tasks. Most of us desire more than living the life of a housekeeper working for seven little men with seven distinct and dysfunctional characteristics. Since we want more, we suffer.

As Christians, we want to be like Christ. We want to hear the story and understand the mission of our lord and savior so that we can be closer to God and to God's people. This is the incarnational invitation. Trying to understand that God is with us is at the heart of our desire. We can desire things, but we must be truthful to ourselves about what we desire and why. Disney has successfully marketed our desires through the "Disney Princess" collection. The marketing strategy is that we can transcend our stories and live their stories with the right accoutrements.

Most of the young ladies in Disney's classic animated tales want more so they suffer. We began with *The Little Mermaid's* Ariel, who wants to be where the people are so her spirit is suffering. She wants to be loved and accepted by people who are different than she is so she must change and become like them. When we do not accept ourselves as the persons God has created, we suffer. When others do not accept us the way God has created us, we suffer. In *The Princess and the Frog*, Tiana wants to be an independent woman in a "man's world" so she is suffering. Instinct tells Tiana that God created all of us as equals so why are there second-class citizens? Some address their own suffering by making others suffer. They abuse their power and sustain a society that discriminates. They believe if I can make you suffer more, I will suffer less. In *Beauty and the Beast*, Belle wants to expand her mind to be a free-thinker. She is not interested in chasing and serving men. Belle has dreams of her own. Free-thinking is often seen as suspect by others. If we step out of line, the whole system, which is running on automatic, might be put out of whack. Belle threatens the system. The townsfolk think she is a freak. Belle suffers because she is seeking freedom and justice. Suffering is the primary characteristic of the Disney princesses.

We desire to live "happily ever after" and we want everything right now so we suffer. If I dress like a Disney princess, will I experience the "happily ever after," right here and right now, and alleviate my suffering?

Marketing, consumerist culture, and modern-day sensibilities have driven the Walt Disney Company through some revisionist history. Snow White was the first Disney princess. She is followed by many, many others. These casts of fairy-tale women are evolving into "modern-day princesses," intelligent and independent, who no longer need men to rescue them with kisses from their lives of suffering. If we change the context, the meaning of suffering shifts and changes also.

In a consumerist culture, we believe we can eliminate suffering through what we buy. We believe we can buy friends and family. We can buy cars and houses. We can buy success. We can buy influence. We can buy happiness. We believe we are what we own.

The colorful "Disney Princess" collection is now available for purchase for young girls of all ages. We can buy the dresses, the crowns, the shoes, and even the hair. As we walk around The Magic Kingdom, we are surrounded by little girls magically transformed into little princesses. But chasing the dreams of fairy-tale princesses can lead to a lot of suffering because, like the fairy tales themselves, we often do not fit into the mold.

A young African-American woman I know has shared with me that when she was in second grade, she dressed up as Snow White for a school costume party. She went to the Disney Store, bought the costume, and proudly donned her Snow White princess outfit.

She loved the film. She loved her princess outfit even more. She marched into school. Her teachers were delighted. Others were impressed by the costume's authenticity.

Then she walked into her math class. A friend of hers, sitting in the front row, yelled out, "Princesses aren't black!"

A hush came over the entire classroom. People stared at her and her once beautiful princess outfit seemed embarrassing and awful. She felt sad. She wanted to cry. She wanted to rip off the costume. She did not fit into someone else's expectations so she suffered for it.

"Princesses aren't black!"

She loved her dress and she still loved Snow White, but suddenly her dreams and desires were in direct conflict with what someone else desired. She shared, "I tried to remember who I was, a black girl, created in the image of God. I tried to respond gracefully. I'm not sure that I did. I tried to forgive. I'm not sure that I have. I hope not to do the same to others. On most days I am able to do this. I pray to be faithful. That's all I can do. But sometimes, it still hurts a lot, even though I say it doesn't."

Princesses suffer when they do not fit into the experiences and expectations of others. We all do.

Suffering has several incarnations. During a lifetime, we have the opportunity to experience them all. We suffer physically. We suffer mentally. We suffer when we seek change. We suffer when we do not like the realities of our lives. We suffer when we want to be someone or somewhere else.

The truth is that there is no degree of suffering that does not hurt. When we suffer, we suffer. We cannot actually say that I am suffering more or less than the person next to me. Suffering hurts no matter the context. C3PO, a golden robot in the film *Star Wars: A New Hope,* while walking around in the desert, says, "It seems I was born to suffer."

Perhaps.

IN THE QUEUE

Is it possible to understand why we suffer?

As we move from here to there, we never know what is going to happen. We try to avoid the present moment by living in nostalgia of the past or by dreaming of a future not yet arrived. I can control what I think I feel by living this way because the past and the future actually exist only in my imagination. I can control thoughts and feelings of the past and the future. The present cannot be controlled. The present belongs totally to God.

Suffering is directly related to free will. We suffer because of the choices we make. Understanding the mystery of suffering is the work of a lifetime.

As with all mysteries of faith, there are times when everything makes perfect sense to us. Then suddenly, within a matter of seconds, everything changes, our understanding shifts or totally disappears, and we are stuck wondering, "What happened?"

We all want to understand why things are the way they are.

In the Hebrew Scriptures, what Christians call The Old Testament, The Book of Job presents the suffering of a "righteous" man. Job is successful. He has a wife, children, and many possessions. His success suggests that he has been blessed by God.

As fate would have it, a colleague of God named Satan questions the faithfulness of Job. Will Job continue to love and extol God through various degrees of suffering circumstances? God believes Job will remain faithful so God accepts Satan's challenge and God acts to change the circumstances of Job's life. Job loses everything, including his physical health and appearance. Job's friends comment on the circumstances of his suffering. Each conversation

reveals a different explanation of suffering. Do we suffer because of our past sins? Do we suffer because of circumstances we create? Or is there no explanation at all for the suffering we experience?

The Book of Job asks these questions and many more. Several explanations are offered. Not one of these explanations is totally satisfying. Ultimately, the book states that God is God and we are not. Only God knows why we suffer.

As you move through the queue, think about suffering in your life and in the world. Move to the "Holy Story" section of your journal. Recall times in your life when you experienced suffering. Write them down. Recall the context to the suffering and write it down. What was the cause of the suffering? Was it physical suffering? Was it emotional suffering? Was it suffering about by circumstances of life? What was it that you desired to be different?

When you feel that you have recalled enough, look at each occasion that you have written down. Consider the presence of God in each circumstance. Did you feel the presence of God while you were suffering or was God totally absent? Did family and friends offer you explanations of suffering in hopes of comforting you? If so, were you comforted? What was said?

Today, as you recall the past, where do you believe God is now?

How are you suffering now? Write in your "Holy Story" section how you are suffering now.

Now, take a moment to reflect on the sufferings of the world. How are others suffering? Are you moved by their suffering?

Personally, I have heard the voice of suffering through others from within their life experiences. I have heard suffering in the voice of a homeless youth whose parents had kicked him out of his home because he was gay. I heard it late one night in a hospital in the voice of a scared young man who had to obey his mother's wishes and terminate her life. I heard suffering one night in the anger of a hungry neighbor who was off his meds and was not making it through the day. This voice, this moan is deep within all of us. I do not want to admit how much I suffer. I do not want to recognize this suffering when I see and hear it in others.

Are you moved by suffering?

We have all heard the voice of suffering. This voice seems as if it is from somewhere beyond. It is a voice that comes from a loved one trying to recover from a stroke. It is a voice that hits us hard from a partner who is angry. It is the voice of an infant that gives us no hint of what must be done or how we are supposed to do it. It is the voice of a parent living with Alzheimer's, telling stories that have no context, no connection, no nothing to the person we used to know and love.

Write down in your "Holy Story" section how you are moved by the suffering of others.

Do you believe God is moved by suffering? Recall stories from scripture and from the teachings of the Church where God seems to be moved by suffering.

Write down in your "Holy Story" section how you see God moved by suffering.

FROM THE BOOK
Job 7:1-21

The Book of Job is part of the "Wisdom" tradition in the writings of the Old Testament. In this tradition, beliefs, circumstances and teachings are passed on to younger generations as a guidebook to life. Common sense assumptions are challenged by life's experiences and Wisdom literature emerges. Books of Wisdom in the Hebrew Scriptures are the Book of Job, Proverbs, and Ecclesiastes.

The Book of Job tells of story of a pious man who seems to suffer unjustly at the hands of God. Satan, acting in the role of a public prosecutor,

challenges God about Job's motivations of piety. What is real? What is manipulative? How can extreme cases of grief and suffering change a person and the faith that person professes? How do our family and friends reconcile our suffering and their own personal suffering? These questions are all addressed within the Book of Job. Through conversations with friends and finger-pointing at God, our beliefs about the personhood of Job are challenged, causing this to be one of the most theologically rich and difficult books to appreciate in all holy writings.

JOB 7:1-21

"Do not human beings have a hard service on earth, and are not their days like the days of a laborer? Like a slave who longs for the shadow, and like laborers who look for their wages, so I am allotted months of emptiness, and nights of misery are apportioned to me. When I lie down I say, 'When shall I rise?' But the night is long, and I am full of tossing until dawn. My flesh is clothed with worms and dirt; my skin hardens, then breaks out again. My days are swifter than a weaver's shuttle, and come to their end without hope.

"Remember that my life is a breath; my eye will never again see good. The eye that beholds me will see me no more; while your eyes are upon me, I shall be gone. As the cloud fades and vanishes, so those who go down to Sheol do not come up; they return no more to their houses, nor do their places know them any more.

"Therefore I will not restrain my mouth; I will speak in the anguish of my spirit; I will complain in the bitterness of my soul. Am I the Sea, or the Dragon, that you set a guard over me? When I say, 'My bed will comfort me, my couch will ease my complaint,' then you scare me with dreams and terrify me with visions, so that I would choose strangling and death rather than this body.

"I loathe my life; I would not live forever.

Let me alone, for my days are a breath. What are human beings, that you make so much of them, that you set your mind on them, visit them every morning, test them every moment? Will you not look away from me for a while, let me alone until I swallow my spittle? If I sin, what do I do to you, you watcher of humanity? Why have you made me your target? Why have I become a burden to you? Why do you not pardon my transgression and take away my iniquity? For now I shall lie in the earth; you will seek me, but I shall not be." [2]

RIDE THE ATTRACTION
The Twilight Zone Tower of Terror

When entering the Walt Disney World Resort from Highway 192, you cannot help but notice an unusual structure looming over Sunset Boulevard at Disney's Hollywood Studios. This unusual structure is the Hollywood Tower Hotel, an unattractive building with half of the hotel missing. All is not well. Something bad, perhaps a fire, must have happened there. Suddenly the doors near the roof of the hotel open. People scream. The doors close. Then the terror repeats itself in just a matter of moments.

The Hotel was built in 1994. The hotel still welcomes guests but you begin to realize that you will become a permanent resident of *The Twilight Zone.*

The *Tower of Terror* is one of the most interesting and ingenious attractions created by the Disney Imagineers. The design of the ride is quite simple. Guests move up the tower in one elevator shaft, travel down a hall, enter another elevator shaft, then drop and rise several times. Imagineers designed the ride to be pulled upwards and downwards, faster than gravity, using a series of hard-working cables. This engineering feat gives guests at the Hollywood Tower Hotel an unusual experience of weightlessness.

Blood-curdling screams from the thirteenth story's exterior opening doors invite the thrill-seeker to check in and stay the night. Guests approach the foot of the tower and enter through the gates. Legend has it that this gathering place for Hollywood's elite became a *Twilight Zone* mystery in the midst of a Halloween thunderstorm. "On October 31, 1939, the luxurious Hollywood Tower Hotel was at the height of its popularity as a Tinseltown gathering place. Then, at midnight, lightning struck the hotel, transporting an elevator car full of passengers to *The Twilight Zone.*" [3]

Guests can see the thunderbolt's scars across several floors of the hotel tower's exterior.

A misty garden invites guests toward the hotel's lobby. Haunting music from another era surrounds the hotel's entrance. Once inside the lobby, guests can see that this once beautiful and magnificent hotel has been neglected. Dust and cobwebs cover valuable antiques.

Guests are quickly escorted into a small library with a television monitor. On the monitor, familiar images from the popular TV Series *The Twilight Zone* begin to appear. Rod Serling welcomes us to the mystery, saying, "You unlock this door with the key of imagination. Beyond it is another dimension - a dimension of sound, a dimension of sight, a dimension of mind. You're moving into a land of both shadow and substance, of things and ideas. You've just crossed over into *The Twilight Zone.*"

The storm approaches and lightning surrounds the little room. On the monitor, we recognize the hotel's lobby. Guests move about freely. We notice a starlet with a producer, a grandmother with a little girl, and a bellman escorting the guests into the elevator to take them up the tower to their hotel rooms.

Mr. Serling sets the scene. "Hollywood,

1939. Amidst the glitz and the glitter of bustling young movie talent at the height of its golden age, the Hollywood Tower Hotel was a star in its own right, a beacon for the show business elite. Now, something is about to happen that will change all that."

The guests enter the elevator. The elevator shuts. We see the outside of the hotel. Lighting strikes. The elevator plunges. Half of the front of the hotel disappears. Where have the guests gone? We are invited to follow in their footsteps.

"The time is now, on an evening very much like the one we have just witnessed. Tonight's story on *The Twilight Zone* is somewhat unique and calls for a different kind of introduction. This, as you may recognize, is a maintenance service elevator, still in operation, waiting for you. We invite you, if you to dare, to step aboard because in tonight's episode you are the star. And this elevator travels directly to *The Twilight Zone*."

We move out of the little library into the boiler room, which looks like something right out of the final scenes of Irwin Allen's disaster classic *The Poseidon Adventure*. Wheels turn. Steam pipes leak. Ancient parts move. A feeling of claustrophobia sets in. We are in tight space.

People enter elevators. Doors shut. They disappear and move upward into the hotel where the mysteries of *The Twilight Zone* await.

Suddenly, the elevator is there to take you upward. You enter. In the elevator, there are three rows of seats. Seat belts are fastened. Then, the bellman sends you on your way.

The smooth move upward is a little unsettling. It appears that, at any moment, everything will drop and shift and the fear of falling will be real in this *tower of terror*.

As quickly as the elevator has moved upward, it suddenly stops. Is this it? Is this where I will enter the twilight zone?

The doors open and Rod Serling continues

to address us. "You are the passengers on a most uncommon elevator about to ascend into your very own episode of *The Twilight Zone*. One stormy night long ago, five people stepped in the door of an elevator and into a nightmare. That door is opening once again and this time, it is opening for you."

The guests from the black and white monitors in the library far below us suddenly appear right in front of us in a ghostly form! They are haunting. They are inviting us to step out of the elevator and follow them down the mysterious hallways of the hotel. Nobody wants to go. Suddenly, the elevator doors close and we continue moving upward to the upper floors of the hotel. We are climbing quickly and the whole time your body is saying stop, stop, stop, stop because you know what is ahead. You witnessed it as you were staring up at the hotel from Sunset Boulevard. But, you are trying to trick yourself into a state of denial!

The doors open again. Rod Serling continues, "You are about to discover what lies beyond the fifth dimension, beyond the deepest, darkest corner of the imagination in the *Tower of Terror*."

Unexpectedly, the elevator is moving forward, heading down the hallway and toward a wall. At the end of the hall, all light sources disappear and you are plunged into darkness. You sit. You wait. You are anxious.

There is a sudden drop and you are out of your seat. The elevator is pulled upward and suddenly you are looking out at Disney's Hollywood Studios park, which seems thousands of stories below you.

What happens next depends on which episode of *The Twilight Zone* you are in. The ride is imagineered so that it is a different experience every time you ride it. You will drop. You will float. You will scream. You will move into The Twilight Zone.

After several rises and falls, the car stops and you find yourself moving backwards. Rod

Serling speaks again, saying, "A warm welcome back to those of you who made it, and a friendly word of warning, something you won't find in any guidebook: the next time you check into a deserted hotel on the dark side of Hollywood, make sure you know just what kind of vacancy you're filling, or you may find yourself a permanent resident of *The Twilight Zone.*"

 FOR REFLECTION

The Dalai Lama, addressing a crowd in Central Park, said, "It is our experience of suffering which connects us to others. It is the basis of our capacity for empathy. But it is not enough to empathize. Feelings aren't important within the reality of the way things are. We must act. We must respond. We must do something. In this way we walk through the suffering."

Suffering is a mystery. Why we suffer, how suffering connects us to God, and how it provides context for our relationships with others has been the quest of spiritual sojourners since the creation of our spaceship Earth. All of the world's religions begin, move through, and end with the mystery of suffering. All the world's religions have a different understanding, a different teaching, a different approach to the significance of suffering within its particular religious context.

Suffering is violent. It changes how we think and feel at any particular moment in time. It challenges our faith beliefs. It is hard to understand the "why."

Suffering often appears instantly and shifts our paradigm of the world just as quickly. Many deny the existence of God because of the amount of suffering in the world. Others see suffering as the doorway into an understanding of the soul.

Not one of us likes to suffer; however, every one of us is suffering.

Because of the incredible diversity of people living and working and worshiping on the African continent, it is difficult to determine a widely-held religious belief on suffering. But our earliest writings about suffering are there. As people and tribes and nations developed across the vastness of the continent so did humankind's search for meaning. How did I get here? How do we relate to each other? How do we relate to people who are so very different from us? Is there a God? How do the spirits of the animal kingdom communicate with the spirits that determine and direct the outcomes of my life? How am I supposed to make sense of things like evil, violence, sickness, suffering and death? Everything has a place. What is my position within place? Across Africa, people of different tribes and culture and language and nations developed legends that invited generations to come into the mystery of suffering.

Hinduism responds to the mystery of suffering by looking at your lot in life, your status in life, your position in society. The caste system is a system that upholds that your position is determined by your level of enlightenment. Your Karma determines the suffering you experience, the suffering you must work through, the suffering you must endure, in order to become an enlightened being. You will suffer through several incarnations of life until you transcend the realities of this world through enlightenment.

Buddhism teaches that all of life is suffering. We suffer because we desire things. We desire to be different from who we are. We desire to have this kind of spouse or that type of car. So all of life in Buddhism is disciplined towards ending suffering. Buddhist say we end suffering by walking "the eight-fold path," by making the best choices in the midst of difficult situations. The choices we make determine the amount of suffering we experience in any given moment.

In Judaism, we suffer because of relationship. Judaism begins by teaching we were created to be in relationship with God and in relationship with each other. We live out life by creating, and breaking, and re-creating, our relationship with God and our accountability to others. We suffer because we break off our relationships, we break covenant, over and over and over again. Within the Jewish tradition, the faithful life is all about living into covenant, getting our relationship with God and our relationships with each other right.

Christianity is different from these faith traditions. Our understanding of suffering begins at the foot of the cross, moves through an empty tomb and into resurrection light. We profess that the cross says something totally different about the mystery of suffering because of the context it is given by a redemptive God. Our walk with Christ, our journey of faith proclaims that, our life with God, our understanding of self, and our relationships with each other, are all about the cycle of life, death, resurrection and rebirth. We celebrate what was and is and is to come, beginning by taking up our cross and following Christ.

What does it mean to take up our cross and follow Christ?

In the Christian tradition, we do this by moving through a prescribed calendar that invites us to pray, walk and act so that our faith beliefs have context and meaning.

The Church calendar begins with Advent, a time where we celebrate hope and expectation based on our desire to know God. Christmas is when God breaks through time and space to be with us. God in a baby invites us to be what we are afraid of the most - being vulnerable. During Epiphany and the ordinary time that follows, we celebrate how the teachings and ministry of Christ are revealed to us. On Ash Wednesday and during the season of Lent, we are called to examine how we have turned against God and against God's people. We are invited to examine our hearts and turn towards God so that we can become the body of Christ in the world.

During the last of week of Lent, during Holy Week, Christians everywhere relive, reenact and reclaim the last days of Jesus' life in order to understand the mystery of suffering and to live into God's promise of new life in the midst of death. We look at suffering so that we can claim it as holy, so that we learn to walk with confidence the way of the cross, so that we might incarnate, and to take on, the ministry and actions of Jesus.

All of us know a thing or two about suffering. We believe all of God's people are suffering, no matter where we are born or our position in society. We believe we suffer because God allows us to make choices in this world. Sometimes we make good choices. Sometimes we make bad choices. Sometimes we may not even know the differences between good and bad but we have to make a choice anyway.

We say that suffering happens when we break off our relationships with God and with God's people, but we proclaim that in the midst of suffering, there is triumph because God breaks through time and space to be with us in the midst of suffering. "When one is in pain, all suffer, and when one is healed, the whole world breathes a bit easier." [4]

In the midst of suffering, in Christ's death, there is new life. This new life has everything to do with our loving our neighbor as Jesus loved us. Jesus asks to take on his very nature, to be loving and forgiving, to be responsible, to be accountable, and to take up the cross and follow him.

After Jesus' resurrection, we celebrate Pentecost, where the spirit of God sets our hearts on fire so that we can be the hands and hearts of Jesus in the world, taking on his nature, not by placing the scars on someone else, but by taking on the mystery of suffering and to be with others in the midst of suffering.

Jesus says, "I give you a new commandment, that you love one another. Just as I have loved you, you also should love one another. By this everyone will know that you are my disciples, if you have love for one another."

Love is not an obscure concept. A brief summary of the two great commandments are love God and love your neighbor. We show love in recognizable actions. Because feelings of love are just feelings, our responses to these two commandments must be visible. Feelings are just personal, inner responses. Recognizable actions reflect our commitments to love God and our neighbors.

Feelings have nothing to do with ministry and action and justice and the cross. Feelings allow me to remain caught up within myself. Jesus on the cross may make me feel bad or sad or hopeless and powerless, but the victory of the cross is to look upon it and to take on the ministry of Christ right in the very midst of the sufferings of the world.

This is victory.

This is power.

This is grace.

"Take up your cross and follow me."

Not a cross of burden, not a cross that is too much to bear, but a cross that reminds us that with God and with each other, all things are possible.

THE E-TICKET

Religion provides a framework to wrestle with the mystery of suffering. What we surround ourselves with gives our lives meaning. A suffering God, a resurrected God, a redemptive God, a living God - these realities help us to understand the mys-

tery of suffering. Because of the immensity of God, one explanation of suffering just is not enough.

When one person suffers, we all suffer. When I suffer, others suffer with me.

As we become a global community, we share and participate in the suffering of sisters and brothers around the world. We are connected by dreams, hopes and experiences. Cultural context is different. Our God-given humanity is the same. "The advancement of mass communications worldwide has brought more and more people of divergent classes and cultures and interests in communication with one another through experiencing the same mysteries… Man does not need religion or cathedrals rising from his fields to remind him of mystery any longer; he is steeped in it from the moment he turns on the television set and witnesses evil at work around the globe to the day he sits in a laboratory and uncovers nature's hidden powers in subatomic particles." [5]

Suffering is meaningless without context. As Christians, the birth, life ministry, death, and resurrection of Jesus Christ provides our context. Followers of Christ meet suffering "in acceptance and hope. He or she confronts it, identifies with those experiencing it, and then struggles through it to grow into a new humanness," [6] allowing us to live, love and walk with others with new confidence, empathy and understanding.

Let us continue working in the "Holy Story" section of your journal.

Recall how suffering is approached from world's major religions. Did any of the world's faith traditions resonate with your personal beliefs? Why?

Is there a time of suffering in your life which makes it difficult for you to find context and meaning?

Gather some index cards and colored pencils. Get a candle.

Light the candle to claim the space. Draw

a cartoon that illustrates this time of suffering. Each card should indicate a shift in the action. Filmmakers call this a storyboard.

Next, create a cartoon or storyboard that illustrates the last hours of the life of Jesus Christ. Perhaps you will draw moments from the Garden of Gethsemane or the trial before Pilate. Maybe you will draw the crucifixion, three crosses on Calvary, with Jesus between the two thieves. Maybe you will illustrate Joseph taking care of the body. Jesus' body placed in the tomb. The descent to the dead, the ascension into heaven. Maybe you will draw all of this. After you have finished, take some of the storyboards from your incident of suffering and begin to compare them to the last hours of Christ's life. Place moments that are similar in your experience with those that are similar with Christ's. Are there significant contrasts? Note these if there are. Are there any new meanings that come to light? What are the implications?

Next, turn to the "Rule of Life" section of your journal. Consider the mystery of suffering. Write down the heading "Suffering," then consider the following statements as you compose your rule.

SUFFERING

Suffering is _____ .

I experience suffering because _____ .

When I suffer, I call on God to _____ .

When God doesn't respond to my suffering, I believe _____ .

When others suffer, I am called to _____ .

When I suffer, I expect others to _____ .

 THE COLLECT

We have reflected on suffering. It is time to write a concluding Collect. We will change the formula a bit.

Start by naming God.

Then write down how God is present or absent in the world of suffering. State what you believe.

Claim and proclaim how suffering is present in your life. Write down what you believe. State where God is in your suffering. Write down what you believe.

Conclude by stating two things. Write a sentence about how God does or does not suffer. Finish the collect by writing why suffering has impacted your life. Finish with "so be it" or Amen.

If you feel you are in the midst of suffering now, write another Collect. Name God. State several characteristics of God as they relate to suffering. Write about how you are suffering right now. Then state what you want God to do about this suffering. Then proclaim what you think God will do about it and why. Conclude by writing by what power God will act. Amen.

✛

ENDNOTES

1 (Taylor, 2000, p. 66)
2 (May & Metzger, 1973, p. OT 632-633)
3 (Gordon & Kurtti, 2008, p. 112)
4 (Jefferts Schori, 2007, p. 48)
5 (Fox, 2001, p. 46)
6 (Williams, 1991, p. 21)

DEATH } *What Happens When I Die?*

 ## MAIN GATE

"Faith makes things turn out right," says Penny from *The Rescuers*.

But, whenever we experience the death of a spouse or partner, family member or friend, neighbor, colleague or distant relative, our faith perspective shifts or can even be challenged. Sometimes we are, as English singer Kate Bush says, "Suspended in Gaffa." Stuck in the mud, trapped in the dark, searching out angels and saints in the star maps of heaven calling out to them to get us back on the journey of faith.

I encounter many people of deep faith who are challenged by everyday realities. Some are hungry. Others are homeless. Some are diagnosed with cancer. Others rest in despair on their deathbed. To some, death happens on the way to work. To others while sitting alone in the living room. A dark spirit creeps into our souls and we find ourselves in the depths of depression. Our faith is challenged. Our confidence about the resurrection promise wanes.

Death is around the corner, ready to change everything we think we know about this world. Death proves there is a lot we do not know. Death is the gateway to something else. Our faith beliefs dictate what we think that something else is.

As a Christian, I believe death leads to new life. As parts of me die, other parts of me are redeemed and, through redemption and grace, I have a more meaningful life. Sometimes our encounters with death are frightening. Other times they are humorous. Jesus says He is the Alpha and the Omega leaving us, the faithful, everywhere in between.

What kinds of death have you experienced? Physical? Emotional? Hypothetical? How often have you stood at the gate of death and wondered what part of you would live on the other side? Are you at the gate alone or is someone by your side?

At the Walt Disney World Resort, several attractions take us through death and beyond. Some are humorous. Others are scary. Some provide hope. Others scare us with the unexpected twists of fate. All four parks at the Walt Disney World Resort have an attraction that invites us to ride into death.

Near the Resort's entrance from Hwy. 192, you can't help but notice the *Tower of Terror*. A fatalistic lightning strike transports elevator riders into the twilight zone. Will they ever return?

Mr. Toad's Wild Ride is no longer a part of Fantasyland at the Magic Kingdom, but is still popular at Disneyland. This dark attraction puts the guest in the driver seat, traveling dangerously fast through the streets of London and into the countryside. Near the ride's conclusion, Mr. Toad meets his death head-on in a collision with a train. Suddenly, Mr. Toad is surrounded by devils. He has gone to hell. No happily ever after for him!

At Epcot, we are challenged throughout the park to wake up and be good stewards of everything God has given us. We are confronted with the realities of how we are killing the land and the sea and the sky and how we must harness the power of the imagination to change the course of our projected path of extinction.

At Disney's Animal Kingdom, we journey hundreds of thousands of years back in time, to the age of the dinosaurs, in hopes of discovering what killed them off so that we can change the realities of this time.

What happens when I die?

It seems like an impossible question to answer. Responding in faith, all of the world's major religions offer an explanation about what happens when we die and beyond. On some days, none of the explanations seems satisfactory. Death is so unknown. And I have no control of what happens next.

When I die, do I cease to exist? Is there a place beyond this? Will I become a ghost? Will I recognize my family and friends and pets?

I cannot imagine non-existence. Maybe there is a reason for that. Have I always existed?

Mark Twain once said, "The fear of death follows from the fear of life. A man who lives fully is prepared to die at any time."

 IN THE QUEUE

We can understand more fully and prepare for death by honoring the dead.

One of Disney's most popular modern animated classics is *The Lion King*. The film follows the childhood of Simba, the lion cub of the recently deceased Lion King named Mufasa. Simba is introduced as future heir of his father's throne at a ritual on Pride Rock at the opening of the film.

According to the *The Lion King*, there is a circle of life and we must find and claim our part in that circle. The film suggests that the world beyond the known, the world we inhabit when we are dead, is part of that circle. The spirit world communicates with us in this world, providing us courage and strength to believe all the promise within us. Simba recalls a conversation with his father. Under the dome of a starlit sky, Mufasa tells Simba that our ancestors watch over us from a part of the created world that is unknown to us.

Like most Disney films, the death of a mother or father causes the protagonist to live into who they are whether they want to or not. Simba feels responsible for his father's death. In order to avoid discerning how death is part of the circle of life, Simba runs away, living on the edge of the kingdom with a pair whose "no worries" attitude empowers Simba to delay trying to find meaning and redemption in his father's death.

As Christians, we celebrate All Saints' Day, a day of hope when we recognize and pray for the dead who have gone before and are watching over us. The celebration recognizes the dead whose lives inspire us to live into the fullness of this mortal life. All Saints' Day invites us to look at the faith of the dead so that we can deepen and strengthen our own faith. Where this Community of Saints actually resides and the impact they have over our individual lives depends on our trust in God's promise to give new life after death.

How do you honor the dead? Do the dead call to you, inspiring you to live into a more faithful life?

The Lion King was adapted to the Broadway stage in 1997 by the brilliant artist Julia Taymor. She was able to inspire and lead a creative team, transforming the beloved animated classic into an incredible night of musical theater. Puppets and an expanded soundtrack inspired by the rhythms of Africa bring the audience right to the foot of Pride

Rock where we pause and look around and ponder the Circle of Life, a circle that moves beyond the Pride Lands and into the heavenly realm.

Do you believe in heaven? Where and what is it? If you believe in heaven, what is an image that captures in essence what it is to you?

The Lion King on Broadway has a powerful musical number about death, resurrection and the community of saints. "He Lives in You" was written by Lebo M. In Act I, Mufasa and Simba gaze at the stars. Mufasa explains to Simba that the great lion kings and ancestors of the past are watching over us, guiding and strengthening us. Mufasa says, "Ingonyamanengw' enamabala. (Here is a lion and a tiger). Night and the spirit of life calling. Oh, oh, iyo, mamela. And the voice, just the fear of a child answers. Iyo iyo, mamela. Ubukhosi bo khokho (Throne of the ancestors). We ndodana ye sizwe sonke (Oh, son of the nation). Wait, there's no mountain too great. Hear these words and have faith. Have faith." Later, Mufasa dies while saving Simba's life.

In the second act of *The Lion King*, Simba decides to claim his place in the circle of life. Rafiki beckons Simba to live into the promise of who he is. He can do this by honoring the legacy of his father. Rafiki sings, "He lives in you, he lives in me. He watches over everything we see. Into the waters, into the truth. In your reflection, he lives in you."

Into the waters…

Into the truth…

Sit aside. Claim some intentional space. Take some time in silence.

Recall those you have loved who have died. Go to the "Holy Story" section of your journal and list those who have died but live in you.

On the next page, write the title "My Community of Saints."

Then jot down some thought about those persons using the questions below as guidelines.

How are you related to this person? What are some of your fondest memories of this person? How did this person open up the world to you? How did this person help you to love more deeply? What did this person teach you about life and God? What is an object that reminds you of this person? What part of this person still lives in you?

Take your time as you look and reflect upon this part of your Holy Story.

FROM THE BOOK
Matthew 27:50 – 28:1-10

Tradition tells us that The Gospel of Matthew was probably written down between 85-95 AD, after the Romans sacked Jerusalem, destroying the temple. The Gospel writer appears to have used the Gospel of Mark as the primary source text, combined with another collection of the teachings of Jesus. It was primarily written for a Jewish audience in hopes that they would come to understand that Jesus was the promised Messiah. It is the only Gospel to use the word *church* so it was likely written for small Jewish communities whose members were followers of Christ. The Gospel is mission-oriented, calling on all believers to "go, therefore, and make disciples of all nations." (Matthew 28:19)

Our passage for reflection presents an interesting road map for the faithful praying about dealing with death and understanding the promise of resurrection. Within a few passages, we experience the death of Jesus, the reaction of the witnesses, the raising of the community of saints, the honoring of the dead through the claiming and care for Jesus' body, and then the promise of new life beyond death through Jesus' resurrection.

MATTHEW 27:50 – 28:1-10

Then Jesus cried again with a loud voice

and breathed his last. At that moment the curtain of the temple was torn in two, from top to bottom. The earth shook, and the rocks were split. The tombs also were opened, and many bodies of the saints who had fallen asleep were raised. After his resurrection they came out of the tombs and entered the holy city and appeared to many. Now when the centurion and those with him, who were keeping watch over Jesus, saw the earthquake and what took place, they were terrified and said, "Truly this man was God's Son!"

Many women were also there, looking on from a distance; they had followed Jesus from Galilee and had provided for him. Among them were Mary Magdalene, and Mary the mother of James and Joseph, and the mother of the sons of Zebedee.

When it was evening, there came a rich man from Arimathea, named Joseph, who was also a disciple of Jesus. He went to Pilate and asked for the body of Jesus; then Pilate ordered it to be given to him. So Joseph took the body and wrapped it in a clean linen cloth and laid it in his own new tomb, which he had hewn in the rock. He then rolled a great stone to the door of the tomb and went away. Mary Magdalene and the other Mary were there, sitting opposite the tomb.

The next day, that is, after the day of Preparation, the chief priests and the Pharisees gathered before Pilate and said, "Sir, we remember what that impostor said while he was still alive, 'After three days I will rise again.' Therefore command the tomb to be made secure until the third day; otherwise his disciples may go and steal him away, and tell the people, 'He has been raised from the dead,' and the last deception would be worse than the first." Pilate said to them, "You have a guard of soldiers; go, make it as secure as you can." So they went with the guard and made the tomb secure by sealing the stone.

After the Sabbath, as the first day of the week was dawning, Mary Magdalene and the other Mary went to see the tomb. And suddenly there was a great earthquake; for an angel of the Lord, descending from heaven, came and rolled back the stone and sat on it. His appearance was like lightning, and his clothing white as snow. For fear of him the guards shook and became like dead men. But the angel said to the women, "Do not be afraid; I know that you are looking for Jesus who was crucified. He is not here; for he has been raised, as he said. Come, see the place where he lay. Then go quickly and tell his disciples, 'He has been raised from the dead, and indeed he is going ahead of you to Galilee; there you will see him.' This is my message for you." So they left the tomb quickly with fear and great joy, and ran to tell his disciples. Suddenly Jesus met them and said, "Greetings!" And they came to him, took hold of his feet, and worshiped him. Then Jesus said to them, "Do not be afraid; go and tell my brothers to go to Galilee; there they will see me." [1]

RIDE THE ATTRACTION
The Haunted Mansion

"Welcome, foolish mortals, to the *Haunted Mansion*."

Our Ghost Host beckons us to enter if we dare into a world beyond our normal experiences. It is world we contemplate every waking moment of our lives. What happens after I die? Is there a place between here and there? If I am afraid to give up this life, can I linger here and party on? If I say "yes," what would be the cost to my soul?

Walt Disney's the *Haunted Mansion* suggests a rather humorous and fun afterlife. But you have to die to get there!

The first *Haunted Mansion* was built in Disneyland. It took nearly twelve years to move from concept to attraction, opening in 1969. A "Help

Wanted" sign invited ghosts from all times and all places to apply. It was written by Disney Imagineer Marty Sklar. The invitation went like this: "Notice! All ghosts and restless spirits. Post-lifetime leases are now available in this *Haunted Mansion*. Don't be left out in the sunshine! Enjoy active retirement in this country club atmosphere, the fashionable address for famous ghosts, ghosts trying to make a name for themselves… and ghosts afraid to live by themselves! Leases include license to scare the daylights out of guests visiting the Portrait Gallery, Museum of the Supernatural, graveyard and other happy haunting grounds. For reservations, send resume of past experience to: Ghost Relations Dept. Disneyland. Please! Do not apply in person." [2]

Upon opening, the *Haunted Mansion* became one of the most popular and beloved attractions at Disneyland so it was included in the original plans for The Magic Kingdom, Walt Disney World, Florida.

We all know a good ghost story. We know people who believe in ghosts. Some of us believe we have encountered ghosts in spooky situations.

What happens when I die? Can I actually remain with the people I love after I have left this mortal flesh? The *Haunted Mansion* answers these questions and playfully invites us to contemplate even more. It is an attraction, allowing the guest to notice something new and unexpected upon every return.

At The Magic Kingdom in the Walt Disney World Resort, The *Haunted Mansion* is the focal point of Liberty Square, just off the banks of the Rivers of America, beyond the Hall of the Presidents. A hearse pulled by an invisible horse invites guests to enter the mansion if they dare.

It is a mansion where ghostwriters have an extensive library and non-stop séances communicate with the world beyond, using musical instruments and magical incantations. Ballroom guests appear and disappear by the illuminating glow of a candle and playful spirits rise from the grave for a swinging wake. It is home to 999 happy haunts, but there's room for a thousand. If you would like to join them, you can make final arrangements at the end of your tour.

Although the mansion and the ghastly property that surrounds it is full of graves, tombs and spirits, the afterlife looks quite fun and celebratory. The *Haunted Mansion* is both dark and mysterious, and playful and upbeat. "Marc Davis, who worked primarily on the characters and gags, wanted a lighter, more playful approach. Claude Coats, a former background painter who focused on settings and atmosphere, favored a darker tone." [3] The ride is a marvelous combination of both.

As you stand in the queue, guests notice the graveyard where the mansion's owner is buried. "Master Gracey, laid to rest, no mourning please, at his request." Buried near Master Gracey is séance queen Madame Leota. Her tombstone reads, "Dear Sweet Leota, Beloved by All, In Regions Beyond Now, She's Having a Ball."

As you mourn the dead, suddenly, the majestic doors creek open and we are invited inside by our Ghost Host.

Our journey begins in a ghostly study. The room is dark and it is hard to maintain a sense of direction. Mansion owner Master Gracey ages right before our eyes as the Ghost Host welcomes us, saying, "When hinges creek, in doorless chambers, and strange and frightening sounds echo through the halls… Wherever candle lights flicker, though the air is deathly still; that is the time when ghosts are present, practicing their terror with ghoulish delight."

Next, we move into a corridor that has no windows and no doors. It is the mansion's Portrait Gallery. Our Ghost Host welcomes us, saying, "Here, in our gallery, you'll see rare paintings of some of our guests as they appeared in their corruptible, mortal state." The four portraits are of a young lady with an umbrella, a distinguished gentleman with a document of some kind, a woman posing with a flower and a smug-looking gentleman. Then, our senses seem to betray us. The room begins to stretch and more of the portraits are revealed. The former guests, content and full of life, appear to be dangling over death. The Ghost Host speaks to us, saying, "Your cadaverous pallor betrays an aura of foreboding, almost as though you sense a disquieting metamorphosis. Is this haunted room actually stretching or is it your imagination?" The Ghost Host suggests that there is only one way of escaping the Portrait Gallery, suicide by hanging!

We escape into a hallway leading to a boarding queue. The Ghost Host apologizes, saying, "I didn't mean to frighten you prematurely. The real chills come later. Look alive and we will continue our little tour." We move onto a beltway and board a moving vehicle called a Doom Buggy. The Doom Buggies will take us deeper into the *Haunted Mansion*.

We pass the portrait gallery hallway and move into the mansion's Library. The collection features some of the best ghost stories ever written. Books are being removed from the shelves by unseen readers. We move through the Music Parlor where a ghost plays soothing music and cobwebs and creaks distract the reader from enjoying a good mystery.

Our Doom Buggies appear to be moving upward. We encounter the Stairway of Infinity. We feel as if we are moving ahead but are we on the road to nowhere? Where all of this is leading is not exactly clear.

Next, our Ghost Host brings us through an endless hallway with floating candelabra. Our Ghost Host interjects, "We find it delightfully unlivable here in our ghostly retreat. Every room has wall-to-wall creeps and hot and cold running chills."

We move into Madame Leota's séance chamber. Floating instruments respond to Leota's commands, hinting at a connection with spirits beyond what we can see. Leota chants, "Serpents and spiders, tail of a rat, call in the spirits, wherever they're at. Rap on a table, it's time to respond. Send us a message from somewhere beyond. Goblins and ghoulies from last Halloween awaken the spirits with your tambourine. Creepies and crawlies, toads in a pond, let there be music from regions beyond! Wizards and witches, wherever you dwell, give us a hint by ringing a bell."

The séance is entrancing. Leota is beguiling. A guest can't help but to begin to be caught up in the spirit world.

Without warning, our Ghost Host bids us farewell for a little while. He says, "The Happy Haunts have received your sympathetic vibrations and are beginning to materialize. They are assembling for a swinging wake and they'll be expecting me. I'll see you a bit later."

As our Ghost Host moves on to join the party, we round the corner and find ourselves on a balcony observing a ghostly party below. There is a long table where ghosts appear and disappear with the blowing out of a candle on a cake. Spirits dance and portraits have a shooting match while a ghostly organist provides music to set the scene.

We move forward and find ourselves moving through the attic of the mansion. It is here where we get a hint about the tragedy that surrounds Master Gracey and the spirits that we are encountering. After traveling by some family portraits we discover a beautiful, ghostly bride, the mistress of the attic, prepared for a wedding that probably never occurred. Is this why the spirits are celebrating?

We move out of an attic window and descend into the graveyard out back. A party is going on as ghosts of all kinds come out to socialize. In this amusing climax through the world between here and there, we meet opera ghosts, tea-tottling ghosts, dueling ghosts and the famous marble-bust quartet. The quartet sings joyfully, "When the crypt doors creek and the tombstones quake, happy haunts materialize and begin to vocalize. Grim grinning ghosts come out to socialize."

As we prepare to leave the festive graveyard, the quartet warns us, singing, "Now don't close your eyes or try to hide or a silly spook may sit by your side, shrouded in a daft disguise. They pretend to terrorize. Grim grinning ghosts come out to socialize."

As we round the corner, three ghosts are asking us if they can hitch a ride out of there! Can they go where we are going? Our Ghost Host catches up with us, warning, "There's a little matter I forgot to mention. Beware of hitchhiking ghosts! They have selected you to fill our quota, and they will haunt you until you return."

A hitchhiking ghost jumps into our Doom Buggy to follow us home. A small ghostly manifestation of Madame Leota standing on the ledge of a crypt begs us to return, saying, "Hurry back. We're just dying to have you. Don't forget your death certificate." We pass below her and suddenly find ourselves returning to the land of the living.

"If you would like to join our jamboree, there's a simple rule that's compulsory. Mortals pay a token fee. Rest in peace or haunting spree? So hurry back, we would like your company."

FOR REFLECTION

What do we expect to happen when we visit a gravesite?

Are graveyards the land of the living or the land of the dead?

Whenever I see plastic flowers I think of my great-grandmother. My mother's mother's mother. My great-grandmother. All of us called her Maw Maw.

My five cousins and I loved Maw Maw very much. Every Tuesday we would go to Maw Maw's house to celebrate chicken night. Maw Maw would sit in her big, green recliner chair and we would run by the chair to see if she could catch us. She could. She would reach out with her skinny arm and stop us in our tracks. Maw Maw was very, very strong.

Whenever I see plastic flowers, I think of Maw Maw. She would say, "When I die, don't you dare put plastic flowers on my grave. Plastic sticks around forever. We don't. I want real flowers on my grave. They are alive. They look beautiful. Then they die. Going back to the ground. Just like we will. And I find that comforting."

Maw Maw died on April 4, 1974. She is buried in the town of Franklinton, Louisiana. Franklinton is about 100 miles north of New Orleans. It is a small town, a country town, a town where everybody knows everybody. It is a small town with a lovely little Catholic church. My great-grandfather, Maw Maw's husband, built the church. We called him Paw Paw.

My Paw Paw was a celebrity in this town because he was known as the man who built the Catholic church.

"That's the man," the town's people would say.

"There he is," is what I would hear whenever I went to the grocery store with my Paw Paw.

I was proud to be his great-grandson.

Franklinton was their town. And so Franklinton is where our family's plot, our family's gravesite is, a beautiful graveyard, full of oak trees, interesting headstones, winding rock pathways, and the Heidelberg Family Gravesite. Our family plot. Surrounded by so many others. So many lives. So many stories.

I hadn't been to the family gravesite in years. It seems like when I was younger we went all the time. It took forever to get out there from New Orleans. To me, it seemed as far as Mississippi.

"Are we there yet?"

"How much further?"

"Are we there yet?"

However, I knew that when I saw Ms. Dorothy's Country Store, we were almost there. Almost to Franklinton, Louisiana.

When was the last time you were at a family gravesite?

Who is buried there? Is it a loved one, a parent, extended family, dearest friend, or, heaven forbid, a beloved little one?

What happens to us when we visit the gravesite?

What do we expect to discover?

My Paw Paw bought a gravesite in Franklinton, Louisiana with 10 plots. He imagined that he would be buried there, with his beloved wife - my Maw Maw - his four children, and the spouses of his children. Ten plots. The Heidelberg Family Gravesite.

The family headstone was in place soon after he bought it. But it would be many, many years before anybody was buried out there.

But I remember the first. And I remember the funeral.

I was only four, but my grandmother loved to tell me about my first funeral. It was my grandfather's funeral. Her husband's funeral. He died in 1970.

We would all be gathered around this big, long table at chicken night at my Maw Maw and Paw Paw's house.

My grandmother would ask, "Kevin. Do you remember that funeral?"

"No," I would say.

We had a routine worked out. She would laugh. And then say to me, "Well you had an ear for listening to priests back in those days. The priest kept saying in the sermon that my granddaddy was alive, but in the middle of the sermon, you looked up at me with big, wide eyes and said,

'Grandmommy, that priest keeps saying that granddaddy is alive, but I looked in that coffin and he is really dead.'"

"He is really dead. . ."

She loved to tell that story. And would laugh hysterically every time she told it to me or to family or to friends.

Four years after my granddaddy died, Maw Maw, the one who hated plastic flowers, would be next.

My Paw Paw, my great-grandfather, lived to be 102. He died in 1997. And we buried him out there in Franklinton, Louisiana, in the gravesite he had bought so long ago.

Most recently, my grandmother joined them. It was time for her to take her place at the family plot.

It had been a long time since I had taken that drive to Franklinton, Louisiana. Although I found myself in deep sadness over my grandmother's death, I was actually excited about returning to the family plot to see how things were out there.

What happens to us when we visit a gravesite?

What was I hoping to discover? What did I think was going to happen when I got there?

I think about the feelings I had throughout my entire body, the tingling in my stomach, the tears in my eyes, the numbness in my head, yet the exciting sound, the thumping, pumping noise of my beating heart. I was going to see my Maw Maw and Paw Paw and Granddaddy, and my Grandmother was going to be with them. But, there was something stirring within me, a restlessness, an exhausted feeling, perhaps mixed in with just a little bit of hope.

What was I hoping for?

Sometimes it is very hard for me to understand the power and the promise of the resurrected Christ. Many days it all makes sense and I feel my faith is secure. On other days, I can't make heads or tails of it, and I feel like I am walking across a tightrope of belief.

I find comfort and peace, realizing that Jesus' disciples' experience of resurrection had nothing to do with faith or belief. For them, it was reality. They saw it. They saw it and were scared, in awe, and in amazement.

Perhaps it is their testimony, handed down to me through faith, that gives me comfort. Their friend Jesus was raised from the dead. Perhaps someday I will be with my loved ones again. I will laugh, walk and tell stories with them again. This is the resurrection promise.

Maybe this was and is what we experience when we go to the gravesites when we visit the resting places of those who loved us as much as God loves us.

Once we look beyond the tears of our grief, we can hear somewhere in the back of our minds the excited voices of the women running from the tomb telling to anyone that would listen to them that their friend had risen and that one day we will all be together again.

My grandmother wanted a large spray of calla lilies on her coffin at her funeral. As we got out of our cars at the Heidelberg Family Plot in Franklinton, Louisiana, I could see the beautiful spray sitting on top of the simple pine box.

As we prepared to put my Grandmother in the ground, my cousins and I removed some of the calla lilies. Together, we walked around in silence. First, we placed a calla lily on the marker for my Granddaddy. I thought about the sermon I heard at his funeral. I thought about how my grandmother loved to tell that story.

Within the power of resurrection is the promise to me that my granddaddy will one day be able to look me in the eye and say, "You see, that priest was right. I am alive."

My cousins and I moved on to the marker for my Paw Paw. And we all placed a calla lily on it.

Within the power of resurrection is the promise to me that my Paw Paw will one day say to me through his laughter, "I spent my life building Catholic churches and you had to go off and become an Episcopal priest!"

Then we moved over to the marker for Maw Maw.

My cousin Billy, the brother I never had, whispered to me, "Remember, I don't want any plastic flowers on my grave."

My other cousins heard it and we all laughed together.

There was beautiful irony in the moment. My Maw Maw's marker was actually slightly split in two. And a beautiful baby oak was pushing its way through her gravestone, reaching up towards the sky.

Nothing plastic for Maw Maw. Because plastic isn't alive.

THE E-TICKET

The Sheltering Sky by Paul Bowles is a powerful book about love, existentialism and mortality. Paul Bowles says, "Death is always on the way, but the fact that you don't know when it will arrive seems to take away from the finiteness of life. It's that terrible precision that we hate so much. But because we don't know, we get to think of life as an inexhaustible well. Yet everything happens a certain number of times, and a very small number, really. How many more times will you remember a certain afternoon of your childhood, some afternoon that's so deeply a part of your being that you can't even conceive of your life without it? Perhaps four or five times more. Perhaps not even. How many more times will you watch the full moon rise? Perhaps twenty. And yet it all seems limitless."[4]

What happens between here and there?

When we die, are we in the presence of Christ immediately? Or do we wait for the Day of Judgment when all will be raised together? Is there an in-between time where I must work out my remaining sins before I enter the kingdom of heaven?

Sit quietly. Open to the "Holy Story" section of your journal and read over the people you honored while "In the Queue." Close your eyes and let the voices speak to you in the present moment.

If you can, gather pictures and objects that remind you of the community of saints that you are remembering. Next, I invite you to build a Day of the Dead altar in order to remember them.

Day of the Dead altars are built to honor loved ones who have passed away. They help us claim a space for them in the land of the living.

Day of the Dead or *Dia de los Muertos* is a tradition in Mexico that moves through 4000 years of history. Instead of fearing life, a day was created to celebrate death and the afterlife which is a continuation of this life. After the Spanish conquest of 1521, this Aztec tradition was blended with the Catholic celebrations of All Saints' Day and All Souls' Day, traditionally celebrated on November 1st and 2nd of each year.

When I served at All Saints' Chicago, as curate for the rector The Rev. Bonnie Perry, the congregation would create Day of the Dead altars around the entire sanctuary for loved ones and hang prayer flags written to the dead. The flags hung between our heads and the roof of the church. For me, this celebration of the community of saints brought the two realms together in powerful ways. The space between me and my loved one suddenly seemed penetrable, accessible, obtainable and believable. I hope by creating your own Day of the Dead altar you may look into this mystery.

First, choose a space for your altar. It can be in a corner. It can be on a section of your desk or counter. It could be on a small table in a hall or in your living room. Whatever the space, claim it as sacred.

Next, decorate the space with objects, photographs or with anything that reflects on the person or people you are remembering on the altar. Be creative. Arrange everything with care. Create different tiers within the space to invite yourself or others into the realm of the person being honored.

Day of the Dead symbols can be placed within the altar space. Candles are common. Marigolds are symbolic in Mexican culture and are believed to help the dead find their way back to Earth. *Papel picado* (perforated paper) are beautiful hand-cut flags that can add color to your altar. You may want to consider incense to be burned from somewhere within the altar.

As you build your altar, spend time reflecting on the person or people you are remembering.

You may choose to do this during the traditional time of the year, the weeks leading up to November 1st or 2nd. Or you may consider building this altar as you do your work through this chapter. Whenever you decide to do it, remember that at some point, you must take down the altar. Save the objects for the next time you construct a Day of the Dead altar. The claiming of space and beauty of preparation make this a powerful discipline for bringing together the spirits of the living with the dead.

Next, turn to the "Rule of Life" section of your journal. Write DEATH and then begin the rule below it. Perhaps you may want to use this formula:

Death

Today is a good day to die.
I prepare for death by doing _____ .
I honor the dead by _____ .
I celebrate the Community of Saints by _____ .
I step in the mystery of the resurrection by _____ .
May the souls of all the faithfully departed through

the mercy of God rest in peace.

 # THE COLLECT

Write a Collect recalling and remembering all who were, and are, and are yet to come. Address God. Proclaim what you believe is God's role during death and what you believe God promises beyond that. State what you believe about the people you have loved who have died. State the truth about what you want to happen after death. Ask in God's name.

✢

ENDNOTES

[1] (May & Metzger, 1973, p. NT 44-45)
[2] (Surrell, 2003, p. 22)
[3] (Wright, Imagineers (Group), & Walt Disney Company, 2005, p. 70)
[4] (Bowles, 1998, p. 238)

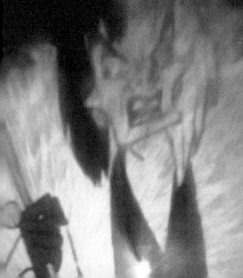
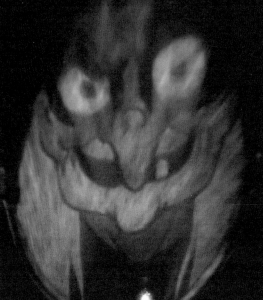

JUDGMENT } *Can I Change?*

 ## MAIN GATE

"What do we do when things go wrong?" asks Snow White in Disney's animated classic *Snow White and the Seven Dwarfs.* In *Snow White,* jealously clouds judgment. Judgment is sacrificed for immediate action. Because things have gone wrong in Snow White's stepmother's eyes, her judgment is unreflective and is reactive. Instead of thinking, she responds. Instead of reflecting, she destroys. Instead of living into the person God created, she becomes the person susceptible to the forces of evil.

Judgment and evil work together hand-in-hand. Judgment is good. Evil is not. We often fall into evil and feel judgment is bad when we do not take the time to ask ourselves exactly what is happening, what is going on. If we ask ourselves these questions and if we take the time to get to the heart of the matter, possibilities are endless and redeemable.

Judgment comes in many forms. Something in us changes with judgment. We hear inner voices urging us to make a decision. We hear the voices of others telling us to do what they want us to do. A judgment is made and we are acted upon. When we respond to our inner voices, we make a judgment and act upon others.

Making a judgment, rendering a decision is the only way to move forward, but the moment of judgment is often overlooked due to our impatience. Because we have all been victims of poor judgment, the word *judgment* has negative meanings for us. However, if I can pause for a moment and clean the slate of meanings, I find that I may be able to formulate the correct questions that will empower me and allow me to move forward.

Often we react when we are exposed to too much information. We become overwhelmed and cannot process all of it. So we render a decision. The verdict is read. Case closed. There exist no gray areas. Everything is black or white. Even though some of us prefer to live in the black or white world, God's world is actually all gray. The good news is that the Holy Spirit works best in the gray. We get trapped in the black and white, rendering the work of the Spirit impossible.

This finality is where we get stuck.

If I am stuck in judgment, I cannot change. I become set in my ways. I believe that my way of looking at the world is the only correct way. I will protect what I believe at all costs, often at the expense of others. I may not realize that my judgment is cloudy. I give in to evil. I repeat sin. Ultimately, I make bad choices to prevent change.

It is only with an encounter with good that we can truly move on. Often, this good comes from God or it may come from someone else. If we have managed to make ourselves vulnerable and open in the midst of cloudy judgment, the good might come from within ourselves.

Many of us see judgment as something

acted upon us, but this is not the case. In the midst of judgment, we are in total control. Judgment uniquely places us in a position of power. A decision must be made. God has given me the power to make the decision and I can choose this or I can choose that. The responsibility is mine. Often I do not want to make the decision so I hesitate. I am still in control, but I feel like the control lies elsewhere. The call is mine, only mine, and the way to move forward is up to me.

I am responsible for my own actions.

If I am going down the wrong road, I can turn around in any given moment. Nothing is done that cannot be undone. It is right here, right now, in this moment that I can move forward or turn my life around.

Often I do not want to be held accountable. I do not want to be accountable to God or to someone else. I do not want to feel that I am a victim to someone else's rules. But we all need rules. We all need guidelines

Many of us carry shame because of past decisions we have made. Some of these decisions have been good. Some have been bad. "Rules require accountability and relationships are always in dialogue in the respectful system. However, in the shame-based system, rules are rigid and require perfectionism."[1] The intention is the key to understanding the judgment made. Did I decide to do what is right? With the choice that I made, did I intend to hurt someone? If I have made a bad choice, can it be undone?

In every second of life, we make choices. In every moment, we have the opportunity to re-up, re-commit, and move forward with confidence or to turn things around in positive and redeeming ways. In *Snow White*, the Queen continues to make judgments based on jealousy, contempt, and fear. But at every moment a decision could be made to walk in the light. It is never too late. Villains are

villains for as long as they choose to be. Whenever we are moved by bad decisions, it seems like the hole we are digging into darkness is getting deeper and deeper. In reality, friends may reach in to pull us out but only we ourselves can stop the digging.

At the Walt Disney World Resort, there are decisions to be made. What park do we go to today? What ride should we fast pass? Is it better to stand in line over here or wait over there? Where should we eat? Should I take a moment to drink some water and take time to notice what is going on around me? The choices are endless and sometimes overwhelming. But it there truly a bad choice? What is the worst thing that can happen?

Judgment is a good thing. Taking time to clear our heads to make good judgments is the biggest gift we can give to ourselves and to others. For many of us the work of the moment is overcoming the shame associated with judgments made in the past. This is difficult and painful work, but this is important work. Shame is an easy excuse to continue to make poor judgments. Often, it is the least painful and/or the simplest route. Therefore, many of us take this route.

Shame is the death of us. It kills our spirit. It clouds our vision. It empowers us to make poor judgments. But we can stop all of that today, right here and right now.

Judgment is the necessary step towards choosing the opportunity or opportunities that turn lives around, leading to new life.

 IN THE QUEUE

The Canterbury Tales, written by Geoffrey Chaucer, states, "For in their hearts doth Nature stir them so, Then people long on pilgrimage to go, And palmers to be seeking foreign strands, To distant shrines renowned in sundry lands."

The journey of the spiritual life is hard to navigate. It is difficult to map out. The direction often shifts, takes a turn, moves in unexpected directions.

Where am I going? Who is accompanying me? How did I get here?

I am lost.

During the journey, I stop and ask, Where is God? I am feeling abandoned. Did I make a bad decision somewhere? And if I did, will I be forgiven? Can this decision be redeemed?

When we judge, God is with us. God's love for us and God's saving and redeeming power is difficult to comprehend. The message we receive from our culture is that bad people make bad decisions. Good people make good decisions. I have made plenty of bad decisions so I must be bad. Sometimes I am overwhelmed, exhausted, disgusted, or just too tired to try to turn my life around by making a good decision, so I pray for God to restore my faith and open my eyes so that I can see that all can be undone.

In the midst of death, I must stop and assess where I am. What does God expect from me? Does God accept me as I am in the messiness of my life?

Experiences of the faithful are all written down for us to see and to pray over in the Book of Psalms.

Is it OK to feel abandoned by God? Psalm 88 says this: "O Lord, my God, my Savior, by day and night I cry to you. Let my prayer enter into your presence; incline your ear to my lamentation. For I am full of trouble; my life is at the brink of the grave. You have laid me in the depth of the Pit, in dark places, and in the abyss." [2]

Is it normal to wish ill will on challenging people in my life? Psalm 137 says this: "By the waters of Babylon we sat down and wept, when we remembered you, O Zion. As for our harps, we hung them up on the trees in the midst of that land.

For those who led us away captive asked us for a song, and our oppressors called for mirth: Sing us one of the songs of Zion. O Daughter of Babylon, doomed to destruction, happy the one who pays you back for what you have done to us! Happy shall he be who takes your little ones, and dashes them against the rock!" [3]

Is some level of paranoia a normal part of human experience? Psalm 31 says this: "Have mercy on me, O LORD, for I am in trouble; my eye is consumed with sorrow, and also my throat and my belly. For my life is wasted with grief, and my years with sighing; my strength fails me because of affliction, and my bones are consumed. I have become a reproach to all my enemies and even to my neighbors, a dismay to those of my acquaintance; when they see me in the street they avoid me. I am forgotten like a dead man, out of mind; I am as useless as a broken pot. For I have heard the whispering of the crowd; fear is all around; they put their heads together against me; they plot to take my life." [4]

When I am confused about my experiences of God with the reality of my life, when I wonder how God is working in the world, when I can not seem to figure out how God is working in my life, I find comfort in the psalms. For me, the Psalms give voice to the depth and breadth of the human experience. They are the human response to trying to understand the realities of life.

Most psalms include a judgment that will hopefully lead to an action. All psalms celebrate the human condition which God ordained when God created this world.

Martin Luther, the great Catholic reformer, said this about the psalms: "Whoever has begun to pray the Psalter earnestly and regularly, will soon leave behind easy, emotional prayers and long for the realness, the juiciness, the anger, the strength, the passion, and the fire found in the Psalter."

The psalms are a unique part of Scripture

because they are prayers to God which have become for us the Word of God. They are addressed to God, from the first person, and have been used continually in the life of the Church and synagogue from long before the life of Christ.

We find psalms of prayers and psalms of praise. Some psalms are laments, full of murmuring, directed towards God because of the believer's discontent. Other psalms are petitions, asking God for things to help with survival. Some are curses, asking God to strike down the evil ones so that the believers triumph.

Scholarship suggests that a majority of the psalms were probably hymns of the Hebrew people used during worship. Tradition ascribes some of the psalms to David, but many are believed to have come from other cultures surrounding the Hebrew people. David and David's kingdom did influence the psalms. This influence is most recognized within the first 41 psalms, but the remaining psalms were probably composed during the divided kingdom. The psalms near the back of the book were songs sung by pilgrims, as they made the journey to a holy site. For us today, the psalms are a source of theology.

In the Psalter, we encounter conflicting views of God. God is portrayed as the judger, the punisher, the deliverer, the good shepherd of the people. The psalms are resources for personal prayer, a voice in times of celebration, a comfort in times of loneliness, a cry for help during times of despair.

Psalm 66 captures the difficulty and the reality of being on a journey with God. The first half of Psalm 66 is a song of praise, but the concluding verses recall the difficulties of understanding the promises of God.

Psalm 66 recalls the 40 years of wandering around lost in the desert, pointing the finger at God and saying accusingly, "You have brought us into the snare; you laid heavy burdens upon our backs. You let enemies ride over our heads; we went through fire and water; but you brought us out into a place of refreshment." [5]

The psalms remind us that wherever we find ourselves on the journey of faith, we are not alone. In the New Testament, Jesus assures us that we are not alone. In the Gospel of John, we encounter Jesus' farewell discourse. The farewell discourse is made up of Jesus' words of comfort to His followers, as He prepares for death, where He tells his friends that He will be with them no longer.

In the psalms, the faithful yell at God, thirsting for justice. They question God, hungering for manifestation. They doubt God because inhumanity seems to cut through the fog. They praise God, because when they look back, they remember where they have been and assess where they are. They may not know where they are going, but God promises through Jesus not one of us is ever alone, even in death itself. As we lie in the stone-cold tomb, the Advocate reaches in and drags us out into new life.

The psalms are full of judgment: judgment for and against God, judgment for and against people, judgment for and against self. Judgment occurs when we realize something in us must change. We may be stuck; we may not know what to do; we may be grasping at something. Recognizing that we must change allows us to change.

Are we asking the right questions?

While we are "In the Queue" let's examine some circumstances and ask some questions.

Turn to the "Holy Story" section in your journal. On the next available page, in light pencil, draw a brick wall. Take your time. Your wall must be recognizable as a wall and it should be drawn lightly. You will be writing on your wall and your writing must be legible and dark enough to be read.

List times in your life when you felt judged. What was the context? What was the situation?

What are your thoughts and feelings associated with being judged? What changed? Did you change? Did someone around you change? How did these times end?

List times in your life when you were judging others. What was going on? What were the circumstances? How did you feel? How did this end?

Looking at the situations you have written down, what questions could you have asked to move you through the situations in a helpful way? List them.

FROM THE BOOK
John 20:10-31

The Gospels of Mark, Matthew, and Luke are called the Synoptic Gospels because they shared circulated sources proclaiming the mission and ministry of Jesus. The Gospel of John differs in tone and narrative structure from the Synoptic Gospels. All of the gospels were written and edited by writers and editors with the agenda of reaching a specific audience for a specific purpose. The Gospel of John appears to have been written by an exiled community for encouragement in the midst of rejection. Ninety percent of the Gospel of John is new content not found in any of the Synoptic Gospels. The Synoptics proclaim Good News through action. The Gospel of John proclaims Good News through love. John Calvin, the sixteenth-century French theologian, believed that Mark, Matthew and Luke revealed the body of Christ. The Gospel of John reveals Jesus' soul. Scholarship suggests that this Gospel was probably written much later than the other Gospels, possibly around 80 AD. Scholarship suggests that the Community of John may have been believers of Christ who had been kicked out of the temple because of their proclamation that Jesus was the long-awaited Messiah. A lot of the anger expressed towards "the Jews" in John was probably expressing anger about community infighting between disagreeing Jewish communities. What is certain about John is that the "beloved disciple" wrote the Gospel so that we might believe.

John 20:10-31
Jesus Appears to the Disciples

When it was evening on that day, the first day of the week, and the doors of the house where the disciples had met were locked for fear of the Jews, Jesus came and stood among them and said, "Peace be with you."

After he said this, he showed them his hands and his side. Then the disciples rejoiced when they saw the Lord. Jesus said to them again, "Peace be with you. As the Father has sent me, so I send you." When he had said this, he breathed on them and said to them, "Receive the Holy Spirit. If you forgive the sins of any, they are forgiven them; if you retain the sins of any, they are retained."

But Thomas (who was called the Twin), one of the twelve, was not with them when Jesus came. So the other disciples told him, "We have seen the Lord." But he said to them, "Unless I see the mark of the nails in his hands, and put my finger in the mark of the nails and my hand in his side, I will not believe."

A week later his disciples were again in the house, and Thomas was with them. Although the doors were shut, Jesus came and stood among them and said, "Peace be with you." Then he said to Thomas, "Put your finger here and see my hands. Reach out your hand and put it in my side. Do not doubt but believe." Thomas answered him, "My Lord and my God!" Jesus said to him, "Have you believed because you have seen me? Blessed are those who have not seen and yet have come to believe." [6]

RIDE THE ATTRACTION
Fantasmic!

At the end of the evening, guests gather at the Hollywood Hills Amphitheater to watch Sorcerer Mickey confront some of Disney's most popular villains including Cruella de Vil from *101 Dalmatians*, Maleficent from *Sleeping Beauty* and Ursula from *The Little Mermaid*. *Fantasmic!* at Disney's Hollywood Studios "features a dream-world battle of good versus evil in which Mickey's imagination comes to life - from the whimsical ways of his colorful friends to the darkness of the menacing Disney villains." [7]

During this popular performance, we are invited to visit the bright and dark spaces of our imagination. What we think and feel during the journey within those cracks and crevices of our hearts and minds impacts everything we think and do. The show combines live actors with animated segments projected on screens of water. The huge amphitheater positions the guests around a wide river. Across the river, on the other shore, is a mountain whose cliffs and valleys will be used as a stage throughout the performance.

The music beckons us to use our imagination to create a fantastic or "Fantasmic" dream. Our host welcomes us, saying, "Welcome to *Fantasmic!* Tonight, our friend and host Mickey Mouse uses his vivid imagination to create magical imagery for all to enjoy. Nothing is more wonderful than the imagination, for in a moment, you can experience a beautiful fantasy or an exciting adventure! But beware; nothing is more powerful than the imagination for it can also expand your greatest fears into an overwhelming nightmare. Are the powers of Mickey's incredible imagination strong enough, and bright enough, to withstand the evil forces that invade Mickey's dreams? You are

about to find out. We now invite you to join Mickey and experience *Fantasmic!*, a journey beyond your wildest imagination!"

Across the river, at the foot of the mountain, Mickey appears. As he did in the Sorcerer's Apprentice, Mickey begins to use the waters of the river to conduct a symphony of the imagination. Colorful fountains rise up and dance to the rhythm of the music. Colorful fountains of reds, yellows and blues invite us to join Mickey in the celebration of the imagination. The water forms a screen and we see Mickey conducting the waters in the animated classic *Fantasia*.

Flowers fall on the screens of water and images beckon us to move forward. "Set it in your mind and you can find in your imagination, mysteries and magic, visions fantastic, leading to strange and wondrous dreams."

The music shifts as we move through the flower stems and turn our attention to the mountain. The water disappears and large, colorful animals inhabit the stage. A barge of gorillas and a barge carrying Rafiki from *The Lion King* floats rapidly by on the river.

The mountain becomes dark and the waters rise up, revealing projected images from *The Lion King*. The water becomes bubbly and we meet the heroes of many of Disney's animated classics. We hear musical themes beginning with "Hukuna Matata" from *The Lion King* and blending into "I Wan'na Be Like You" from *The Jungle Book*. The seven dwarfs travel across the water projection as we hear "Hi Ho" from *Snow White and the Seven Dwarfs*. *Snow White* gives way to *Alice in Wonderland* and *Hercules* which leads to Pinocchio's recalling that he has no strings to hold him down. The Genie from *Aladdin* reminds us that we have never had a friend like him. Mulan travels by reminding us of what many are willing to do to live into their God-given created nature. The mice from *Cinderella* move by us followed by the love felt by *Lady and the Tramp*. Bambi in the forest gives way to the dancing plates from *Beauty and the Beast's* "Be Our Guest." The bubbles then invite us to life under the sea as we dance with the seahorses and lobster from *The Little Mermaid*.

From Pinocchio, Jiminy Cricket appears in a bubble of water, gets swallowed up by a whale, whose tail splashes up Mickey Mouse, struggling within the waves of the water. Mickey asks, "Hey, what's going on? Uh-oh!"

A cannon blast puts us temporarily into darkness that moves us into the next live-action scene on the mountain. We see the settlers from *Pocahontas* surrounding the British flag. The leader belts out, "I hereby claim this land in the name of his majesty King James the First. The people celebrate as Native Americans paddle across the river in the shadow of the declaration. The resources of the land are stripped as the conquering peoples "dig and dig and dig." The water projections return, conjuring up the spirits of the native peoples while the conquerors take up arms and fire upon them with the intent to kill. John Smith, because of his love for Pocahontas, disobeys orders and appears on the mountaintop with her. Mother Willow declares, "What a dream!" reminding Pocahontas that she must listen to the spirits for guidance.

Within the projected animation, the eyes of John Smith and Pocahontas meet. The music continues, "See it in your mind and you can find in your imagination, tales of enchantment, beauty and romance, happily ever after." We see Cinderella dancing with Prince Charming, and Aladdin and Jasmine traveling across the sky on the flying carpet.

The waters for projection disappear and three barges appear on the river. Floating by are Belle and the Beast, Ariel and Prince Eric, and Snow White and her Prince.

Belle and the Beast dance as we hear, "Tale as old as time. True as it can be. Barely even friends then somebody bends unexpectedly… Certain as the sun rising in the east, tale as old as time, song as old as rhyme, Beauty and the Beast."

Their barge moves away, revealing another barge with Ariel and Eric, "What would I give if I could live out of these waters? What would I pay to spend a day warm on the sand? Bet you on land they understand, bet they don't reprimand their daughters, bright young women sick of swimming. Ready to stand."

Snow White and her prince appear. "Some day my prince will come. Some day we'll find true love. Tale as old as time. Song as old as rhyme. . ."

The barges disappear just around the river bend. The music and lighting shift. The Wicked Queen from *Snow White* appears onstage. She beckons the Magic Mirror. She looks at herself in the mirror, disappointedly waving her arms, conjuring up dark spirits, saying, "Slave in the magic mirror, come from farthest space. Through wind and darkness, I summon thee! Speak! Let me see thy face."

The Magic Mirror responds, declaring, "Famed is thy beauty, Majesty. But hold, three lovelier maids I see. And here, in Mickey's imagination, beauty and love will always survive."

The Wicked Queen yells, "No!" in response to the mirror's declaration. She stirs up a potion, saying, "A Magic Spell in the black of night with a scream of fright and a bolt of light. Turn my hair to white!" The bubbling pot explodes and the Wicked Queen has been transformed into the familiar Wicked Witch. Cackling through her teeth, she declares, "Now I'll turn that little mouse's dream into a nightmare fantasmic! Imagine this! Magic Mirror on the wall, all the forces of evil I call."

The Magic Mirror appears, saying, "You have the power," but morphs suddenly into the Wicked Witch, who finishes the thought saying, "to control his mind…"

And then, like magic, the classic villains of Disney films appear within the waves of the water. Ursula chimes in, "Oh, yes! How exciting!" Cruella de Vil from *101 Dalmatians* chimes in, "Tonight! Let's do the job and take his spirit tonight!" Scar from *The Lion King* roars out, "Yes! Perfect!" Scar morphs into Frollo from *The Hunchback of Notre Dame,* who adds, "It's too late, coward!" He begins to hiss like a snake as he turns into Jafar from *Aladdin*. "It's time to say goodbye to Mickey! Enter the Cave of Wonders!"

Jafar tosses Mickey into the Cave of Wonders. Mickey is on the flying carpet, flying through the cave at perilous speeds. Fire erupts. Jafar appears with his serpent's tongue, proudly declaring, "And now you will see how snake-like I can be!"

Suddenly, the waters part and a huge snake appears across the river on the mountain stage. It is immense and scary and smiles towards the guests. Mickey appears on the other side of the mountain, moving cautiously towards the snake. As he moves about the Cave of Wonders, he encounters Aladdin's magic lamp.

Mickey exclaims, "Look, a magic lamp! Maybe if I just rub it and wish!" We are tossed into darkness as the villains appear, declaring that the universe is theirs to command! And the villains promise a huge finale that illustrates the power of evil in the world.

Hades from *Hercules* taunts us, declaring, "You will love this! One more thing!"

We are in darkness. Then suddenly, the devil Chernabog from *The Night on Bald Mountain* segment from the Disney animated classic *Fantasia* appears. He calls on the restless spirits to arise and they begin to traverse the dark night to enhance the power of the nightmare.

The spirits step aside to reveal Maleficent, armed and ready to take on Mickey Mouse. She taunts Mickey, saying, "Now you will deal with me! Hello the powers of my imagination!"

As she rises towards the heavens, she summons the darkened powers of fire and water. A fire-breathing dragon appears and the villains of the Disney films laugh with glee!

"Imagination!" The villains cackle and laugh and mock and celebrate as the fire-breathing dragon takes over the entire mountain stage. Mickey seems powerless as the dragon sets the entire river ablaze.

Mickey, full of courage and empowered by the spirit of imagination, faces the dragon, claiming, "You may think you are so powerful. Well, this is *my* dream!"

Mickey begins to summon the waters just as he did as the sorcerer's apprentice. As the waters quench the fires, Mickey recovers a sword and places it in the stone, reminiscent of *The Sword in the Stone*. The villains are destroyed. The powers of evil have been defeated.

Tinker Bell sprinkles some magic pixie dust and a steamboat appears, carrying all of the Disney heroes. They wave at the guests celebrating the triumph of Mickey's imagination. They sing, "See it in your mind and you will find in your imagination, mysteries and magic, visions fantastic leading to strange and wondrous dreams. Dreams are make-believe but could they all come true? In your Imagination! Deep in your mind it's magic you'll find! When out of the night the forces ignite to blind you with frightening speed. You use your might to brighten the light creating a night of wondrous dreams!"

Mickey appears on the top of the mountain concluding *Fantasmic!*, boldly asking, "Some imagination, huh?"

FOR REFLECTION

Ripley's *Believe It or Not* began in 1918, when artist Robert Ripley produced cartoons that were entertaining and slightly off-center. The cartoons presented scenarios that could be true but were difficult to believe. The Ripley's brand name has expanded into a host of attractions that are just a little bit more high-end than attractions you would encounter at Coney Island during its heyday.

Do I believe it or not? A judgment has to be made in order to move forward.

How many conversations in your life have begun with the phrase "I'm going to tell you something but you are not going to believe it."

Many times, a family member or a friend has shared a story or told an incredible tale that is just too impossible to believe. The facts do not seem to add up. The story is hard to believe because the circumstances are totally ridiculous or absurd. Other times, what is shared is too horrific, too unbearable; the level of suffering is too much to stomach, so we choose not to believe.

Thomas said, "Unless I see the mark of the nails in his hands, and put my finger in the mark of the nails and my hand in his side, I will not believe."

This passage from John is often referred to as the "Doubting Thomas" passage. But I do not think Thomas was doubting at all. I think Thomas was standing in the middle of a confrontation with unbelievable circumstances within the context of suffering.

In the midst of suffering, we must render judgment - a judgment toward belief or a judgment of unbelief.

We have all experienced suffering. When we experience suffering, everything we think we know about God, and everything we think we know about how the way the world works, is significantly challenged. Something traumatic has happened and our eyes see things differently. Our anxiety level and our fear about what is next skyrockets out of control. We are unable to remember what hope feels like. We are suffering. We have a decision to make.

In order to understand what is going on around me, often I must shift the context. I must remember who I am. I must recall who God is. I must believe the promises God makes to all of God's people. Then, I must render judgment. We make these decisions every day. I can choose to turn towards God and embrace hope. I can choose to turn away from God and continue to experience suffering with no context or meaning. I must render a judgment.

Jesus' friends are in the midst of death. Do they believe all that has been spoken about the power of God to heal and reconcile the world? Or, do they believe the voices surrounding them that death is the final answer and God has truly abandoned them?

Judgment is needed when we have hit a brick wall, when something has happened that challenges the way we see the world. What we choose to do next will either support everything we believe or will challenge everything we believe. The good news is decisions are never final. They can be rethought, rejudged and redone.

We have all experienced severe degrees of suffering after the death of a family member or a beloved friend. When facing death, we cannot help but have something within us change, something within us altered. After any death, our relationship with God shifts. And our own suffering becomes overwhelming, unbearable. We cannot stand to be with ourselves. We cannot stand to be with others. In the midst of suffering, it often becomes difficult to remember a different reality, another way of living. As we move through grief, our belief system will be challenged. The foundations of our personal beliefs will compel us to see the world in one context or another. We judge the circumstance. We decide the context. We act on our beliefs.

Are these decisions based on faith beliefs or are they choices influenced by the cynicism and doubt of the world?

Thomas is suddenly caught unaware, unprepared, when normality is breached through by a truly unpredictable encounter with a friend's suffering and death. Thomas does not want to believe Jesus suffered. He denies it. And by denying Jesus' suffering, he denies his own. How much suffering can Thomas accept? How much suffering can any of us accept? However he answers that question and however he chooses to act determines what comes next.

There is no doubt here. There is just a fear of making the wrong judgment in the midst of suffering. Am I willing to have so much trust in God that I can allow everything I believe to shift? Thomas says, "Unless I see the mark of the nails in his hands, and put my finger in the mark of the nails and my hand in his side, I will not believe." Sometimes we believe that if we make the wrong judgment, God will abandon us forever. "My God, my God, why have you forsaken me?"

We all feel forsaken, forgotten and abandoned. But it is within these moments of despair that we must examine the context within which we are making our judgments.

Barbara Brown Taylor, in her book entitled *Suffering: God in Pain,* says this about our fear in the midst of challenging circumstances, "The worst is the utter silence of God. The God who does not act. The God who is not there. The God who - by a single word - could have made all the pain bearable who did not speak. Not so Jesus could hear. The only voice (Jesus heard on the cross) was his own, screaming his last, unanswered question at the sky,

"'My God, my God, why have you forsaken me?'"

We must shift the context. As we encounter the crucified Christ, we must remember the context of the empty tomb and the resurrection stories. Suffering circumstances cloud our judgments. When we are in the midst of suffering, we often feel guilt, shame, and sometimes even more sadness, for feeling the way we are feeling. We feel as if we are faithless, an unbeliever, a traitor to God. Many of us are ashamed of our suffering. We are ashamed of being human. But God will judge us based on our human condition - a condition Christians confess is redeemed by a God who understands our suffering in the midst of the realities of this world.

Gilda Radner, the great comedian from the original cast of *Saturday Night Live,* played a memorable character named Roseanne Roseannadanna. Roseanne Roseannadanna was a broadcast journalist. She would always end her news reports with the phrase, "You know, it's always something. If it is not one thing it's another." If you are not suffering this way, then you are suffering in this other way. She was a talented comedian.

Gilda Radner fell in love and married actor Gene Wilder. But, Gilda suffered a lot throughout their married life together. She lived through two miscarriages, and then was diagnosed with ovarian cancer in 1986. She shares her story of living with cancer in her beautiful, humorous and poignant book *It's Always Something*. Gilda says, "I wanted a perfect ending. Now I've learned, the hard way, that some poems don't rhyme, and some stories don't have a clear beginning, middle and end. Life is about not knowing, having to change, taking the moment and making the best of it, without knowing what's going to happen next."

It's always something. I must make the best judgment within the context of my life.

A young person, a prince, led a sheltered life. He lived in a gated community. But, one day he snuck out of the gates and ventured out. In the city he saw a man sitting on the side of the road, starving, hungry, on the brink of death. Then, he encountered a young woman, blind from birth, wandering the city streets, hitting walls and bumping into people, while the crowds walked by, trying not to get involved with the woman's disability. Then he was stopped on the road by a funeral procession moving through the marketplace, while few took notice. "Remember you are dust and to dust you will return." He realized he was living in the midst of a city of people not willing to talk to each other. He decided to renounce the material life and pray for an end to all the world's sufferings. Suddenly he realized that suffering was just a part of the world's noble truth. Through prayer, the Buddha discerned that "All of life is suffering." The Buddha taught that we can end suffering if we examine the context of our lives. If we deny the context, ultimately this denial causes madness.

Suffering is suffering. There are no degrees of suffering. Suffering is suffering. And it hurts. All of it hurts. Maybe, there is some comfort in knowing that we do not suffer alone. God suffers with us. Jesus' death on the cross confirms that God does indeed suffer. Jesus dies on the hard wood, feeling abandoned and betrayed.

But, that is not the end.

Jesus appears to Thomas and the others, behind locked doors, in the upper room, with scabs on his hands, with pierced scars in his side. God is with Thomas in his suffering. Thomas is with God in the Lord's suffering. This is the context of our lives. We stand beside Thomas, beside Jesus, and with the disciples in the upper room in the midst of all that was and is and is to come. We are called to make a judgment and to move forward. Whatever we decide, God invites us near, invites us to come closer, promising healing and promising new life.

Thomas is full of life and full of love for his friend. He does not want to see his friend suffer. He does not want to believe that his friend had died the way he did. Thomas said, "Unless I see the mark of the nails in his hands, and put my finger in the mark of the nails and my hand in his side, I will not believe."

Jesus, reaching out towards Thomas, says touch and see. Believe in love. Believe in life. Believe that God loves you. You decide. You be the judge. Believe it or not.

THE E-TICKET

Film directors make creative decisions. Financial administrators make business decisions. Airplane pilots make navigational decisions. Christians make life-giving or life-denying decisions. When Christians make life-giving decisions, they have stepped towards God. When Christians make life-denying decisions, they have turned away from God and from God's people. A judgment must be made.

Life happens at an alarming pace. We are standing still in one place and then suddenly, and without warning, everything changes. The road ahead cannot be seen and the twists and the turns come from nowhere. In the midst of everything we are called to act. We can risk it all and make a leap of faith. We can react in fear and deny the joyfulness of creation. William S. Burroughs, in his book *Junky*, says, "When you stop growing, you start dying."

To pray without ceasing is to invite God to be with you in every decision made throughout the day. Prayer is associated with intentionality. During our movement through this travel guide, we have claimed sacred space in hopes that the presence and the spirit of God can be felt as we contemplate and act upon what really matters in life.

We associate prayer with sacred space, intentional time, silence, a celebration of sacraments.

Then we move out into the world to do the work God has given us to do.

Prayer is actually about movement. It is about claiming intentional space, listening to the spirit of God, and moving through the realities of life, profoundly aware of and respectful of the presence of God's spirit in every moment of our lives. This is what it means to pray without ceasing.

Prayer is movement. Prayer is about being aware of the power of God. Prayer is about being aware of our relationship with all of God's people. Prayer is about making the Gospel choice in everything we do because everything we do matters.

When we pray, when we are truly alive, we must know who we are. We must ask the right questions. We must rely on the power of the spirit. We must make the right judgment call. If we can do all this, our judgments will be fair and our actions life-giving.

Judgment is life-giving. Judgment is necessary. Judgment is the fork in the road. Our judgments either bring us closer to God or tear us away from God.

Move to the "Holy Story" section of your journal. Consider the following questions around judgment. Write down your reflections.

How has judgment been used in your life? Think about when you have judged yourself. Think about when you have judged others. Were you brought closer or were you pushed away because of the judgments you made? The power of God actually moves through God's people in judgment. How can judgment be healing and transforming in your life and in the lives of the people you know and the people you do not?

Next, move to the "Rule of Life" section of your journal. Contemplate and write down your Rule about judgment.

JUDGMENT

Judgment is _____ .

When I am judged, I _____ .

When I judge others, I _____ .

To claim the spirit of God in every judgment made, I must _____ .

To me, God and judgment and all of my actions are _____ .

 THE COLLECT

One of my favorite Collects from the Episcopal *Book of Common Prayer* is a beautiful prayer for rest after a day of work.

"O Lord, support us all the day long, until the shadows lengthen, and the evening comes, and the busy world is hushed, and the fever of life is over, and our work is done. Then in thy mercy, grant us a safe lodging, and a holy rest, and peace at last. Amen." [8]

All of us work and live and move through a lot of personal experiences throughout the day. We have had to make decisions. Judgment calls have been made.

Open the "Holy Story" section of your journal and accept what has been done and what has been left undone. Remember the simple steps and write a Collect to gather your thoughts and reflections.

1. Address God
2. Describe an action or several actions of God
3. Ask God for something
4. Thank God

ENDNOTES

[1] (Tigert, 1999, p. 69)

[2] (Episcopal Church., 1979, p. 712)

[3] (Episcopal Church., 1979, p. 792)

[4] (Episcopal Church., 1979, p. 623)

[5] (Episcopal Church., 1979, p. 674)

[6] (May & Metzger, 1973, p. NT 157-158)

[7] (Gordon & Kurtti, 2008, p. 108)

[8] (Episcopal Church., 1979, p. 833)

REPENTANCE } *Is It Possible to Turn Things Around?*

MAIN GATE

"You must not let anyone define your limits because of where you come from. Your only limit is your soul," says Gusteau in *Ratatouille*. When we are on a spiritual journey, as we move through the chances and changes of this life, we take a few wrong turns. So, we must turn around and find our way back. Sometimes the path back to God begins in an instant. New perspective has been informed by the context of hope so love surrounds you as you find your way back. Other times, this new perspective can take days, months or years. In the midst of this wilderness time, highs and lows may be experienced compounded with depression, despair, anxiety and the search for truth. We must constantly look towards God and God's people during these dark nights of the soul.

Sin turns us away from God. *Repent* literally means "turn around." Repent turns us back towards God. To remain in sin, to get stuck in judgment, narrows our vision and focus on self. We are in survival mode. Sometimes this is all we can do. It takes every bit of our energy to breathe and to make it through the day. Repentance demands that we look beyond the tips of our noses to see the truth in the world around us. We move over the walls or past the boundaries that isolate us, stepping into dangerous but transforming territory. This movement is dangerous because it will change us but we do not know how, nor can we control it. God is in charge. Do I want God to be in charge?

When we travel forward between Point A and Point B, we may not have a clue of what is ahead. Our past journeys and current realities influence our spiritual actions and reactions. We can build up our spirits through faith, believing that we are created and are beloved by God, or we can listen to messages surrounding us, telling us how much we fall short. One reaction draws us closer to God. The other separates us from the love of God.

To know and not to act is not to know. After we have formulated and asked ourselves the right questions, we need to act. We need to respond. If we do not respond, we remain in judgment and little, if anything, changes. Repentance is all about turning around, affecting change, and bringing about the kingdom of God.

In judgment, we claim what has turned us away. We confess. We speak to our heart. We may seek out a friend or family member and speak to them. Some of us may seek out a pastor for confession. We must remember that God is with us. Turning around takes claiming the truth, seeking others for love and support and direction and above all, trusting God to be with us as we make our way out.

At the Walt Disney World Resort, we turn around and go back many times.

On *Maelstrom* in Norway at Epcot, we

jump in Dragonship and hit the water. As we prepare for our journey, we are told to remember where we have come in order to claim our context. "You are not the first to pass this way nor shall you be the last. Those who seek the spirit of Norway face peril and adventure but more often find beauty and charm." Suddenly, we find ourselves sailing forward seeking the Seafarers. We are in Norway's past. Trolls suddenly appear before us and are angry to find us trespassing. "What's this? How dare you come near! This is troll country! Away! Be gone! I will cast a spell on you! You will disappear! Disappear! Back! Back! Over the falls!" We suddenly forge backwards, plunging into Norway's present, discovering that sometimes we must go back in order to turn around.

On *Expedition Everest* in Asia at Disney's Animal Kingdom, there are many dead ends. The tracks have been destroyed and we must back up in order to return to continue on the journey. Once we face forward again, we must try to escape the Yeti by falling through the mountain, reassessing our journey the entire way.

As we travel around World Showcase at Epcot, we make decisions, hear stories and celebrate the journeys of everyone on this Spaceship Earth. "Nationalism is not, one could argue, an unmitigated evil. It provides a bonding force to unite highly diverse tribes and peoples. It finishes a sense of collective identity capable of drawing people out of themselves and their family groupings into a larger whole. It is one of the sole forces capable of standing up against the economic onslaught of the transnational corporations."[1] As we make ourselves vulnerable by sharing our stories, we can see how decisions in the past have led others.

Wherever we find ourselves on the journey of faith, God's blessings are with us. When we are judging, we must make a decision of how we will move onward. If we choose to repent, our decision has been to face toward God. This willingness to make the journey back to God and to God's people requires vulnerability. We cannot control it all.

As God-lovers, we are called to live our lives within tension. We hear the words of God. We learn and discover the history of God's people in Holy Scripture. We see a faithful God. We discover unfaithful people. Who am I in the midst of this story and what am I willing to think and do? What journey do I need to be on to receive love through the power of grace?

The spirit of God connects me with people and circumstances that transcend time and space. This connection is an overwhelming context. But it is also an overwhelming and generous gift. Many have passed this way before. What questions did they ask? How did they respond? How were they able to move forward?

I want to shape my own destiny. I want to control what happens to me. That does not seem like too much to ask. I want to live the Gospel truth with integrity but I often don't want to do what is required of me. Knowing and not acting dead-ends at hypocrisy. To know and not to act is not to know.

Repentance starts by examining and recognizing what is holding me back. I need to be aware of the disconnects. Am I acting in any way that does not truly exhibit my faith beliefs? If I do not know what my faith beliefs are then this lack of knowledge is probably what is holding me back. I must be aware of this division within myself in order to get any Gospel work done.

Maya Angelou, the brilliant writer and spiritual thinker, once shared that she is scared of the God we must face in the midst of repentance. "I believe in God. I believe in whatever people call God. I believe in life. I believe in will. I believe in good. I believe that right wins out. It may sound naive, but I believe in those things…"[2]

IN THE QUEUE

Sometimes when we are in the queue, we feel lost. We are not aware of where we are going. We seem to be going back and forth and back and forth, not really going somewhere. At some point, we will need to make a decision that delivers us from the world of "back and forth," onto a path of clear decision. The actions that follow indicate our understanding of the implications of the choice or choices we have made.

We often confuse repentance with feeling better. We have moved past hurt and anger and are feeling better so we associate better feeling with the good. "In popular culture, to forgive means to overcome feelings of anger and resentment... Emotional healing is a good thing and there are many paths that may lead to it, but emotional healing is not the main purpose of forgiveness. To forgive means to forgo a rightful claim against someone who has wronged us."[3] We have been hurt or we may have hurt somebody else. Often, we associate feelings with the need to change. We often forget the act that caused us to feel that way.

All actions have context. Inappropriate actions are not the whole story. To repent means to place ourselves within a larger context than just the offending act. Feelings often present us from doing that. Our focus narrows and we are more stuck than we realize. Episcopal priest Martin L. Smith, when speaking of repentance and reconciliation, says, "Focusing solely on our own pain over wrongdoing, and the pain we feel in sympathy with those we have wounded, only deals with the outer edge, as it were, of the mystery of repentance. The heart of the experience is that we sense the pain of God. The true grief experienced in repentance comes from being admitted into the feelings of God."[4] An act of repentance is cause for celebration. In the wonderful hymn "There's a Wideness in God's Mercy," we sing this beautiful verse: "There is no place where earth's sorrows are more felt than up in Heaven; There is no place where earth's failings have such kindly judgment given."

In the "Holy Story" section of your journal, you are going to create a road map for repentance.

At the top of the next available page, write "Repentance Road Map Prep." Then consider and write down your responses to the following:

When do I need to repent? What happens? What makes repentance necessary? What are the signs that I have done injury to myself, to God, and to God's people? What is the purpose of repenting? What do I need to repent? What resources are needed to help in the turnaround? Moving beyond my feelings, and the feelings of others, how do I know if repentance has been accomplished?

After you have finished answering these questions, move to the next page of the "Holy Story" section of your journal. At the top of the page, write "Repentance Road Map."

Illustrate in a road map or mind map, the steps and resources you outlined above. If you feel called to be creative, illustrate the steps.

FROM THE BOOK
Luke 15: 1- 32

The Gospel of Luke was the third Gospel to be written. Tradition teaches us that Luke was an artist, a physician and scholar. Perhaps Luke was a traveling companion of Paul's. Scholarship suggests that the Gospel of Luke and the Book of Acts are one volume, one continuous book, one continuous story, discovered on two separate scrolls. It appears that the Gospel of Luke and The Book of Acts were to be part of a trilogy. Perhaps a third volume was in the works but we have no record of it. The Book of Acts ends without much of an ending. It is sort of like the ending of *The Empire Strikes Back* - a lot has happened but there is still a lot more to come. And we are more than two-thousand years later.

During the introduction to the Book of Acts, the writer sums of the Gospel this way: "In the first book, Theophilus, I wrote about all that Jesus did and taught from the beginning until the day when he was taken up to heaven, after giving instructions through the Holy Spirit to the apostles whom he had chosen. After his suffering he presented himself alive to them by many convincing proofs, appearing to them during forty days and speaking about the kingdom of God. 'This,' he said, 'is what you have heard from me; for John baptized with water, but you will be baptized with the Holy Spirit - not many days from now.'"

Like the Book of Acts, the Gospel of Luke is addressed to Theophilus, or "God-lover." According to themes that emerge throughout Luke's Gospel, a lover of God worships, builds community, reaches out to people excluded from society who are living on the margins and seeks to do the will of God in all things. The Gospel appeals to a diverse crowd of seekers because it includes details about women disciples, offers testimony of life-changing conversion experiences, and calls on us to develop our spirituality through worship and prayer, all within the context of steadfast love.

The story of the prodigal son is one of the most beloved in all of the Gospels. It is unique to the Gospel of Luke. Because of the parable's complexity, there are many ways in which to enter the story.

LUKE 15:1-32
THE PARABLE OF THE PRODIGAL AND HIS BROTHER

Jesus said, "There was a man who had two sons. The younger of them said to his father, 'Father, give me the share of the property that will belong to me.' So he divided his property between them. A few days later the younger son gathered all he had and traveled to a distant country, and there he squandered his property in dissolute living. When he had spent everything, a severe famine took place throughout that country, and he began to be in need. So he went and hired himself out to one of the citizens of that country, who sent him to his fields to feed the pigs. He would gladly have filled himself with the pods that the pigs were eating; and no one gave him anything. But when he came to himself he said, 'How many of my father's hired hands have bread enough and to spare, but here I am dying of hunger! I will get up and go to my father, and I will say to him, "Father, I have sinned against heaven and before you; I am no longer worthy to be called your son; treat me like one of your hired hands." ' So he set off and went to his father. But while he was still far off, his father saw him and was filled with compassion; he ran and put his arms around him and kissed him. Then the son said to him, 'Father, I have sinned against heaven and before you; I am no longer worthy to be called your son.' But the father said to his slaves, 'Quickly, bring out a robe—the best one—and put it on him; put a ring on his finger and sandals on his feet. And get the fatted calf and kill it, and let us eat and celebrate: for this son of mine was dead and is alive again; he was lost and is found!' And they began to celebrate.

"Now his elder son was in the field; and when he came and approached the house, he heard music and dancing. He called one of the slaves and asked what was going on. He replied, 'Your brother has come, and your father has killed the fatted calf, because he has got him back safe and sound.' Then he became angry and refused to go in. His father came out and began to plead with him. But he answered his father, 'Listen! For all these years I have been working like a slave for you, and I have never disobeyed your command; yet you have never given me even a young goat so that I might celebrate with my friends. But when this son of yours came back, who has devoured your property with prostitutes, you killed the fatted calf for him!' Then the father said to him, 'Son, you are always with me, and all that is mine is yours. But we had to celebrate and rejoice, because this brother of yours was dead and has come to life; he was lost and has been found.'" [5]

RIDE THE ATTRACTION
World Showcase

Just a short monorail ride from the Transportation and Ticket Center is Epcot, a park made up of two themed areas, World Showcase and Future World. World Showcase is a permanent celebration highlighting the people and traditions of several countries including Mexico, the People's Republic of China, Norway, Germany, Italy, the United States, Japan, the Kingdom of Morocco, Japan, France, the United Kingdom, and Canada. During the journey around World Showcase Lagoon, guests are invited to encounter food, artists, exhibits, films and thrill rides that capture the spirit of each pavilion.

Just beyond *Spaceship Earth*, beyond a dancing fountain, is a peaceful promenade leading to World Showcase. Host countries sit at the edge of the lagoon inviting the adventurer to come and see. If we listen carefully, we can hear the story, share in the struggle, overcome the doubt and move boldly into the future. World Showcase is a tribute to our finding the way in a world full of joys and tears.

The great faiths of the world are represented. Voices from the Judeo-Christian tradition, Islam, Buddhism, Taoism, Shintoism, and Native American spirituality can be heard and experienced. All of the faith traditions have a theological framework to help the faithful respond to the world around them. What is the world like? What is expected of me? What goes wrong? What needs to change? How do I find my way back? What happens when I do?

Like the journey around World Showcase, the path of the faithful is full of choices and turns, moving forward and turning back, all in hopes of living and acting and playing faithfully in God's world.

As we move beyond the promenade and arrive at the edge of World Showcase Lagoon, we cannot help but notice The United States Pavilion. *The American Adventure* is an incredible multimedia show reminding us of what the United States is made of. It is hosted by Mark Twain and Ben Franklin, who recall our history with humor and insight. Ben Franklin uses the words of John Steinbeck to give context to the American adventure. "America did not exist. Four centuries of work, bloodshed, loneliness, and fear created this land. We built America and the process made us Americans… A new breed, rooted in all races, stained and tinted with all colors, a seeming ethnic anarchy. Then, in a little time we became more alike then we were different, a new society, not great, but fitted by our very faults for greatness."

The presentation moves through history remembering the quest for freedom, the difficulty with manifest destiny, the struggles for equality, and the unending hope for building a better future for all. Ben Franklin uses the words of Thomas Wolfe to hold out the vision that all Americans hope to live into: "To all people, regardless of their birth, the right to live, to work, to be themselves, and to become whatever their visions can combine to make them. This is the promise of America."

As we exit *The American Adventure* and move around the lagoon, the turning points stand out - the hope experienced through a heavenly harvest, the struggle to control water so that a nation can be fed, the quest to capture within musical composition the yearnings of the human spirit, and the attempt to communicate with the gods by understanding the stars and movements with the heavenly realm.

As we walk around the lagoon, the spirit of adventure is sparked within our souls. It is usually when we journey into a context different from our own that we are able to clear our hearts and minds, remembering who created us and for what purpose. The journey takes time, patience, persistence and the building of character.

The Mexico Pavilion celebrates the *Rio de Tiempo*, the river of time, the obsession with movement, the manifestation of the Aztec calendar. Inside the pavilion, a boat ride takes us through a journey through life, celebrating the Day of the Dead and the joy of the human spirit. Stepped pyramids climb toward the stars where native peoples gazed, seeking our clues and patterns in hopes of unlocking the secret of how this world works. What is next? What guides me? And what is our place within this vast mystery?

At the center of the pavilion for People's Republic of China is the Temple of Heaven. It is a circular structure inviting the traveler into a Circle-Vision 360° film entitled *Reflections of China*. Taoism emerged from within this nation's borders and its spirit is prevalent throughout the film. Earth, water, fire, wind and wood are elements that shaped and are influencing the history of the Chinese people. We hear the story of dynasties rising and dynasties falling. We hear the story of peasants revolting and peasants rising, leading to a People's Republic. We see the Great Wall, walk amongst the Terracotta Soldiers and ride with the Mongolian herdsman, finding our place in the struggle to understand the human condition.

Next to China is Norway. A traditional stave church invites the seafarer to celebrate the spirit of Norway. Stacked vertical wooden boards, or staves, come together to create a church's walls. Within Norway's Pavilion, we hear of the quest to conquer and navigate through a beautiful, but sometimes brutal, environment. But the people offer the best of what they have to create a nation of innovation and gratitude. Resources are harvested to sustain life in the harshest of climates.

As we stand at the shore of the Norway Pavilion, a heavenly beat beckons us to discover and take note of the spirits surround us. Just beyond the beautiful *bermilion torii,* a red gate modeled after the gate at the ancient Itsukushima Shrine, guests are invited to move into the Japanese Pavilion. Drummers call out to the gods at the foot of the elegant *goju-no-to* or five-story pagoda. It is modeled after the pagoda of Horyuji Temple in Nara. Each of the pagoda's levels represents the five elements Buddhists believe are the foundations of all things of this world - earth, water, fire, wind and sky. A Japanese garden beckons to move through and listen to what the world around us is telling us.

Just over the horizon, at the foot of the Eiffel Tower, is France's Pavilion. Beyond the bakery and wine shops is an intimate 350-seat movie theater showing a beautiful film entitled *Impressions de France*. This cinematic journey highlights the city of Paris and moves through the charm and beauty of the provinces, featuring the music of some of France's best-known composers, including Debussy and Satie. We see sacramental celebrations of marriage and baptism, gathered people feasting on food and partaking in wine, walking through mansions of history and getting on board hot-air balloons, enjoying the surrounding of mist and mountains.

As we continue to journey around World Showcase, we see St. George slaying the dragon within the borders of the German Pavilion, we stroll through St. Mark's Square past Tivoli Fountains at the center of the Italian Pavilion, and stop to enjoy tea, beer or biscuit at in the United Kingdom's Pavilion.

Native American Indian totem poles welcome us to explore Canada. Each totem pole tells the story of the past. They are depictions of family trees, rooted in the ground, standing firm in the present, but reaching skyward towards the heavens preparing for the world we have yet to see. A French gothic building is the focal point of the Canadian pavilion, modeled after the Chateau Laurier in Ottawa. Canada is a lifetime of journeys for the traveler.

A minaret from Marrakesh invites sojourners to the Moroccan Pavilion. Beautiful tiles and winding streets beckon us to move beyond *Bab Boujeloud* into the street bazaar. As we move away from the lagoon and further into the streets of Morocco, we turn left and we turn right, we move backwards and we move forwards, but we are reminded that several times a day, no matter in which direction our lives may be turning, Muslims stop and turn toward Mecca, turning toward God, giving focus and context for everything that is experienced in this life.

To repent means to turn back to what gives life purpose and meaning. We move beyond what pulls us apart and separates us from each other and from God, turning back to the center, claiming the holiness of our created state so that we can do the work that God has given us to do.

The Irish blessing reminds us that "Life is short. We do not have much time to gladden the hearts of those who travel the journey with us. So be swift to love and make haste to be kind. And may God continue to bless us in all that we do and all that we are."

FOR REFLECTION

On most days, the idea of God's grace just does not make any sense. Grace is very difficult to understand and even more impossible to comprehend.

We sing about grace - "Amazing Grace, how sweet the sound, that saved a wretch like me." We talk about grace as if there is some fatalistic aspect to it. We have all heard or even said, "There but by the grace of God, go I." We declare a lack of grace when someone's life circumstances have suddenly changed for the worse - "Fallen from grace."

The grace of God is central and essential to our journey of faith. Why is grace so difficult for me to understand? What is grace anyway?

"The Prodigal Son" is probably one of the most well-known Gospel parables. It is all about grace. But, personally, I do not want to accept what grace is as seen in this parable. If I truly accept the grace of God, I have to look at how I act, show gratitude and examine what I truly think about actions of God. When I repent and turn towards God, how must I change? How must I live my life?

"The Prodigal Son" is probably not a good title reference for this parable. It focuses our attention on the sinful actions of only one son and not on the reactions of the other. The son who leaves and lives a life of debauchery, caused by fulfilling every desire of the flesh, is much more interesting than the son who stays home and seems angry and resentful at his brother's return.

Instead of calling it "The Prodigal Son," we should consider entitling it "The Prodigal Son, the Waiting Father and the Angry Brother." This title follows the shifts and the actions within the parable as the story unfolds. We need to follow the actions

and thoughts and feelings of the son who leaves. Then we need to examine and reflect on the father who gives the prodigal son everything he has asked for and then waits. Finally, we need to understand and absorb the thoughts and feelings of the son who stays.

All three of the subjects of this parable exhibit grace at one time or another. Who we relate to the most gives us a glimpse of how we believe the grace of God works in the world. The beauty of this story, as Jesus tells it to us, is that deep down inside we can relate to the decisions and actions of all three.

The prodigal son is eager to get away. By asking for his inheritance from his father, the prodigal son has declared that his father is as good as dead to him. He wants to get away, to get out and to see the world. He is a rebellious adolescent. He leaves his country and lives and works and plays with foreigners. These foreign people do not look or think or even believe like him. They raise and eat pig, drink a lot, and enjoy a multitude of bodily pleasure. It sounds as if it is Mardi Gras every day in this foreign land. As fate would have it, famine hits the land and desperation and death take hold. The pigs the prodigal son is feeding are eating better than he is. In the midst of swine, he remembers who he is. He is a person beloved by God. He is a son who is loved by his father. He is desperate. He is alone. He has made many mistakes.

Is it possible to turn this desperate situation around or will I be swine all of my life? Who knows me? Who remembers me? Who loves me as I really am?

Elbert Hubbard, a successful salesman with the Larkin Soup Company, and a popular evangelical theologian, said this, " We are punished by our sins, not for them."

The waiting father is desperate for a sign of a long-missed loved one. He sits at the window. He waits at the end of the driveway. The father is a man with a generous heart and a gracious spirit. He prays to live into grace as exhibited by God, "I give because I love. I give because I trust. I give because I can give. I am generous because I am generous. I am thankful so I give."

Victor Hugo wrote, "When grace is joined with wrinkles, it is adorable. There is unspeakable dawn in happy old age."

The angry son is hardworking and diligent, but is resentful of the love shared equally and freely by the father of the two brothers. The angry son, disgusted at the wastefulness of his brother, has done everything right. He loves based on merit. He shares his love and concern with people who have earned it. He prayed his truth: "I have followed the established rules. I understand the boundaries. I have lived and am living within the parameters set down by the law. I have obeyed all the expectations of me."

But all of this "righteous living" has filled him with anger and resentment. Resentment narrows focus. Resentment invites us to focus on self often at the cost of the humanity of another. Resentment helps us to lose ourselves, forget who we are, where we come from or even what we stand for. Resentment closes doors and locks us in a chamber with no windows and no doors.

From where is my help to come?

Anne Lamott says, "I do not at all understand the mystery of grace —only that it meets us where we are but does not leave us where it found us."

For me to begin to understand grace, I must repent and turn and face God. By facing God from within the totality of who we are, we can get a glimpse of how grace works.

I have a hard time understanding grace.

Jay Bakker, an inspirational evangelical and congregational leader, has taught me some things about grace. In his book, *Fall to Grace: A Revolution of God, Self & Society,* Bakker approaches the powers of grace through God's overwhelming generosity.

Jay Bakker lives in Brooklyn, where he is co-pastor of Revolution Church, a church that meets in a bar and has a nationwide online following. He speaks to congregations and other groups all over the country about faith, grace, and his experiences with the underside of life and Christianity.

Jay Bakker is the son of Jim and Tammy Faye Bakker. Jim and Tammy Faye Bakker were hugely successful televangelists on the PTL Network. PTL stands for "Praise the Lord." They rose to fame and power in the late 1980s appealing to their nationwide living room congregation to support their quest to build a religious theme park based on a time-share model. Through seedy backroom transactions, and tactics pushing through and beyond blackmail, revelations of accounting fraud led to prison time.

When speaking of the Parable of the Prodigal Son, Jay Bakker points out that "The mistake of the prodigal son is that he thinks he squandered his father's love along with his inheritance through his bad behavior. It's not like he's repenting out of genuine regret. He's crawling back because he is hungry. The good son's mistake, by contrast, is that he gets so caught up in his own good works and deeds, in his self-righteousness, that he thinks he has earned his father's love and inheritance. Grace is all about acceptance. By accepting grace, we accept God, we accept ourselves, we accept each other."

As a person struggling to understand grace, acceptance is a good place to start. I must accept who I am and turn around and look at God face-to-face. Who and what have I accepted? Who and what have I rejected? And why?

As I pray to God to understand the "why," and as I pray to God to understand the "how," it is somewhere in that struggle, in my inability to answer, that I get a brief glimpse of what grace is all about.

When we are in relationship with God and with each other, we can truly redeem the wrong. We have the courage to confess our sins. We can embrace the truth and with God's help and with the help of God's people, we can learn to accept and to recognize God's grace.

We usually learn to demand our rights before we learn to value our relationships. This is why grace is so difficult to understand Is there anything I need to do? There must be something.

Meister Eckhart once said, "If the only prayer you ever say in your entire life is 'thank you,' it will be enough."

THE E-TICKET

Repentance is about the U-turn. We have made a judgment and have decided to act upon that judgment. When we truly repent, we turn back towards God to accept responsibility for our actions. God is waiting for us at the turn-around lane. That is grace. We are changed.

Jean-Paul Sartre, in his classic existential book *Nausea*, observes, "But I must finally realize that I am subject to these sudden transformations. The thing is that I rarely think; a crowd of small metamorphoses accumulate in me without my noticing it, and then, one fine day, a veritable revolution takes place."

It is difficult to define repentance. It is an action that involves change and relationship. We need relationships to understand God, to understand the other, and to understand self.

Take a few minutes to reflect upon what you believe repentance is, then turn to the "Holy Story" section of your journal.

You are going to move through a

repentance brainstorm.

Set a timer for one minute. When you begin the timer, write down as many words as possible that come to mind about what you believe repentance is. Be quick. Try not to think too much. But think enough so that you actually get some words written down on the paper!

When the timer goes off, stop writing. Sit in silence for a moment. Then slowly read over the words you have written.

After a brief amount of time, set the timer again for one minute. When you begin the timer, quickly jot down times in you life when you feel you have repented. Use key words that trigger the incidents. Do not write the entire context.

When the timer goes off, sit in silence for a moment. Read over the key words and reflect on the incidents you have recorded. Then, let's consider one of the incidents that still has some energy around it.

In the "Holy Story" section of your journal, write out the details of the incident. What was good about the incident? What went wrong? How did you feel and what did you think as you tried to turn things around? What resources did you need to make a decision? What happened after you made the decision to turn back? Where did you receive grace? Where was grace given to you? How did repentance play out for you in this incident?

Next, consider if there is something that you still need to repent. If so, what is the context? What went wrong? What is holding you back? What do you need to do to repent and move on? If it involves other people, what do you think they need to do? What does God want you to do right now?

Finally, turn to the "Rule of Life" section of your journal. Reflect and write using the following formula.

REPENTANCE

Repentance is _____ .

When I repent, I _____ .

When I repent, God _____ .

After repentance, I believe _____ .

 # THE COLLECT

We have reflected on repentance. It is time to write a Collect.

Remember the parts of a Collect. Address God. Describe an action or several actions of God. Ask God for something. Why do you want God to do this? Thank God.

Record your new Collect in the "Holy Story" section of your journal.

✛

ENDNOTES

[1] (Wink, 1986, p. 87)

[2] (Hewitt, 1996, p. 442)

[3] (Volf, 2005, pp. 168-169)

[4] (Smith, 1985)

[5] (May & Metzger, 1973, p. NT 106-107)

RESURRECTION } *Where Is the Laughing Place?*

 ## MAIN GATE

"Nothing's impossible!" says the Doorknob in Disney's animated classic *Alice in Wonderland*. Tea parties are celebratory. What is discovered through the looking glass is dependent upon the context of what we have experienced and truly believe. The journey of faith is difficult, but there are clear signs while we fall through the mud, walk down the hall, get lost a little, and make our way through the narrow door to the tea party. Resurrection occurs after we work through theological truths. We were created by God. We mess up. We have a decision to make. The choice we have is to turn and face God and move into new life, or we can turn away from God and from God's people. The choice determines the destination and outcome. God opens the door, rolls away the stone at the tomb's entrance, and then invites us to jump beyond the clouds into the starlit heavens.

My personal life choices and experiences are given new contexts and new meanings when considered side-by-side with the promise of resurrection and new life. Life's journey, one of hits and misses, helps us to somewhat understand the power and love of that promise. "The story of redemption is like a great symphony that embraces all our errors, our bum notes, and in which beauty finally triumphs. The victory is not that God wipes out our wrong notes, or pretends that they never happened, but that God finds a place for them in the musical score that redeems them." [1]

God's love for the world is illustrated by the promise of new life in the midst of death. For those who have been touched by the power of redemption and resurrection, our work on Earth is to deliver ourselves and everyone else from this world of inequality, victimhood and destruction. What we do during every moment of our lives matters. All work, all play, times of leisure, moments of love, and even moments of hate, are filtered through promise - a promise that every bit of our souls and spirits will be made anew by the power of God. This is grace. This is the promise of resurrected life.

"I can't go back to yesterday because I was a different person then," says Alice through the pen of Lewis Carroll. Change happens. Minutes pass. Am I thankful or not? If I am thankful, how am I going to give thanks to God?

Jesus' response is simple. If you love me, take care of my people. When they hunger physically and spiritually, feed them. When they thirst for righteousness and justice, organize with others to quench these thirsts. When they suffer for loving, surround them with love. All it takes is all we have.

Our choice as people of God is quite simple. Make people free or create more victims. Since victimhood is something we can create and control, we often lament the culture of the victim.

We look at injustice and know it is not fair. We see victims of violence and pray for the dead. We see people homeless and hungry and feed the displaced. But we must do more. We must hold accountable the political and social systems which sustain victimhood.

We hold on to and claim the times when we have been made the victim. We seek out the victims in our world and we feel good when we can redeem the victim through liberal thoughts. But, to understand resurrection, we must do more than think about it. We must act. It is through acting together in intentional community that we begin to get a glimpse of power and of the promise of resurrection.

We are called to change the system. That is what Jesus did. Jesus loved the law. Jesus loved the temple. Jesus changed the laws and when our laws and institutions are creating victims, we are called to change them.

From *Alice's Adventures in Wonderland* by Lewis Carroll:

"But I don't want to go among mad people," Alice remarked.

"Oh, you can't help that," said the Cat, "we're all mad here. I'm mad. You're mad."

"How do you know I'm mad?" said Alice.

"You must be," said the Cat, "or you wouldn't have come here."

Catholic theologian James Alison, Anglican theologian and former Archbishop of Canterbury Rowan Williams, and Evangelical theologian Rob Bell have all implored us to remove victimization from the world. Our victim, the crucified LORD, will rise up, and break the chain of oppressor-victim by reaching out to the oppressor with open arms. From beyond the grave, our LORD and savior invites us to explore, to have a closer look, to come and see the goodness of the LORD beyond our narrow-mindedness. This is the path to loving God, loving self and loving neighbor as God loves us.

We are born into a world where distinctions exist based on race, class, nationality, religious beliefs and so on. Distinctions create human-made order and human-made comfort. Stereotypes are invented to support distinctions and to keep barriers in place. It is in response to individual needs that we create victims and hierarchies, which we believe will place us closer to God and keep others at a distance. But God travels to the outer regions, to those living on the edge, to the victims created by the lack of love and concern by others; God says I will love you and redeem you and give you power. But you must use your power, to bring everyone in from the margins. There are many rooms but only one house.

God entered the world through a young unwed woman. All the messages that surrounded her told her what was expected of her. But because of her belief in the power of God, she turned off the voices and said yes, going against everything she had been taught or led to believe. She was on the edge. She was misunderstood by her people. But she mattered to God. We all matter to God. No exceptions.

God with us in Jesus healed the sick, fed the poor and gave sight to the blind. We need the law so that we have a common language, a common understanding of how to live together. But we need God's grace to empower us to love as God loves us.

The world tells us that we are unworthy, incomplete, inadequate and even unlovable. But in the midst of a violent, destructive and often unforgiving world, Jesus on the cross called on God to forgive. God took Christ from the tomb of death and resurrected Him to new life, saying humankind can continue to kill and destroy, but I love you and can save you. Love as I love. God's love is good news for me, for you, and good news for all people.

All love makes sense within the context of the resurrection. God calls us to love God, love self and love neighbor. We must create communities to transform in the name of love. Dr. Martin Luther King, Jr. said, "Injustice anywhere is a threat to justice everywhere. We are caught in an inescapable network of mutuality, tied in a single garment of destiny. Whatever affects one directly affects all indirectly."

Resurrection does not happen in a vacuum. New life is not instantaneous. It is a journey, a process with God, and a walk done with others. We cannot walk it alone. What God promises is that death is not the answer. Evil does not overcome good. Love wins. We want to touch and see and confirm and believe. "My Lord and my God."

When we proclaim resurrection, even if we cannot understand it, grasp it, or sometimes through periods of doubt, believe it, we take on the redemptive work of God. This means we are willing to feed the hungry, heal the sick, care for the neighbor, support the poor in spirit and deliver the people of God. If we do not care for ALL of God's people, we have not accepted the Good News. If we do not love ALL of God's people, we do not believe in the teachings of Jesus. If we do not feed ALL of God's people, we have rejected the blessings of God given so freely to us.

Resurrection is a call to wake up, regroup, reassess and react. What am I willing to do to give thanks to God?

From *Alice's Adventures in Wonderland* by James Carroll:

"Would you tell me, please, which way I ought to go from here?"

"That depends a good deal on where you want to get to."

"I don't much care where –"

"Then it doesn't matter which way you go."

Through the resurrected Christ, God has shown us where we are going. Do you believe it? If you do, then live and work and play like it matters.

IN THE QUEUE

Our personal experiences inform our beliefs and attitudes about the faith journey. We live. Something happens. We have choices to make. Things get better or worse.

The resurrection of Jesus Christ assures us that God redeems and gives new life. Often, we do not see this or the outcome was not what we had hoped for or expected, so we move forward, disappointed.

While we walk "In the Queue," we are going to take some time to recall, to remember and to recognize redemptive experiences that we may have overlooked or may not have given God thanks for.

Jesus' Sermon on the Mount is probably one of the most easily recognizable Gospel passages. What Jesus proclaims are beatitudes. *Beatitude* comes from a Latin word that means "fortunate," "blissful" or "happy." You are going to reflect upon your life experiences through the promises of the Beatitudes.

Take a moment. Claim some space. Center yourself. Then read Jesus's Sermon on the Mount from the Gospel of Mathew.

MATTHEW 5:1-12

When Jesus saw the crowds, he went up the mountain; and after he sat down, his disciples came to him. Then he began to speak, and taught them, saying:

"Blessed are the poor in spirit, for theirs is the kingdom of heaven.

"Blessed are those who mourn, for they will be comforted.

"Blessed are the meek, for they will inherit the earth.

"Blessed are those who hunger and thirst for righteousness, for they will be filled.

"Blessed are the merciful, for they will receive mercy.

"Blessed are the pure in heart, for they will see God.

"Blessed are the peacemakers, for they will be called children of God.

"Blessed are those who are persecuted for righteousness' sake, for theirs is the kingdom of heaven.

"Blessed are you when people revile you and persecute you and utter all kinds of evil against you falsely on my account. Rejoice and be glad, for your reward is great in heaven, for in the same way they persecuted the prophets who were before you." [2]

Take a moment. Sit in silence. Then read the passage again slowly. What does the passage seem to say about your life experiences?

Turn to the "Holy Story" section of your journal. On the top of the page, write "When I Was Redeemed."

In order to get an understanding of how God is working in your life, you are going to take some time to claim redemptive experiences in your life. You will use the Beatitudes to provide stepping stones through this meditation.

Recall a time when you have felt "poor in spirit." Write down the circumstance. What was the context? Did that feeling change? If yes, what caused it to change? If not, what needs to happen so you no longer feel poor in spirit?

Recall those in your life whom you have loved and who have died. Write down words or phrases that express how you felt about them during life. What do you miss? What is your hope for them and for you? What does God want for you? What does God want for the persons you miss?

What injustices in the world do you witness and see and experience? Who are the victims? Who are creating victims with the choices they make? Recall a time when you have felt you were treated unfairly. What happened? Was the circumstance redeemed? If yes, what happened? If no, what does God need to do to redeem it? What do you need from God to know that redemption has come to this circumstance?

What does mercy mean to you? When have you been given mercy? When have you granted mercy? What do you need right now?

When have you found peace in your life? Think of the times. Write them down. Where is peace needed in the world?

Recall a time when you have been persecuted by someone else for who you are and what you believe. What was the context of this experience? Have you ever persecuted others because of who they are or because of what they believe? Has anything changed to cause you to think and act differently?

How do people react when they discover that you are on a journey of faith? Have people questioned your integrity or your state of mind?

During this time, have you noticed any redemptive acts in past instances that you felt were unredeemable?

FROM THE BOOK
Ezekiel 37:1-14

The prophet Ezekiel spoke to the people of Israel during a time of exile, six hundred years before the birth of Christ. Like most prophets encountered throughout the Hebrew Scriptures, Ezekiel was a bit of a personality. Some might describe him as a mystic. Others might describe him as a voodoo priest. Author William Burroughs would probably call him a junky. Ezekiel spoke from a realm beyond the grasp of many of us through dreams, visions and trances.

Ezekiel believed in a living, powerful God. He was afraid that the people he lived amongst were asleep, "out to lunch," and unaware of the miraculous things going on around them.

His call was prophetic. Wake it. See reality. Discover God. Make yourself ready. Do the work that God is demanding you to do. If you are courageous enough to accept this work, you will discover new life. According to Ezekiel, the good and the bad news about all of this is that God will be with you always. Live and act like that matters to you.

Ezekiel proclaims that we are responsible for our actions or lack thereof. In a culture that encourages blame of the other over and above accepting the responsibility of one's actions, the prophetic message was not and is not a popular one. Faithful communities are where we experience God and where God's reconciling power can be felt, manifested and transformative.

As blunt and frightening and mystical and overwhelming as Ezekiel's message is, in the midst of it all, in spite of the mess, "The Lord is There."

Ezekiel 37: 1 – 14
The Valley of Dry Bones

The hand of the Lord came upon me, and he brought me out by the spirit of the Lord and set me down in the middle of a valley; it was full of bones. He led me all around them; there were very many lying in the valley, and they were very dry. He said to me, "Mortal, can these bones live?" I answered, "O Lord God, you know." Then he said to me, "Prophesy to these bones, and say to them: O dry bones, hear the word of the Lord. Thus says the Lord God to these bones: I will cause breath to enter you, and you shall live. I will lay sinews on you, and will cause flesh to come upon you, and cover you with skin, and put breath in you, and you shall live; and you shall know that I am the Lord."

So I prophesied as I had been commanded; and as I prophesied, suddenly there was a noise, a rattling, and the bones came together, bone to its bone. I looked, and there were sinews on them, and flesh had come upon them, and skin had covered them; but there was no breath in them. Then he said to me, "Prophesy to the breath, prophesy, mortal, and say to the breath: Thus says the Lord God: Come from the four winds, O breath, and breathe upon these slain, that they may live." I prophesied as he commanded me, and the breath came into them, and they lived, and stood on their feet, a vast multitude.

Then he said to me, "Mortal, these bones are the whole house of Israel. They say, 'Our bones are dried up, and our hope is lost; we are cut off completely.' Therefore prophesy, and say to them, Thus says the Lord God: I am going to open your graves, and bring you up from your graves, O my people; and I will bring you back to the land of Israel. And you shall know that I am the Lord, when I open your graves, and bring you up from your graves, O my people, I will put my spirit within you, and you shall live, and I will place you on your own soil; then you shall know that I, the Lord, have spoken and will act," says the Lord. [3]

RIDE THE ATTRACTION
Splash Mountain

Splash Mountain is a delightful journey through unexpected twists and turns, climaxing with a plunge into the Briar Patch, and then immediately followed by celebration of new life. It debuted in Frontierland in 1992 and "is based on the 1946 Disney film *Song of the South*, which in turn was based on characters created by Joel Chandler Harris. That movie, with its mix of live action and animation, related the stories of Br'er Rabbit and Br'er Fox as told by Uncle Remus." [4]

Splash Mountain invites us to move through the Laughing Place, a place of mischief, of carefree days, of comedy, of danger and of community, into what is real. But, in order to get there, we have to leave our comfort zone, have faith, get into a log, and let the current take us where it may.

Song of the South takes place after the Civil War during the Reconstructionist Era. Racism, classism and inequality have stolen the identity of the characters in the film. Where is home? What happens when I leave? How do I overcome what has happened to me? If the only home I know is oppressive and abusive, how do I create a new identity for myself? Because of the film's racist undertones, it is a hard film to watch and discuss. Disney has not released *Song of the South* in the United States through popular media channels. In spite of this, "the film had three of the key ingredients that Imagineers looked for in potential them park attraction: beloved and colorful characters in Br'er Rabbit, Br'er Fox, and Br'er Bear; lush, richly detailed settings, from Br'er Fox's lair high atop Chick-a-pin Hill to the thorny bowels of the briar patch; and memorable music that included the Academy Award-winning "Zip-A-Dee-Doo-Dah."[5]

From the outside, the scope of the ride is deceiving. Guests watch logs plunge from the top of *Splash Mountain* into the Briar Patch, round a curve and then disappear towards the back of the mountain. However, the journey to the plunge is complex, mysterious and exciting. Like the journey of faith, *Splash Mountain* invites us to step from Point A to Point B, to step and turn away from what we know and love, in hopes of being transformed into something else.

Once we board our floating log, we begin to make a slow ascent to the top of the mountain. We round the bend and find ourselves on the outskirts of the Briar Patch where we get a bird's-eye view of other logs making the 50-foot plunge down the side of the mountain. We move beyond the patch, further up the mountain, floating through a birdhouse village perched on the side of *Splash Mountain*.

Just below a rickety mountain bridge, we make our first plunge into the world of Br'er Rabbit. Frogs and birds welcome us, singing, "How do you do? Mighty pleasant greeting. How do you do? Say it when you're meeting. How do you do? With every one repeating, pretty good, sure as you're born."

Br'er Rabbit's home is beautiful. The color is vibrant and the mood is festive. He sings platitudes to entertain us as we prepare for our journey. "What goes up is sure to come down. A penny lost is a penny found. How do you do? Fine. How are you? How you come on? Pretty good sure as you're born. And here's a hearty back of a little bit of this and a little bit of that. Stop jumping around! You'll run out of breath! Why don't you sit back and calm yourself? You can hurry on now if you must. We'll do what we like because that suits us!"

But Br'er Rabbit is looking to get out and see the world. Br'er Rabbit sings, "I'm looking for a little bit more adventure. He's heading for a little bit of fun now. I'm hoping for a little more excitement. Time to be moving along."

A baby rabbit sweeps her steps and she notices that Br'er Fox has tied up Br'er Bear at a tree just around the bend. As Bear tries to get out, we hear a warning: "Hey, Br'er Rabbit, you better mend your ways. Yep. He's making his way to the Laughing Place. Time to be turning around."

But Br'er Rabbit hops on past us, beckoning us to move into the Laughing Place. We move past celebratory frogs, carefully hung lanterns at Porky Pine and beyond Br'er Rabbit and Br'er Fox trying to retrieve honey from a bee-infested tree. "Boy, are we in luck! We're visiting a laughing place! Hee hee hoo ha hoo hoo! Everybody's got a laughing place, a laughing place to go. Take a frown, turn it upside down and you'll find yours, we know. Honey and rainbows on our way where everyone is worth his weight! Boy are we in luck! We're visiting a laughing place! Everybody's got a laughing place to go. Come on in, give us all a grin and you'll find yours, I know. Laughing has always been our game. Honey fun is what we bring. Boy, are we in luck! Take a frown. Turn it upside down! And you'll find yours, we say we think."

We plunge past the swarming bees into a laughing place of dancing waters and flowing waterfalls. Br'er Rabbit jokes that all of the bees in the laughing place are going to give us hives. Singing frogs delightfully taunt us as we pass signs that warn us of danger ahead. The celebratory music disappears and we find ourselves in a dark place.

The only light we can see appears to be a stream of heavenly light up ahead past the heavens. But how do we get there?

Two crows suddenly appear above us, perched on a tree branch. They seem to delight in our dilemma of doom. They say to us as our log starts the long journey to the top, "Time to be turning around. If only you could. If you finally found your laughing place, how come you're not laughing? Everybody's got a laughing place. Maybe this one is yours!"

The log ascends in darkness toward the light. It seems as if we are climbing and climbing and climbing some more. Then, we find ourselves at the top.

In the midst of terror, we get a quick glimpse of Cinderella's Castle and then we take the final plunge - the fifty foot drop past the laughing place into the Briar Patch. But this is not the end.

Our log moves beyond the Briar Patch, down a small ravine and into a festive celebration. We have been delivered and everybody gathers to celebrate. Just above us is a sign that says, "Welcome home, Br'er Rabbit" and we move into the party.

On the riverboat, everyone sings, "Zip-a-dee-doo-dah, zip-a-dee-ay. My, oh my, what a wonderful day! Plenty of sunshine heading my way! Zip-a-dee-doo-dah, zip-a-dee-ay. Mister Bluebird on my shoulder. It's the truth. It's actch'll. Ev'rything is satisfactch'll. Zip-a-dee-doo-dah, zip-a-dee-ay. Wonderful feeling, wonderful day!"

We pass the celebration and Br'er Rabbit relaxes in his home. He sings, "Home sweet home is the lesson today. I'm through with moving on now. The Briar Patch is where I was born and the Briar Patch is where I'll stay! I'm back in my home now and I'm sure going to stay. Don't you worry, Mr. Bluebird. I've learned my lesson. Mr. Bluebird on my shoulder. It's the truth. It's actual. Everything is satisfactual. Wonderful feeling. Wonderful day."

FOR REFLECTION

Do we miss resurrection? Is resurrection so common, so familiar, so "happening all the time" that we walk right past it, not even noticing it? Can we take resurrection for granted?

Things around us are constantly shifting and changing, dying and disappearing and then transforming into something else. Is it possible for us to walk right past resurrection without giving it second notice? Do we take resurrection for granted?

The prophet Ezekiel, speaking to the people when they felt they were abandoned by God, proclaimed that God was always faithful and working in the world even when we are not.

Can God leave things unredeemed? Is it possible for God to ignore the cries and suffering of the people, leaving them bewildered in the middle of the valley in a heap of dry bones?

For those of us who have stood in the valley of dry bones, we know there are times when only God knows.

My first trip back to New Orleans, after the levees failed, following the landfall of Hurricane Katrina, was to gut my mother's house. It was just over a month after the storm had passed and just over three days after the water had been drained from my mother's neighborhood. The air was heavy, and sadness and death moved around the streets and neighborhoods just as freely as the humidity.

My mother had four feet of water in her home and everything on the first floor, just about everything of sentimental value, was soaking in a state of decaying muck. Nothing looked familiar.

My colleagues and I from the Youth Outreach Team of The Night Ministry, an agency serving homeless youth residing on the streets in the city of Chicago, traveled to New Orleans to begin the work of mucking out and gutting my mom's house. I did not know much about gutting back then. None of us knew what we were doing. But we knew that everything had to go.

Five of us worked removing the contents, scraping out mud, dismantling and discarding appliances and electronics, knocking down walls and pulling out wet Sheetrock. Four days later, it was done. All had been cleared out.

I remember the day we left my mom's neighborhood. Homes were all buried behind piles of debris. Life no longer existed. All was dead or hidden parked on the curb or beyond our view, covered, looking like bombed-out Beirut, buried in dust, white powder. We left the neighborhood wondering what was next. Would life ever exist on these streets again?

I thought about the words of Ezekiel, the conversation the prophet had with God. God asked Ezekiel, "Mortal, can these dry bones live?" Ezekiel, not knowing what to say, said that only God knew the answer to that.

At All Saints' Chicago, a church just north of Wrigley Field, people were coming together.

Congregations were organizing and building partnerships with others.

Two months later, I returned to New Orleans with a crew of Episcopalians from Chicago. But I have to admit I was a little apprehensive. I wanted to show off the city that I loved but I did not know what was going to be there when I returned. I felt like the city that care forgot was now a heap of dry bones in Ezekiel's valley.

But people who thought new life was possible came together. We are all related and there was work that needed to be done. We began to muck out and gut houses. During our free time, we toured the city to see the extent of the damage. I had not done that when I had come down to begin the work on my mom's house. There was not time.

Pictures and all the video coverage in the world did not capture the extent of the devastation. Communities along the Gulf of Mexico in Mississippi were literally dragged into the water. Nothing remained. Most of New Orleans was underwater and had remained that way until the city was able to pump it out, almost two months later.

In the lower ninth ward, houses were piled up on top of cars. The majority of houses had been shoved off their foundations and had been pushed down the block, crashing and smashing everything between here and there.

In the middle of a neighborhood pile of rubble was a church. It was locked up and the smell coming from inside was incredibly putrid. From our vantage point on the street, there was nothing but water-tossed mayhem inside. We could not go in.

Outside, next to the church's door, was a handwritten sign. It contained a quote from Ezekiel 37:1. "The Lord set me down in the middle of a valley; it was full of bones. Can these bones live?" The sign captured the resurrection doubt all of us encounter when we encounter the power of death.

Death interrupts the routine, throws us out of the comfortable and then deposits us into a pile full of doubt, fear, and anxiety.

For those of us from Chicago, the valley of dry bones became a question, a scriptural entryway into the New Orleans we were encountering, a question of resurrection hope for our trip.

We gutted. We mucked out. We cooked our meals. We talked to people. We were invited into the sacred spaces of people's lives. We talked about life in the middle of death. We wondered where the hope was and questioned if there would be life on the other side.

During a break from our work, I returned to my mother's neighborhood to see that all of the garbage had been removed. Sitting within the frame of my mother's gutted house, there was a pile drywall stacked on the concrete slab. The wood frame was being treated and the smell I remembered from two months before was not as prevalent. It looked like people were working in the homes but it was obvious that nobody was living there.

We returned to Chicago and told people the story. We asked people to pray about joining in on the work and to pray about the recovery of New Orleans and the central gulf coast.

During Advent of the following year, we returned. We had more people with us. We were grateful to be back. The worked continued. We mucked out. We gutted. But on that trip, we also primed and painted a house that had been gutted, treated, raised, and was nearly ready for the homeowner to move back in. Can these bones live?

We visited the lower ninth. For the most part, the houses and debris had been completely removed. There was a lot of green space, and nature had begun to settle in. Where were all the people who had lived there? Would they come back? These were property owners. There had been communities there. Would they return to build a new community?

The Ezekiel church was open. We went inside. The church had been gutted. Sunlight streamed in from the windows and open doors. It was a wide-open space. On the steps, at the entrance of the church, someone had built a small memorial, using plates and dishes and water, commemorating those who had died in the neighborhood.

Just inside the church on the left, there was a striking piece of artwork of John the Baptist baptizing Jesus in the Jordan.

As our relief team mucked out and gutted and did the work of restoring what had been, we were thrilled to hammer in drywall, prime and paint more houses, visit a music club and eat at a restaurant that had recently reopened. We were overwhelmed by the possibility and promise of new life. We could not take it all in.

The city was greener. People were laughing. Music was returning to the streets. Stores were beginning to open. Restaurants once again had food and walk-in refrigerators. There seemed to be new life just beyond death.

We continued to return. Building. Painting. Hearing more stories. Claiming our place in the story. Through our trips together to New Orleans, we could truly see and track resurrection. We saw dry bones being raised and made anew.

In the middle of life, as we move about in our comfort zones, as we re-establish our daily routines, do we fail to notice the presence of God through multiple resurrections?

Sometimes, it is only when our life has been thrown totally out of whack, when routine has been totally removed, when the world as we know it is totally destroyed, that we begin to seek out and notice the resurrection in our lives.

When the resurrected Christ stood in front of Thomas, and Thomas was able to place his finger in the holes of Christ's hands, and feel the piercing in Christ's side, Thomas was finally able to exclaim, "Lord, I believe."

Community helps us to notice resurrection. Story reminds us where we have been. Proclamation helps us claim as sacred the times when we have sinned. Neighbors and friends and family remind us of our faith journey when our faith is lacking. We gather in community and call on God to be known to us in the simple and through the ordinary. Within the spirit of God there is nothing simple and ordinary about any of this. All of it matters. All of it can be redeemed. All of it will be resurrected and given new life.

For me, returning to New Orleans is returning to something new and familiar. Katrina killed aspects of that. But through the gracious hearts of many people and through the power of God, a valley of bones can stand up, reconstitute and get life.

As I drive into New Orleans, changing the music from Sirius XM to WWOZ, I notice all the blue flags with the fleur de lis and the powerful words, "Rebuild, Renew, Rebirth."

I cannot help but wonder, is it possible that resurrection is happening all the time and we do not even notice it?

 # THE E-TICKET

In order to recognize the redemptive work of God in our lives, we must take a moment, look around, see what was and is and is to come, notice it, and then proclaim it. We need to learn, understand and share a language that empowers us to describe the redemptive work of God in our lives. This is the work of theology. In Steven Spielberg's brilliant film *Close Encounters of the Third Kind*, music became the shared language of people from very different cultures, contexts and backgrounds.

As we move through life, we want to know how to live and how to respond to God and God's people in faithful, meaningful ways. When we speak to others, we encourage others wherever they are on their journey and we are inspired by others to continue moving forward on ours. How do we share our experiences of God so that we can do the work that God has given us to do?

The School of Theology of the University of the South has a theological program called Education for Ministry (EfM). The program is a four-year journey that utilizes theological reflection to make connections with scripture, tradition, history and theology. By studying holy scripture, by understanding the passions and desires of theologians throughout all time, and through empowering us to examine how our personal experience inform our beliefs, the EfM program teachers that we all live through a Doctrine of Humanity.

The Doctrine of Humanity is a journey of faith. The Doctrine of Humanity begins by defining the created world we live in. What is the world like? Then we are asked to contemplate what goes wrong in that world. We move past sin into judgment. In judgment, when we encounter an "a-ha" moment, we realize how we have participated in the sin of the world. Then we have a choice to make. If we choose to respond to God's call and hope for us, we turn back toward the created world, repenting, with a new awareness of how the world works. By placing ourselves before God with this new awareness, we are redeemed. The Doctrine of Humanity is creation, sin, judgment, repentance and redemption.

Disney's *Splash Mountain* is an excellent attraction to map out the Doctrine of Humanity. If you are using this guide while visiting the Walt Disney World Resort, ride *Splash Mountain*. After you have experienced the attraction find a place to sit and ask yourself the following questions:

What kind of world is the world of *Splash Mountain* (creation)?

What goes wrong in this world (sin)?

What changes your view of this world (judgment)?

What changes (repentance)?

What is there to celebrate (redemption)?

After you have spent some time meditating on the ride, take a moment to examine some significant moments in your life. In EfM, we call them stepping stones, events that shaped who we are as people of God. Write about these five moments. Then apply the Doctrine of Humanity to these five moments by answering the following questions about each moment - What is the world like? What went wrong? What was the "aha" moment? How did you journey back? How did you celebrate?

God holds out the reality of the resurrected Christ for us to live into, hope for, strive for and prepare for, so when we walk into it, we are as ready as we can be.

After you have spent some time doing this, turn to the "Rule of Life" section of our journal.

Write a rule about resurrection. Use the formula before.

RESURRECTION

Resurrection is _____ .

I have experienced resurrection in my life when _____ .

I have noticed resurrection when _____ .

I proclaim resurrection to others by _____ .

 THE COLLECT

Turn to the "Holy Story" part of your journal.

Gather your thoughts on resurrection. Think for a minute about things as they are created by God. What circumstances and life experiences separates them from God, forgetting who or what it was and who had created? When and what was a decision that needed to be made? What changed and turned things around? What part of that was transformed and brought to life?

You are going to write three Collects about redemption and resurrection.

First, write a Collect about the resurrection of Jesus. Address God. Identify God's relationship with Jesus. Name what God did through the life of Jesus. Write about what happened on the cross, in the tomb and through the resurrection. Give thanks.

For the second Collect, give thanks for the power of resurrection in your life. Address God. Recall a time when things were wrong. What did it feel like? What changed? Where did that change come from? What was new? How did it happen? Give thanks.

For the final Collect, ask God to grant new life to someone or something that died. What new life will God grant through the power of resurrection?

✠

ENDNOTES

[1] (Jones, 2005, p. 199)
[2] (May & Metzger, 1973, p. NT 6)
[3] (May & Metzger, 1973, p. OT 1,107-1,108)
[4] (Wright, Imagineers (Group), & Walt Disney Company., 2005, p. 56)
[5] (Surrell, 2007, p. 82)

NEW LIFE } *Where Am I Going?*

MAIN GATE

"It's the Circle of Life and it moves us all through despair and hope, through faith and love, until we find our place on the path unwinding, in the Circle of Life." The journey of faith is wonderfully summed up in Tim Rice's lyrics from Disney's *The Lion King*. At its essence, *The Lion King* is all about new life found within community. Community gives us context. Community gives us support. Community either builds us up in the spirit or takes us down in the name of principalities and powers. Community calls us out and ultimately helps us discern who we are supposed to be.

In *The Lion King*, Simba leaves his community where he is destined to be King, traveling beyond the margins, to where the forgotten and the outcasts struggle for existence. Within the struggle, two animals live within an existential response of "no worries." Others gather together to plot to overthrow the status quo because they are hungry.

Christian community calls us to be people of God, to focus on mission. This same community gives us the power to affect change. Many of us find Christian communities within traditional religious institutions. Others seek out non-traditional communities where intention is clearer and hearts of community members are more accessible, making it easier for all members of the community to build and maintain trust.

Vibrant communities repeatedly move through the cycle of being created. These communities must struggle with discovering how to move the mission forward while encountering many pitfalls, how to make decisions based on the community's vision, how to move forward to discover new opportunities on the other side of the struggle. If a community is not struggling, it is probably not living into its mission.

Communities have functional responsibilities. These are the elements that keep the community organized - bylaws, the upkeep of the gathering space, the accessibility of community meetings, the nuts and bolts of what is needed to for the community to work.

Communities have relational realities. Relationships are sometimes most difficult to establish, but it is within these relationships that the true work, the mission of the community gets acted upon. As Kennon Callahan, the talented pastor and church community researcher, reminds us, the modern institutional church is failing because it often focuses solely on the functional. We spend most of our time in meetings tending to the maintenance of buildings, dealing with property issues and unhappy neighbors, and addressing financial realities of the church. These discussions interfere with time that should be spent getting to know each other, developing our spiritual lives and building community to act upon the Gospel commission. The Gospel commission demands one resource – God's people. We need relationships to do the work God has given us to do.

Community reminds us who we are. Community sustains us in times of trouble. Community stabilizes us during times of change.

We all belong to several communities. We move from community to community to make sense of the context of our lives. We seek out community to affirm and to challenge what we believe in order to be motivated to act. We need community to hold ourselves accountable and to encourage us along the journey. Some of us find accountable community in a church congregation. Others find accountable community within a tight-knit group of friends.

Communities have been called different names throughout history. Gangs are "street communities." Every one of us is in a gang. We all have gang affiliation. During biblical times, gangs were called the tribes of Israel – like-minded people who gathered together for power, protection, a place to belong, and the worship of one God. Popular gangs today include political parties, religious denominations, such as the Episcopal Church, gyms, social clubs, fraternities or sororities, and even alumni organizations.

People of faith must build community wherever they are. Early followers of Christ met in small groups, sharing meals in remembrance of Jesus. These communities raised up leaders, helping to organize and to connect with similar communities of faith. As the politics of the empire and the mission of Church began to co-mingle, it became extremely difficult to separate one from the other. Holy persons who struggled with the dynamic relationship between politics and religion sought to be set apart, moving to the desert, residing in solitude in caves and makeshift huts. These desert mothers and fathers were sought out by the faithful who were trying to hear and to respond to the voice of God in noisy metropolises. Eventually, within the city itself, monastic communities emerged. Monasteries were made of a group of the religious who were set apart and who felt called to help God speak to citizens in the midst of the business of everyday city life. Julian of Norwich was a solitary monastic who lived in a hut attached to the city church. One window looked into the church at the sacramental presence at the altar. The other window looked out onto the city square, seeking presence of the holy and the sacred within the work of the day.

Members of monastic communities listened to hear and to respond to the voice of God through intentional disciplines. A Rule was established to organize the community and leadership emerged to help the community live into and respect the Rule. The Rule held the community accountable. The community focused on the mission of the monastery by adhering to the Rule and by being in relationship with the others who had taken on the vows of the community.

Many question the integrity of institutions because of the politics involved, but it is through the leveraging of these community relationships that the mission of the institution gets accomplished.

New monasticism has emerged to open the doors of the monastic life to people who are not necessarily set apart but are intentional in how they live within societal and institutional structures. In 1935, Dietrick Bonhoeffer wrote a letter to his brother suggesting that "the restoration of the church will surely come only from a new type of monasticism which has nothing in common with the old but a complete lack of compromise in a life lived in accordance with the Sermon on the Mount in the discipleship of Christ. I think it is time to gather people together to do this."

New monastic communities may live together in a house, develop a Rule and create a worship structure that honors its work and calls the community members to remember how God is working and present in everything they do. Some new monastic communities have a vision of sustaining the community for the long term. Other new monastic communities intentionally gather for a specified period of time, for a specific purpose, create a rule, listen to God, fulfill the mission and then disband.

Today, faithful people continue to set themselves apart, forming community, establishing rules and responsibilities to build trust, empowering the faithful to act upon the blessings of God. Rooted in the monastic movement, these God-seekers push community creators deeper and deeper into the culture we live in. Traditional monastic walls are replaced with houses, store fronts, mobile vans and hotel conference centers. These communities, like the monastic communities before them, are set apart and are intentional.

We can create vibrant communities anywhere. We should be creative in how, why, and for how long we will gather. God wants to be with us.

I suggest that a Disney Monastic is a person of faith who enters the theme park experience with the intention of discerning the voice of God at the place where dreams come true. At the Walt Disney World Resort, we join one of the largest gathered communities in the world. On that property, there are permanent communities: the employees who work there, the characters who entertain there, and the artists who create there. On that property, there are temporary communities. Guests who enter the gates of a particular theme park become a temporary intentional community. People who stay at one particular hotel or another become a temporary community. Even people who load onto a boat in the Seven Seas Lagoon, or bravely take a seat on a Dooms Buggy in the *Haunted Mansion*, or get welcomed aboard Monorail Red or get blasted off within a rocket ship at *Space Mountain* become

a temporary community. "There is a ceremonial, even ritual aspect, to any form of play in which the playtime and play space are clearly marked as separate and distant from everyday routine. Whether we go to a Disney park or a ball game, there is always the excitement of deciding to go and planning what to take and what to wear, the anticipation of arrival, and the pure pleasure of walking through the entrance with the intention to play." [1] During our shared experience, we become travelers on the journey. We are connected to others in ways we may not be aware of or even imagine.

Through this travel guide, I have invited you, the monastic, to claim intentional space, to pray, to engage scripture, to participate in the culture, and to reflect on your life experiences, all in hopes of helping you to discover what God is calling you to do. Then I hope you feel empowered to seek out others to create God-centered communities to get the work done.

Riding rides at Walt Disney World is purely functional. Taking time to be with others, to listen to what stories are being told, relating them to personal experiences and the experiences of others, then prayerfully discovering how our common experiences are similar and different from the situations handed down through Holy Scripture, just might inspire us to create God-centered communities to change the world.

God created us so that we could be in relationship with God. God came to us in Jesus Christ so that we could understand how to be in relationship with God and with God's people. The spirit came down in a fiery flame to give us the power to establish communities to open our eyes to see God's hand at work in the world.

As followers of a living God, we are called to create communities that teach us how to love and how to be holy. God meets us where we are. We are called to meet and greet each other wherever we are.

"When two are three are gathered in my name, I will be in the midst of them."

Whenever we choose to move through the Main Gate, we enter community. The gates we enter mark and identify the community we seek. Our intention as we pass through creates and captures the space for what we hope happens next. The journey never ends. We get on the ride. We experience the attraction that becomes part of our shared experience. We get off the ride. We walk past the queue with others waiting to get on and we find ourselves back in the fray. We have more decisions to make and many journeys to plan. Where am I going? We need God and we need each other to figure that out.

 IN THE QUEUE

What surrounds us gives our lives meaning. Communities provide context. Different communities allow us to see things from different vantage points. We need community to help us to see God and to determine what God wants us to do. People organize to get things done. Institutions emerge to keep the organization focused on its mission. Institutions fail when the relational aspect falls away and the community collective becomes focused on maintenance, survival and keeping it together without change. Communities need to identify shared passions over and over and over again. This keeps relationships strong and keeps the mission of the organization fresh and alive.

Throughout this spiritual guide, we have been examining the contexts of our lives, beginning with the heart of the matter and then praying to shed light on all that is around it. "In the early days of Disney Feature Animation, Walt and his animators instituted a technique of story development that would become a cornerstone of the process. Rather than work from a traditional screenplay, as would be done by live-action production, they worked from storyboards, a series of sequential sketches illustrating the flow of the action."[2] These sketches, when combined with others, provided context and meaning.

Lev Kuleshov was a Russian filmmaker who experimented with context and meaning. He believed that whatever surrounds an incident, whatever the context, gives it meaning. Shifting the context, by changing what surrounds the image itself, causes new meanings to emerge. The Kuleshov Effect proves that how we combine singular images into an organized whole provides context and meaning.

In the early days of filmmaking, filmmakers would set up a camera, point it at the action, and let things happen. The camera never moved. The action moved in and out and within this stable frame. Audiences would have the same vantage point throughout the film.

Lev Kuleshov believed that storytelling through film could be more powerful and compelling by moving the camera around and combining the images together. He said a film's story could be conveyed through editing by how shots were arranged and put together. To illustrate what he meant, Kuleshov made three short films and showed them to three separate audiences. He took his camera into an empty room and filmed a close-up of the expressionless face of a famous Russian matinee idol. The actor was just staring off into space. Then, he used the exact same shot of the actor's face in three separate films.

In the first film, he cut together a shot of a bowl of soup. Then, he edited it together with the shot of the matinee idol's expressionless face, cutting back to the shot of the bowl of soup. He showed this short film to an audience who thought the matinee idol was brilliant. They said it was obvious that the film was about a man who had not eaten for days - that his face portrayed starvation, hunger and a whetted appetite.

In the second film, Kuleshov took a shot of a little girl, dead in a coffin. He cut together the shot of the dead girl with the same shot of the matinee idol's expressionless face. He then cut back to the shot of the little dead girl. He showed this second film to another audience who thought the matinee idol was brilliant. It was obvious that the actor was in deep grief, that he lost his daughter in a freak accident and was on the verge of a nervous breakdown.

In the third film, Kuleshov took a shot of a little boy playing on a playground. He cut together the shot of the little boy playing on the playground with the shot of the matinee idol's expressionless face. He then cut back to the same shot of the little boy playing on the playground. He showed this third film to another audience who thought the actor was brilliant, saying that he was watching the little boy playing and was full of nostalgia, missing his youth, longing for days from the past.

Same face. Different context. Different meaning.

What surrounds us gives our life meaning.

When we forget our context, others provide it. This is the beauty of worship. This is the beauty of creative teams. This is the intentionality of monasticism. New monastics seek new meaning through intentional community.

Dr. Richard Chartres, Bishop of London, said this during his sermon for the Royal Wedding of Prince William to Catherine Middleton: "As the reality of God has faded from so many lives in the West, there's been a corresponding inflation of expectations that personal relations alone will supply meaning and happiness in life. This is too great a burden to our spouses and partners. We are all incomplete. We all need the love which is secure, rather than oppressive. We need mutual forgiveness in order to thrive. But as we move towards our partner in love, following the example of Jesus Christ, the Holy Spirit is quickened within us, which offers the best conditions where we overcome fear and division and incubate the coming world of the spirit whose fruits are love and joy and peace."

We need others to live into the life God created for us. Take a moment to reflect upon communities you are involved in. Then take a moment to reflect upon a community or communities that God may be calling you to join, create or build.

Turn to the "Holy Story" section of your journal.

List all the communities that you are involved in. Perhaps you will begin with spiritual communities. Then move to work communities. Make sure you consider your communities of friends. Then, list your communities of play. Conclude by listing any other communities that you are involved with.

Use the next few pages of the "Holy Story" section of your journal to examine each community individually. Write down what you believe is the mission of the community. Perhaps you are aware of a mission statement. If it is a community of friends, what is its mission? Next, what context does this community provide in your life? Is the community functional, relational or both? How is or is not the community intentional? How does the community respond to what you need? How does the community respond to what the people of God need? What keeps the community together?

Next, spend some time in silence. Think about your passions. Think about the people you know. Think about what is missing in your life. What do you dream of accomplishing?

Pray.

Then consider what God may be calling you to do. If you could build any type of community, what would it be? Make sure that your community is something you are passionate about. Make sure the opportunities for creativity and play are unlimited. What would be the mission of the community? What would it do? Who do you know that you would like to reach out to and build it? Who do you not know but think should be in this community? What would you do together? What would you hope to accomplish? What do you need to successfully build this community?

 ## FROM THE BOOK

Revelation 1:8

Revelation is a book for the imagination. Nowhere else in the Old or New Testaments combined do we get such sensory overload.

To early Christians, the Book of Revelation was a book of hope. It was a call to dispersed communities across the vast Roman Empire to come together in Christ, creating a new community, the kingdom of God.

The Book of Revelation is often used to scare people into submission by guilt and fear. But the writers intended to build community through love for the benefit of Christ's kingdom.

Church teaching attributes the writing of the Book of Revelation to the same writer of the Gospel of John. John's community, tossed aside by those they loved, examine relationships through dialogue, illustrate God's hope for God's people through imagery, such as the Vine, the Light or Salt of the Earth.

The descriptions within Revelation could be used to describe some of Walt Disney World's most beloved attractions.

"After this I looked, and there was a great multitude that no one could count, from every nation, from all tribes and peoples and languages, standing before the throne and before the Lamb, robed in white, with palm branches in their hands. They cried out in a loud voice, saying,

'Salvation belongs to our God who is seated on the throne, and to the Lamb!'

And all the angels stood around the throne and around the elders and the four living creatures, and they fell on their faces before the throne and worshiped God, singing,

'Amen! Blessing and glory and wisdom and thanksgiving and honor and power and might be to our God forever and ever! Amen.'

Then one of the elders addressed me, saying, 'Who are these, robed in white, and where have they come from?' I said to him, 'Sir, you are the one that knows.' Then he said to me, 'These are they who have come out of the great ordeal; they have washed their robes and made them white in the blood of the Lamb.

For this reason they are before the throne of God, and worship him day and night within his temple, and the one who is seated on the throne will shelter them.

They will hunger no more, and thirst no more; the sun will not strike them, nor any scorching heat; for the Lamb at the center of the throne will be their shepherd, and he will guide them to springs of the water of life, and God will wipe away every tear from their eyes.'"[3] This passage could describe part of the journey through *It's a Small World*.

"For three and a half days members of the peoples and tribes and languages and nations will gaze at their dead bodies and refuse to let them be placed in a tomb; and the inhabitants of the earth will gloat over them and celebrate and exchange presents, because these two prophets had been a torment to the inhabitants of the earth."[4] This passage could capture the sensation of riding the

Doom Buggy through the graveyard in the *Haunted Mansion*.

"'See, I am making all things new.' Also he said, 'Write this, for these words are trustworthy and true.' Then he said to me, 'It is done! I am the Alpha and the Omega, the beginning and the end. To the thirsty I will give water as a gift from the spring of the water of life. Those who conquer will inherit these things, and I will be their God and they will be my children."[5] This could be a summary of the popular end-of-the-night show Fantasmic! All of these rides celebrate community beyond the realm of the imagination in the same way that the Book of Revelation calls us into community with God through Christ and through each other.

The writers of Revelation rejoice extolling, "See, the home of God is among mortals. God will dwell with them and their God; and they will be God's peoples, and God will be with them; wiping away every tear from their eyes." [6]

Revelation 1:8

"I am the Alpha and the Omega," says the Lord God, who is and who was and who is to come, the Almighty. [7]

RIDE THE ATTRACTION
Horizons

When Walt Disney imagined the Disney World Resort, he was most excited about EPCOT - the Experimental Prototype Community of Tomorrow. At EPCOT, guests would reside for extended periods of time, creating a temporary community of Imagineers. Their task was to use their imaginations to push technology to the limits in hopes of creating sustainable, enjoyable life here on Earth, in space, to infinity and beyond.

The Walt Disney World Resort promises to inspire us to dream, to reach out to each other, and to leave a legacy. The EPCOT Walt Disney envisioned has evolved into Epcot, a remarkable theme park with the Future World and World Showcase. In Future World, just beyond Spaceship Earth, was once a pavilion called *Horizons*. This attraction invited people around the world to remember where we came from and to ponder and claim the science and technology of the present, so that we could imagine the cities of tomorrow.

Upon entering the pavilion, we were surrounded by voices inviting us to dream and do. The voices sang, "If we can dream it, then we can do it. Yes we can! Have you ever looked beyond today into the future picturing a world we have yet to see? The wonder of finding new ways that lead to the promise of brighter days.

"Have you ever dreamed the dreams of the children? Just imagine the magic their minds can see. Horizons, all shining and new. Horizons, where dreams do come true. And it will be a future built with care for you and me. A world we all can share. For today holds the challenge to make this world a better place to be. New Horizons for you and for me If we can dream it, then we can do it...."

The Director of Music for Walt Disney Imagineering, George Wilkins, wrote the delightful words and music for the Horizons Pavilion. The Horizons Pavilion dared us to dream of underwater cities, communities in the desert and sustainable life out in space.

For those who loved the vast expanse of the ocean, the city of Sea Castle beckoned. "Sea Castle, the newest and most exciting floating city in the Pacific, invites you and your family to come away with us to the sea. Convenient daily departures by Seatrain and Skylift."

Deserts have always been expanses of space and possibility. For those called to the desert, Mesa Verde would be the ultimate destination.

"Mesa Verde, the most advanced desert reclamation complex in the western hemisphere, invites you to explore its wide range of career possibilities. Mag-lev express service to Mesa Verde leaves every thirty minutes."

If we wanted to defy gravity and explore the deep recesses of space, Brava Centauri awaited. "Brava Centauri, newest of the exciting Centauri series of space stations, offers remarkably rewarding opportunities in Earth- support vocations. Come up to Brava. Space shuttles depart daily."

A vehicle was pulled around to take us deeper into the pavilion. "People have been dreaming about the future for centuries." First, we journeyed to the past to remember how yesterday's artists and visionaries thought today's and tomorrow's worlds would look like. We have a dream and follow it. That is the start. We follow that dream with mind and heart until it becomes a reality. Tomorrow promises to be great and beautiful.

Our vehicle moved around a corner and we found ourselves in the present moment. "With what we know and what we're learning to do, we really can bring our dreams to life. It takes a lot of work, but the truth is, if we can dream it, we can do it. Tomorrow's horizons are here, today!

"Crystals. Inspired by nature, now engineered by man for an ever growing role in micro-electronics.

"The world of liquid space. Oceans of minerals and food ready to fuel tomorrow's needs. What you've just seen are the building blocks for the future up ahead. And while it may look fantastic, remember: it's all possible.

"The DNA chain - life's molecular blueprint. Decoding its secrets is leading us to dramatically improved health.

"The sun. Today we're learning ways to harness its limitless energy.

"Colonies in space. Habitats where people live and work. This is no distant dream, we're at the threshold now.

"A computerized view of earth - Landsat photography providing vital data on agriculture, resources, and ecological concerns.

"The cityscape. A living tribute to our richest resource - people.

"Here's a new kind of cityscape - the microprocessor. An entire computer on a tiny silicon chip."

These are the building blocks of the future which were just ahead. The car turned another corner and we got to visit the cities of tomorrow. "One of the nice things about traveling into the future is that the journey's just beginning. If we can dream it, we really can do it. And that's the most exciting part."

Horizons' inspiring vision of the future began to collapse on its own weight. The pavilion was rapidly deteriorating and eventually needed to be dismantled. *Horizons* was replaced by *Mission: Space.*

Of all the imaginative pavilions and enchanting foreign lands encountered at EPCOT, the *Horizons* Pavilion seemed to encompass Walt Disney's dreams for EPCOT and for the vision of the Walt Disney World Resort.

FOR REFLECTION

The conversation began with a simple supper. We were underground, in an old fall-out shelter, left over from World War II, built when the Japanese invaded China, bombing and killing everyone and everything in their path. This leftover shelter was now one of the most popular restaurants in the City of Xi'an, the People's Republic of China.

There must have been 3000 people jampacked in this overgrown tunnel. It was about fifty feet below ground. Everybody was eating. My Chinese friend had brought me here. His name is Jiang Qin.

To eat in this underground tunnel was to join others in ritual. You walked in. You were given a bowl. You were handed four large pieces of hard French bread. You took your bowl and bread and found a table to sit down. Once seated, the ritual and the waiting began. You removed the four pieces of bread from the bowl. Then you took the bread, broke it in half, and then into smaller pieces. You broke the small pieces into even smaller pieces. Finally, you put these pieces back into the bowl.

It was a slow process. The bread was hard. The atmosphere was enthusiastic. The conversations around me in that underground shelter were deafening.

When you had finished breaking all the bread into small pieces, you took the bowl to the counter. A smiling old lady, stirring a big pot of soup, would ladle the soup on top of the broken bread pieces.

I sat down to eat. It was the most delicious soup I had ever tasted.

My friend Jiang smiled then said, "We're eating *yong roe pou moe*. It was Nixon's favorite food when he visited China - when he came here to Xi'an. This is what he ate when he came to my hometown."

Jiang was thrilled that he could introduce me to Nixon's favorite food in all of the People's Republic of China.

Yong roe pou moe.

We sat. We ate. We talked about Jiang's fiancée. We talked about their hopes to get married. I learned about their dreams of the future. Their hopes to have the one child they were allowed to have. It seemed as if the more we talked, the hungrier we got.

Jesus said to the people, "I am the bread of life. Whoever comes to me will never be hungry, and whoever believes in me will never be thirsty."

As we sat in that underground shelter, I experienced a vision of community, an invitation to the table, a glimpse of heaven underground, a preview of new life in a bomb shelter, a promise of things to come.

What was surprising to me was that it all felt so familiar. An understanding of resurrection and a knowledge of the heavenly realm were totally possible, right here, right now, in this moment.

This vision was a vision of new life.

Hours later, we were on the streets.

Ahead, darkness cutting through thick fog. The air was cold and crisp. The streets of Xi'an were dark and misty. We could barely see beyond the front tires of the bicycle. It was as if we were floating through clouds. In this city of millions upon millions of people, the streets were empty.

Every now and then, out there in the foggy darkness, we would hear the bell ringing of another bicycle, warning all of us navigating blindly, that someone, some thing, was out there, moving about.

I was sitting on the back of Jiang's bicycle, holding onto him, as he pedaled us forward into the darkness.

Jiang broke the silence.

"I want to believe Jesus, but I don't know how. It is not allowed."

What was this?

I was struck by the depth of hunger expressed in his simple words. Something was calling him out from deep within his soul. He was reaching towards something beyond himself, something heard about, but unknown to him, something that could possibly provide context and meaning to the circumstances of his life.

He was yearning for community. He wanted to tell me something. He had been betrayed in the past. Could he trust me? Could he trust others? Community had let him down.

"I want to believe in Jesus, but I don't know how. It is not allowed."

A Japanese poem says, "*Furu ike ya - kawazu tobikomu - mizu no oto*"

"Old pond - a frog jumps in - water's sound"

This poem, a haiku, is one of the most famous, written by Matsuo Basho, a Japanese poet, who lived during the Edo period, about 1700 years after the death and resurrection of Jesus Christ. "Old pond - a frog jumps in - water's sound"

In the middle of nowhere, through the leap of a frog, by a leap of faith, we glimpse the power action.

There is action and then reaction. How far will the ripples of water travel, touching and changing everything in its path? Even though the frog appears isolated and alone, through action, the frog claims its direct relationship with everything around it and beyond it. Realizing that we are connected to others and doing something about it is the beginning of trust.

Action. Reaction.

In intentional community, we are connected with those from the past, those we see in this world, and those who are yet to be born. In communities of faith, we are invited ask the deepest questions of life. Does my life have meaning? What does God think of me? What does God want me to do? What happens to me when I die? Can I possibly be saved in spite of myself?

"I want to believe in Jesus, but I don't know how. It is not allowed."

When Jesus gathered with the people on the mount, he spoke to them about the journey of faith. The temporary community, gathered together to hear His words, was forever changed. Today, when these words are heard in community, we are still changed.

God wants to be with us. God wants to work through us in communities of faith. God wants to meet us where we are, as we are, right here and right now.

Jesus said that there will be days when we feel down, depressed, poor in spirit, but that we should not worry. Through the power of God, we will all be welcomed in heaven. Jesus said that there will be days when we suffer and mourn and feel overcome with grief and despair. But through the power of God and through the work of God's people, we will find comfort. Jesus said there will be days when we need to be forgiven and when we need to forgive others. Do not worry because, through acts of grace, we will see God. Jesus' Sermon on the Mount gives us a glimpse of the difficulties of our journey of faith, but it also provides us with hope in times of loneliness and despair.

We need to create, find and build communities of support that empower us to love God and to love God's people. We need to seek out others, organize, and do the work of bringing about the kingdom of God right here and right now.

When Jiang said, "I want to believe in Jesus, but I don't know how. It is not allowed," I was scared that night for many reasons.

Jiang studied English. I was studying Mandarin Chinese. I was scared because my pronunciation progress was slower than I had hoped, and Jiang's English was better than mine.

I was scared that night because we were both out past curfew. Our studies had distracted us from the time, and Jiang was desperately pedaling me to the bus stop in hopes there would be a bus to return me to my university, so that I would not get

into trouble.

I was scared that night because Jiang's wife weighed ninety pounds and I was twice her weight. I was sitting in her place on the bicycle. Jiang had insisted. I was scared that I would break the bike and wear him out.

But I was scared that night most of all, because when he said, "I want to believe in Jesus, but I don't know how. It is not allowed," I did not know how to respond.

Since I had left behind my faith community in order to study in China, I had no support when a crisis of faith appeared. I was in the middle of a faith crisis.

I had journeyed to China in hopes of encountering the country I had read about in history books – the land steeped in Taoism, a land influenced by the teachings of the Buddha, a land of people seeking out the justice of Confucius. Instead, I encountered the traumatic reality of The People's Republic of China, post-Cultural Revolution.

The Cultural Revolution was Mao's historic revolution of ten years, 1966-1976. The Cultural Revolution was a time when the people were re-educated. Communities were destroyed. Trust was broken. Relationships were replaced with the institution of the Communist Party. Intellectuals and the religious were persecuted and shot. Those who spoke the truth were forced to walk the streets wearing dunce caps. Neighbors betrayed neighbors and the secret police, the Red Army, was waiting just down the hall.

Jiang's parents were intellectuals, teachers at a college in Southern China. They had been sent off to a re-education camp when Jiang was a little boy. He remembered the day they left. He was only four. His last image of them before they died was of them being paraded through the city streets, mocked for their knowledge, robbed of dignity, put onto a bus, and then disappearing around the corner and out of his life forever.

"Blessed are those who mourn, for they will be comforted." From where is my help to come?

I was scared that night because I was hungry for God's justice in the world. But to whom could I reach out to help get it done?

The conversation Jiang and I had during our study time together kept coming up in my busy mind.

Two hungry friends pedaling in the fog through the night. It was dark, and the clock was ticking, and the questions of faith were many.

"Blessed are the poor in spirit, for theirs is the kingdom of heaven."

A dear friend once said to me, "I want to believe in Jesus, but I don't know how."

Weeks later, Jiang and his fiancée said they wanted to go to church. Sunday was just like any another day in China. There was always plenty of work to be done and China's biggest resource, her people, were up and about just like they had been yesterday and the day before that.

I had been told that there was a Christian church in downtown Xi'an just to the left of the Friendship Store. Jiang and his fiancée and I got off the bus to a street packed to capacity. We walked through the crowd, not realizing that the people we were walking through were part of an overflow crowd. They could not fit inside the church. The next service was about to begin and there was no more room. Speakers had been placed along the wall leading into the outer courtyard and then out onto the crowded street so that those who had not been able to fit in the church could hear the message. We were told by an elderly lady who greeted us at the door that it is best to get there early because the church was always full during its eight services.

The opening hymn began. It was one of my personal favorites, "Holy! Holy! Holy!" The song and the order of worship were completely familiar to me. There was an opening hymn. There was the reading of scripture. A reflection was offered. And then the people of God received bread and wine so that their hunger was fed and that they could go out and do the work that God had given them to do.

As we sang "Holy! Holy! Holy!" the context in my mind shifted. I was transported to worship communities of the past, where we had sung this hymn during the celebration of Trinity Sunday. I recalled the religious community of my childhood - the priest, the people, the music, and the questions we asked together. I remembered all their sacred stories. Their faces began to appear on a screen in my mind. I remembered how they connected their sacred stories to the Holy Story and I remembered how God had changed all of our lives through time. Suddenly I saw all of those people sitting or standing on the crowded road, gathered beside me and beside Jiang and beside his fiancée. We had descended time and space through the power of God.

Darkness came and I remembered being on the back of a bike on a foggy evening in that crowded city.

"I want to believe in Jesus, but I don't know how."

Love stems from a longing in the heart. Community starts when we trust enough to reach out and share that longing with others. Faith begins when we invite God to be with us. Sacrament receives power when we believe God is made present with us in the familiar, the common, the ordinary, in the things that we take for granted.

When I think of community, I often remember a bomb shelter, underneath a city, in the People's Republic of China, where people eat and drink together, and laugh and love. Then they leave, pedaling away on their bikes, moving about in the darkness, fed, but forever hungry for more.

I remember. I hope Jiang remembers.

THE E-TICKET

When Christians come together in community to worship God, they are fed by the power of the spirit to sustain the faith of the community. When my faith is lacking, others sustain me. When someone else's faith is lacking, my faith and the faith of others sustains them. We are fed within intentional communities so that we can live and work and play in the world, restoring God's creation to a place of love, justice and good news for all.

Some Christian communities profess faith beliefs through the words of The Nicene Creed. The creed proclaims how the gathered community understands how God created the world and works in the world, teaching us how to take care of each other through the example of Jesus Christ, sustained by the power of the spirit to do the work God has given us to do.

We seek out community that supports our belief statements, or at least creates intentional, sacred, safe space where we are able to examine them and live them out. Even though our culture emphasizes the power of the individual, this power is not what being Christian is all about. It is, instead, about the work and the mission of the entire gathered community. Everything we do alone, with our work colleagues or with others matters. God is with us at every living moment. "Life in Christ for Paul was not primarily about a new personal identity for individuals. Paul's understanding was very different from a widespread understanding of the role of 'religion' and the purpose of 'spirituality' in modern Western culture, where they are often thought of as primarily private, individual matters, even though many Christians would say that being Christian also means being part of a church. For Paul, life 'in Christ' was always a communal matter.

This was so not simply because 'it's important to be part of a church,' but because his purpose, his passing, was to create communities whose life together embodied an alternative to the normalcy of the 'wisdom of the world.'" [8]

When the intentional time is over, a leader in the community sends the people out of the doors and into the world to continue the prayer and to continue the work. In the Episcopal Church, we often say, "Go in peace to love and serve the Lord."

Worship is over. The service begins.

The mission has been stated. How quickly we forget it.

How can we incorporate that mission into everything we do? If we try, if we create the intentional space, we can truly transform ourselves, our communities, and the world in God's name.

Turn to the "Holy Story" section of your journal.

List the communities that you are involved in. An example of some communities may be family, work, a book club, a fantasy football league, a church, or a gym.

What communities are you active in now? What communities were meaningful to you in the past but you are no longer a member of? List those communities, too.

Next to each community, write briefly what the intention of the group was. Was the intention stated? Was it assumed? Perhaps a book club's intention would be "to read a book, understand the story's context and meaning, share insights and connect with personal experiences." A workplace's intention could be "to assemble a talented group of people who create products to make money for our constituents who have a share in the company."

Spend some time thinking of the intention.

After some time, come back to this page and conclude by doing the following.

Take a moment and create some holy space.

Mark the space by lighting a candle or by playing some music or by praying a prayer, calling on God to be with you where you are. You are going to write some belief statements based on the work you have done in this travel guide.

Review the statements you have written down in your "Rule of Life." Some you may still believe or agree with. Others may look totally foreign. Do not worry. Nothing done cannot be undone. These are not your definitive belief statements once and for all. You will continue to live. You will continue to experience God. You will continue to live with and love God's people. Based on all of this, your beliefs will probably shift and change. This is inevitable.

We proclaim a living God.

If you have moved through this travel guide from start to finish, you have created a workbook full of belief statements based on your personal experiences.

On the next page of the "Rule of Life" section of your journal, write "A CREED IN THE MOMENT." Then answer the following questions:

Where am I going? I believe _____ .

How did I get here? I believe _____ .

How does story help me understand God? I believe _____ .

How do I find my place in the story? I believe _____ .

How do I know my neighbor? I believe _____ .

How do we live together? I believe _____ .

How do I feed myself and my neighbor? I believe _____ .

Can I be loved in spite of myself? I believe _____ .

Why do I suffer? I believe _____ .

What happens when I die? I believe _____ .

Can I change? I believe _____ .

Is it possible to turn things around? I

believe _____ .

Where is the laughing place? I believe _____ .

I believe I am called to _____ .

The Creed is finished for the moment. As we move past the Main Gate and leave the Walt Disney World Resort, guests pass a sign that says "Buckle up. See you real soon!" And then our focus and attention shifts.

The 8th-century Chinese poet Li Bai hosts the beautiful film *Reflections of China* in the China Pavilion located in World Showcase at Epcot. In an older version of the film, the poet concluded the attraction, saying, "This is the place where we must sever. You go thousand of miles, my friend, once forever. Like the floating clouds, we drift apart. The sunset lingers like the feeling of my heart."

Go in peace to love and serve the Lord.

THE COLLECT

If you have moved through this travel guide from Chapter One to this chapter, this is your concluding Collect. If you started this guide looking for new life, this may be the first time you are writing a Collect.

In this Collect, give thanks for the communities in your life.

Write the Collect using the traditional formula. Begin by addressing God. Then list attributes about God's relationship to community. Acknowledge and give thanks for the communities you are involved in. Give thanks for what these communities mean in your life and how they sustain you. Consider what God may be calling you to do. Conclude by giving glory to God.

As I conclude the writing of this travel guide, I have the privilege of serving on the clergy staff of St. Chrysostom's Episcopal Church in Chicago. As the author of this travel guide, I am, therefore, offering up a prayer attributed to St. Chrysostom. I feel God's blessing every time our congregation prays it together. It is a wonderful prayer about the power of God in the midst community.

A Prayer of St. Chrysostom

Almighty God, you have given us grace at this time with one accord to make our common supplication to you; and you have promised through your well-beloved Son that when two or three are gathered together in his Name you will be in the midst of them: Fulfill now, O Lord, our desires and petitions as may be best for us; granting us in this world knowledge of your truth, and in the age to come life everlasting. Amen.

✢

ENDNOTES

[1] (Hench & Van Pelt, 2003, p. 65)

[2] (Wright et al., 2005, p. 84)

[3] (May & Metzger, 1973, p. NT 372)

[4] (May & Metzger, 1973, p. NT 375)

[5] (May & Metzger, 1973, p. NT 385)

[6] (May & Metzger, 1973, p. NT 385)

[7] (May & Metzger, 1973 p. NT 365)

[8] (Borg & Crossan, 2009, p. 186)

BIBLIOGRAPHY } *A Disney Monastic*

Abingdon Press. (1994). The New Interpreter's Bible : general articles & introduction, commentary, & reflections for each book of the Bible, including the Apocryphal/Deuterocanonical books. Nashville: Abingdon Press.

Alison, James. (1998). Knowing Jesus (New ed.). London: SPCK.

Allen, Diogenes. (2010). Theology for a troubled believer : an introduction to the Christian faith (1st ed.). Louisville, Ky.: Westminster John Knox Press.

Anderson, Philip Longfellow. (1999). The Gospel according to Disney : Christian values in the early animated classics (1st ed.). La Canada, Calif.: Longfellow Pub.

Beard, Richard R., & Disney, Walt. (1982). Walt Disney's EPCOT center : creating the new world of tomorrow. New York: H.N. Abrams.

Bondi, Roberta C. (1987). To love as God loves: conversations with the early church. Philadelphia: Fortress Press.

Borg, Marcus J., & Crossan, John Dominic. (2009). The first Paul : reclaiming the radical visionary behind the Church's conservative icon (1st ed.). New York: HarperOne.

Bowles, Paul. (1998). The Sheltering Sky. New York, NY: Ecco Press.

Callahan, Kennon L. (2010). Twelve keys to an effective church : strong, healthy congregations living in the grace of God (2nd ed.). San Francisco: Jossey-Bass.

Collins, John J. (2007). A short introduction to the Hebrew Bible. Minneapolis: Fortress Press.

Disney Institute. (2001). Be our guest : perfecting the art of customer service (1st ed.). New York: Disney Editions.

Dorotheus, & Wheeler, Eric P. (1977). Discourses and sayings. Kalamazoo, Mich.: Cistercian Publications.

Education for Ministry (Program). (1998). Common lessons & supporting materials. Sewanee, Tenn.: University of the South.

Episcopal Church. (1979). The Book of common prayer and administration of the sacraments and other rites and ceremonies of the church: together with the Psalter or Psalms of David according to the use of the Episcopal Church. New York & Greenwich, Conn.: Church Hymnal Corp.; Seabury Press.

Farnham, Suzanne G. (1991). Listening hearts : discerning call in community. Harrisburg, PA: Morehouse Pub.

Findlay, John M. (1992). Magic lands: western cityscapes and American culture after 1940. Berkeley: University of California Press.

Fjellman, Stephen M. (1992). Vinyl leaves: Walt Disney World and America. Boulder: Westview Press.

Foglesong, Richard E. (2001). Married to the mouse: Walt Disney World and Orlando. New Haven: Yale University Press.

Fox, Matthew. (1982). Meditations with Meister Eckhart. Santa Fe, N.M.: Bear.

Fox, Matthew. (2001). Prayer : a radical response to life (1st Jeremy P. Tarcher/Putnem ed.). New York: Jeremy P. Tarcher/Putnam.

Friedman, Richard Elliott. (1987). Who wrote the Bible? Englewood Cliffs, N.J.: Prentice Hall.

Giannetti, Louis D. (2002). Understanding movies (9th

ed.). Upper Saddle River, NJ: Prentice Hall.

Gordon, Bruce, & Kurtti, Jeff. (2008). Walt Disney World: Then, Now and Forever. New York Disney Editions.

Grover, Ron. (1991). The Disney touch : how a daring management team revived an entertainment empire. Homewood, IL: Business One Irwin.

Hench, John, & Van Pelt, Peggy. (2003). Designing Disney: imagineering and the art of the show (1st ed.). New York: Disney Editions.

Hewitt, Hugh. (1996). Searching for God in America. Dallas: Word Pub.

Hiaasen, Carl. (1998). Team rodent : how Disney devours the world (1st ed.). New York: Ballantine Pub. Group.

Imagineers (Group). (2003). The imagineering way (1st ed.). New York: Disney Editions.

Imagineers (Group), & Walt Disney Company. (1996). Walt Disney imagineering : a behind the dreams look at making the magic real (1st ed.). New York: Hyperion.

Jefferts Schori, Katharine. (2007). A wing and a prayer : a message of faith and hope. Harrisburg, PA: Morehouse Pub.

Jones, Alan W. (2005). Reimagining Christianity : reconnect your spirit without disconnecting your mind. Hoboken, N.J.: John Wiley & Sons.

King, Martin Luther, & Washington, James Melvin. (1991). A testament of hope : the essential writings and speeches of Martin Luther King, Jr (1st HarperCollins pbk. ed.). San Francisco: HarperSanFrancisco.

Kurtti, Jeff. (1996). Since the world began : Walt Disney World, the first 25 years (1st ed.). New York: Hyperion.

Lynch, William F. (1973). Images of faith; an exploration of the ironic imagination. Notre Dame Ind.: University of Notre Dame Press.

Mackenzie, Ross, & University of the South. School of Theology. (1988). Education for ministry.

Sewanee, Tenn. USA: University of the South.

Marling, Karal Ann, & Centre canadien d'architecture. (1997). Designing Disney's theme parks : the architecture of reassurance. Montréal Paris;: Centre canadien d'architecture/Canadian Centre for Architecture ; New York: Flammarion.

May, Herbert Gordon, & Metzger, Bruce Manning. (1973). The new Oxford annotated Bible with the Apocrypha (Rev. standard, containing the 2d ed.). New York,: Oxford University Press.

Miles, Margaret R. (1996). Seeing and believing: religion and values in the movies. Boston: Beacon Press.

Moyers, Bill D. (1996). Genesis: a living conversation (1st ed.). New York: Doubleday.

Palmer, Martin, & Wong, Eva. (2001). The Jesus sutras: rediscovering the lost scrolls of Taoist Christianity (1st ed.). New York: Ballantine.

Peace, Jennifer Howe, Rose, Or N., & Mobley, Gregory. (2012). My neighbor's faith : stories of interreligious encounter, growth, and transformation. Maryknoll, N.Y.: Orbis Books.

Peterson, Monique. (2001). The little big book of Disney (1st ed.). New York: Disney Editions.

Powell, Mark Allan. (2009). Introducing the New Testament : a historical, literary, and theological survey. Grand Rapids, Mich.: Baker Academic.

Price, Harrison. (2004). Walt's revolution!: by the numbers. Orlando, Fla.: Ripley Entertainment.

Project on Disney. (1995). Inside the mouse : work and play at Disney World. Durham: Duke University Press.

Revenson, Judy. (2006). Expedition Everest. Legend of the Forbidden Mountain. The Journey Begins. New York: Disney Editions.

Sartre, Jean-Paul, & Alexander, Lloyd. (2007). Nausea. New York: New Direction.

Smith, Dave. (1994). Walt Disney Famous Quotes. Lake Buena Vista: Disney's Kingdom Editions.

Smith, Martin Lee. (1985). Reconciliation : preparing for confession in the Episcopal Church. Cambridge, MA: Cowley Publications.

Smith, Martin Lee. (1985). Reconciliation : preparing for confession in the Episcopal Church. Cambridge, MA: Cowley Publications.

Society of St. John the Evangelist. (1997). The rule of the Society of St. John the Evangelist : North American congregation. Cambridge, Mass.: Cowley Publications.

Stone, Bryan P. (2000). Faith and film : theological themes at the cinema. St. Louis, MO: Chalice Press.

Surrell, Jason. (2003). The Haunted Mansion : from the Magic Kingdom to the movies (1st ed.). New York: Disney Editions.

Surrell, Jason. (2007). The Disney Mountains : imagineering at its peak (1st ed.). New York, NY London,: Disney Editions.

Taylor, Barbara Brown. (2000). Speaking of sin : the lost language of salvation. Cambridge, MA: Cowley Publications.

Taymor, Julie, & Greene, Alexis. (1997). The lion king : pride rock on Broadway (1st ed.). New York: Hyperion.

Thomas, Bob. (1994). Walt Disney : an American original (1st ed.). New York, N.Y.: Hyperion.

Tigert, Leanne McCall. (1999). Coming out through fire : surviving the trauma of homophobia. Cleveland, Ohio: United Church Press.

Volf, Miroslav. (2005). Free of charge : giving and forgiving in a culture stripped of grace. Grand Rapids, Mich.: Zondervan.

Williams, Rowan. (1991). The wound of knowledge: Christian spirituality from the New Testament to St. John of the Cross (2nd rev. ed.). Cambridge, Mass.: Cowley Publications.

Wink, Walter. (1986). Unmasking the powers : the invisible forces that determine human existence. Philadelphia: Fortress Press.

Wright, Alex, Imagineers (Group), & Walt Disney Company. (2005). The imagineering field guide to the Magic Kingdom at Walt Disney World : an Imagineer's-eye tour (1st ed.). New York: Disney Editions.

Wright, Alex, Imagineers (Group), & Walt Disney Company. (2007). The imagineering field guide to Disney's Animal Kingdom at Walt Disney World : an Imagineer's-eye tour (1st ed.). New York: Disney Editions.

Wright, Alex, Imagineers (Group), & Walt Disney Company. (2010). The Imagineering field guide to Disney's Hollywood Studios at Walt Disney World : an Imagineer's-eye tour (1st ed.). New York, New York: Disney Editions.

Wright, Alex, Imagineers (Group), & Walt Disney Company. (2010). The imagineering field guide to Epcot at Walt Disney World : an Imagineer's -eye tour (2nd ed.). New York: Disney Editions.

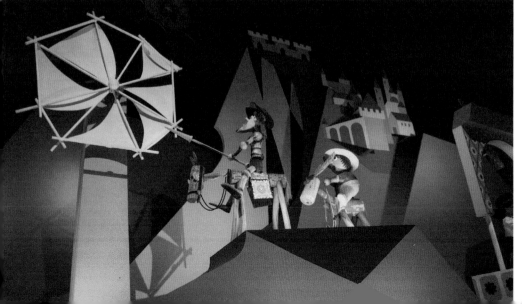

PRODUCTION CREDITS } *A Disney Monastic*

THE CREATIVE TEAM

THE REV. KEVIN M. GOODMAN | AUTHOR

Kevin is an Episcopal Priest, a fan of Kate Bush, and a lover of films and television. As a frequent guest of the Walt Disney World Resort, he finds particular joy riding monorails, walking around World Showcase Lagoon, and sipping a glass of wine on late afternoons at the California Grill. His ministry has pushed him onto the streets to serve with homeless youth and through the halls of injustice advocating for immigration reform and marriage equality. He has been a recorder of sacred story for the people of Renk Diocese, the Republic of South Sudan and a television producer capturing seekers celebrating the spirit of life. A native New Orleanian, he is definitely a Saints fan, a lover of Gumbo, and a connoisseur of the spirits of the Crescent City. He seeks God in the cracks and crevices of popular culture and is always looking for a good margarita.

CONSTANCE WILSON | DESIGNER

Elegant use of fonts and negative space is one of Connie's trademarks. She has been a graphic designer since 1992, influenced by clean type and classic layout. Connie studied art education but soon gravitated to studio art producing textiles for public spaces and handcast paper works. With a love for travel, she seeks out textiles and interesting photo subjects to inspire new work in the studio. Following a recent trip to India and Nepal, Connie has added a love of paisley, Chola sculptures of Shiva as Nataraja - Lord of the Dance, and elephants to her passion list.

CHARLIE SIMOKAITIS | PHOTOGRAPHER

Charlie nurtures a life-long fascination with the art of story-telling. Whether traveling to Central America or South Sudan for humanitarian assignments or creating still life images in his home, his work is always influenced by literature. For the past 15 years he has utilized his background in photography and film to serve his advertising, design and not-for-profit clients.

GINNA FRANTZ | EDITOR

Ginna is a long-time entrepreneur, having founded and run four business in her career. She currently is the owner of Grand Prix Equestrian, a world-class dressage training and boarding facility outside Chicago. Riding, traveling and writing have been lifelong pleasures she enjoys. She has a busy life with husband Jeffrey Breslow, a sculptor. The two enjoy life in Chicago and Vermont where they have homes.

MARGARET GOODMAN | COPY

Although Margaret was born in Brooklyn, New York, in the 1940's, she is a New Orleanian through and through, After graduating from Southeastern Louisiana College in Hammond, Louisiana, Margaret began a thirty-three year career In the Jefferson Parish School System as a teacher, a K-12 English Consultant, a Director of Adult and Community Education, and an assistant principal. She is currently a substitute teacher in an elementary school. Margaret is a Saints fan, a dog lover, a needlepointer, and a grandmother.

KARLA KATE | PROOF
Karla has worked on the product development team of a major educational publishing company for ten years. Before that she drove an ice cream truck, managed a fudge shop, and taught in elementary classrooms both in the United States and Germany. She has also published several feature articles. Karla considers herself an artist, an athlete, an explorer, an observer and, most importantly, a participant.

THE REV. SARAH K. FISHER | FORWARD
Sarah is a native of Athens, Georgia. A graduate of the General Theological Seminary, Fisher has served churches the Dioceses of Chicago and Atlanta, as well as a sojourn as a chaplain in a Level 1 Pediatric Trauma Center. She is passionate about thrift-store shopping, liturgy, laughing, Jerusalem, Buffy the Vampire Slayer, coffee, the Camino de Santiago, and finding the perfect pair of socks.

ACKNOWLEDGMENTS
A great wisdom writer spoke, "For everything there is a season, and a time for every matter under heaven: a time to be born, and a time to die; a time to plant, and a time to pluck up what is planted; a time to kill, and a time to heal; a time to break down, and a time to build up; a time to weep, and a time to laugh; a time to mourn, and a time to dance; a time to throw away stones, and a time to gather stones together; a time to embrace, and a time to refrain from embracing; a time to seek, and a time to lose; a time to keep, and a time to throw away; a time to tear, and a time to sew; a time to keep silence, and a time to speak; a time to love, and a time to hate; a time for war, and a time for peace."

This is my time to give thanks.

My mom, Margaret Goodman, took me to Walt Disney World or Disneyland every Thanksgiving. When Walt Disney World opened in October 1971 we were there during Thanksgiving a month later. We arrived at the Contemporary Hotel at around 7:00 PM. From our window we saw the Tiki Room. We were in The Magic Kingdom twenty minutes later. Because of her Disney World became a place of wonder and retreat for me. But as time went on, we made the pilgrimage to recover, to heal, to deal with anger, to deal with sorrow, to move through divorce and also to fall in love. This has been my experience of the place that Walt built. And I still love going there. I have gone with friends, coworkers, and seminarians and even by myself. But, on each journey, my mom and the spirit of my grandmother are always with me.

I met my partner, Anton Pulung, at Downtown Disney during Y2K. He was working as a Cultural Representative in Animal Kingdom's Asia section. It was his day off. It was my day to relax. I went to the cafe at Virgin Records on the West Side. (It is now closed and has been transformed into a bowling alley restaurant.) I was preparing for an adult seminar called EfM, Education for Ministry. He walked up and asked me if I was actually reading a Bible at Walt Disney World. The answer was "yes." He asked if I was a Christian. The answer was "yes." The rest is an incredible story. We have been talking about God together ever since.

My good friend The Rev. Michele Morgan inspired me to write this book. We became friends while studying together at The General Theological Seminary in New York City. After we graduated seminary and were ordained in the Episcopal Church, she invited me to accompany her and her youth group to Walt Disney World for a youth group faith-based experience. I created some of the exercises that are now contained in this travel guide on those willing or not-so-willing young people.

Their reactions and Michele's support encouraged me to continue. On my deathbed, I would trust my passing soul to the pastoring of Michele. Her love, generosity, and knowing what to say has always given me a glimpse into the grace of God.

The Diocese of Chicago's Renk Media Team is Connie Wilson, Charlie Simokaitis, The Rt. Rev. Jeff Lee and The Rt. Rev. Joseph Garang Atem. Connie and Charlie and I worked with our Bishop on a documentary project in our companion diocese, the Diocese of Renk - the Episcopal Church of Sudan, now in the Republic of South Sudan. We encountered and documented the stories of Christians of great faith. We came back and told their stories to anyone who would listen in hopes of making apparent the Spirit of God n that rising nation. I reached out to Connie and Charlie, asking them to join the creative team for this project. I had no money. I could only offer a few laughs, some change for margaritas, a trip to Disney World and a good time. Connie and Charlie said yes. I am truly blessed and forever grateful.

Ginna Frantz, a former parishioner-turned-friend and fellow spiritual sojourner once observed that I appeared stressed. I shared that I was creatively exhausted. She asked why. I told her about this project. Her words of support often moved me beyond the writer's block. She offered her incredible editing expertise in exchange for spiritual direction. I think I got the best end of that deal. Her words of strength during of times of doubt helped to keep me moving forward. I am thankful for her patience and commitment.

Karla Kate and I met while I served as Curate at All Saints' Chicago. She was a parishioner of the church and an outreach volunteer at our homeless and hunger ministry called Ravenswood Community Services. We became good friends when we discovered common past experiences that made us the people we are today. Between margaritas, we search for good theater in Chicago or get together to plot vacations or the next getaway. She works in the publishing industry and was very gracious to lend her professional expertise for the completion of this project. When will I see you in church?

The Rev. Sarah K. Fisher and I were Lily Curates in the Diocese of Chicago. We traveled together to the Great Church Conference in Beverly Hills, California. We decided to go a few days early so we could explore Disneyland. She had never been. Later, she shared that she had written about our day at Disneyland in a short story workshop. If I had inspired her once to write about Disney, perhaps I could inspire her again to write the forward. She said yes. I am sorry she moved away. I miss her laughter and words of wisdom every day.

My dream is to lead retreats and build spiritual communities at the Disney Parks. I hope this book allows me to do just that. For the first retreat, I have assembled and incredible group of people who patiently watched this thing come together. I would like to thank the inaugural Disney Monastics retreat faculty who agreed to be a part of this vision while it was still a work in progress - Judy Newman, The Rev. Sam Portaro, The Rev. Jackie Cameron, The Rev. Michele Morgan, The Rev. M.E. Eccles and Lynn Bowers. All of you have been inspirations on this incredible E-ticket ride.

I would like to thank the pastors and priests and holy people who shaped and formed me: Bill Morris, Iona Burrell, Ben Wren, Susie Gaumer, Susan Davidson, Jane Henderson, Bonnie Perry, Katherine "Kitty" Clark, Jake Bradley, Jen Rude, Jennette Defriest, Ruth Frey, Joey Sylvester, Larry Dieckmann, Terry Heyduk and Wes Smedley. To be surrounded by such a great cloud of witnesses is a blessing.

I would like to thank my good friends Judy Hills and Lynn Murrell, who invited me take up residence at beautiful Murrell Farm in South Woodstock, Vermont. Their gift created the space for me to complete this vision. I would like to thank my lawyers from Sidley Austin - Tim Payne and Marjorie Baltazar. You both provided me with faith when mine was lacking. I can never thank you and your firm enough.

A special thanks to those who believed in this idea and were willing to support it. I didn't get funded! But these people were willing! Thanks to Valerie Balling, Debra K. Bullock, Kay Collins, Dean Corrin, M.E. and Katie Eccles, Sarah Fisher, Margaret S. Goodman, Marilyn Granzyk, Michael Kozubek, David and Melanie Dickson Lemburg, Jennifer Lloyd, Paul Mallatt, Phyllis Neilson Malone, Elizabeth Masterson, Carole G. Mills, Kim Milone, Ciritta Park, Juleigh Ruby, Delia Saeta, Barbara Stott, Brenda Teague, and Andrea Wright.

And I would like to thank Dan Massa, the go-between, whose faith and commitment continually inspires me.

Now I'm going to Disney World! Hopefully, I will see you there.

DISNEY MONASTICS RETREATS

If you have enjoyed the work of this spiritual travel guide, consider joining a monastic community at Walt Disney World! Our retreats create a God-seeking community at the place where the dreams come true.

Spiritual sojourners PRAY daily. READ God's Holy Story. PRACTICE spiritual disciplines. DISCERN how God speaks through popular culture. IMAGINE and create a Rule of Life. Then ACT to change the world.

Discover God and love God's people through creating and claiming intentional space while riding Disney's most popular theme park attractions. On each retreat, a professional faculty is on hand to enhance community life. Spiritual Directors work with retreat participants to help them find God in their reflections and experiences. Academics provide lectures designed to increase knowledge of history and theology of God's Holy Word.

If you would like more information about upcoming retreats, link to Disney Monastics.
www.disneymonastics.com
therevkevin@disneymonastics.com

Proof

Made in the USA
Charleston, SC
17 February 2014